The Research Journey of /
Therapy (ACT)

The Research Journey of Acceptance and Commitment Therapy (ACT)

Nic Hooper
Lecturer in Psychology, University of the West of England, UK

and

Andreas Larsson
Licensed Psychologist, Karolinska Institutet and Stockholm County Council, Sweden

First published 2015 by
PALGRAVE MACMILLAN

Palgrave Macmillan in the UK is an imprint of Macmillan Publishers Limited,
registered in England, company number 785998, of Houndmills, Basingstoke,
Hampshire RG21 6XS.

Palgrave Macmillan in the US is a division of St Martin's Press LLC,
175 Fifth Avenue, New York, NY 10010.

Palgrave Macmillan is the global academic imprint of the above companies
and has companies and representatives throughout the world.

Palgrave® and Macmillan® are registered trademarks in the United States,
the United Kingdom, Europe and other countries.

ISBN 978–1–137–44015–0 hardback
ISBN 978–1–137–44016–7 paperback

This book is printed on paper suitable for recycling and made from fully
managed and sustained forest sources. Logging, pulping and manufacturing
processes are expected to conform to the environmental regulations of the
country of origin.

A catalogue record for this book is available from the British Library.

A catalog record for this book is available from the Library of Congress.

To my parents, thank you for giving everything to me. And to my wife Amy, who has been patient for every step of this journey, I love you very much

NH

For Therése and our son, Tage, for being the salt of my life. With heartfelt thanks to Lena Seglert, my mother-in-law, who minded Tage while I worked on this during my parental leave

AL

CD = comprehensive distancing
CT = Cognitive therapy
EA - experiential avoidance

Contents

Part III   The Journey Ahead

Figures and Tables

Figures

Tables

Foreword

And what a journey it has been

There is something implausible about this book. If you step back and ask "how did *this* happen?", the answer is far from obvious.

It is not every day that an approach changes the conversation and research agenda in evidence-based psychotherapy. This book is focused on only a portion of the research agenda impacting ACT and its larger community – nevertheless, it is hard to look at the extraordinary research journey it documents and not conclude that something unusual is happening before our very eyes. Chapter 3 of the present volume describes the history of ACT, but it seems worthwhile to add a few details that might make sense of what we are seeing today.

When I began my academic career in 1976 at the University in North Carolina, Greensboro, I had an issue in mind given to me by the late Willard Day: to understand human language as it is actually used. Fresh from a clinical internship year at Brown University with David H. Barlow, I arrived convinced that what Willard was talking about – "human language as it is actually used" – was at the core both of human psychopathology and psychotherapy. I had no idea how to put these ideas together into a single coherent whole. I had no idea how to begin to research this topic.

Luck had put me into a department with wonderful behavioural thinkers including the late Aaron Brownstein, perhaps the best basic behaviour analyst I ever met, and Rosemery Nelson-Gray, a systematic clinical researcher with a grasp of the entire field of behaviour therapy. My first graduate student, Rob Zettle, saw immediately the importance of the question and the need for an adequate answer within the behavioural tradition. In just a few years, a small handful of my clinical graduate students began to do research on rule-governed behaviour and the social context of cognitive change in traditional cognitive behaviour therapy. We had an agenda and an approach that was focused on both basic and applied research. But we did not really have a new strategy or approach, either applied or basic.

Those came from two sources. One was just luck, if you can call it that: I developed an anxiety disorder. After my first panic attack in 1978, I bounced along for a few years struggling with anxiety until it began to balloon into a much larger problem that threatened to destroy my life and my career. I questioned everything just in an effort to survive and I learned to pivot towards the anxiety instead of away from it. Acceptance and commitment therapy (ACT) came together from the flotsam and jetsam of behaviour analysis, Eastern thought, the human potential movement and humanistic psychology (it would not be called "ACT" for years yet to come of course). The ACT journey thus for me was not just about clients and disorders and data – it was personal.

ACT enabled me to pull the plug on unwillingness – that needless postural energy source that turned anxiety into panic. It got me to question the dominance of literal meaning and reason-giving. It focused me more on meaning and purpose. As my students and I applied these ideas to clients, we began to see transformational change.

ACT became part of a larger research agenda in a more academic way. Rob Zettle and I realized early on that understanding verbal rules required a new approach to verbal stimuli (Zettle & Hayes, 1982). Following the lead given by stimulus equivalence, Aaron Brownstein and I realized that a world of possibilities opened up if we thought of relating as an operant. In 1984, I wrote what became the first outline of ACT, relational frame theory (RFT) and their relationship (Hayes, 1984) and the next year Aaron and I presented a fairly detailed account of RFT (Hayes & Brownstein, 1985). Aaron died soon after, which greatly slowed the development of RFT until Dermot Barnes-Holmes arrived on the scene.

In the years that followed, I moved to the University of Nevada, and my lab and a handful of colleagues began to construct the contextual behavioural science (CBS) research program in earnest. People are usually shocked to hear from 1986 to 2000 no ACT randomized trials were published. Instead the work focused on developing measures such as the Acceptance and Action Questionnaire, a task that took nearly a decade (Hayes et al., 2004); developing functional contextualism; laying a solid foundation of RFT research, which did not fully happen until the mid-1990s; creating the early ACT protocols and components; working out the psychological flexibility model; and similar tasks. I deeply believe that this "silent" part of the ACT research journey was a major key to its success. It was slow because there were many things to do and the community doing the work was tiny.

Finally in 1999, the first ACT book was published, co-authored by Kirk Strosahl (who had contacted the work in 1986 at a workshop I gave at the University of Washington), and Kelly Wilson, a graduate student of mine who began working with me in 1989. By the year

2000, only five studies on ACT had been published and the entire ACT research community consisted of several small handfuls of colleagues, former students and their students. But we had laid the groundwork. Labs around the globe began exploring ACT; popular books were written (and tested in randomized trials) – these books allowed people to see for themselves if ACT helped; and professionals were moved personally and professionally by training workshops.

These processes were self-amplifying and allowed the ACT research journey, already at least 20 years old, to increase in intensity and scope. Fourteen years later, Drs Hooper and Larsson have gathered in this volume 265 empirical investigations with 10,080 participants: 108 randomized controlled trials, 36 pilot studies or open trials, 67 studies on ACT processes or components and 54 small studies with $n < 10$ (single-case designs, multiple baselines and so on). Approximately two-thirds of the literature on ACT has been published in the last four years; last year a new randomized controlled trial appeared every 12 days. As of this writing, the Association for Contextual Behavioral Science – the professional and scientific society that is guiding ACT development – has about 7,500 members worldwide. ACT is the overnight sensation . . . the one that took 35 years to construct.

Explosive growth came because the foundation was well and truly laid. When the time came, people saw the heft of the work and it empowered them to modify the methods and take them in new directions. They could do so without contradicting their assumptions, because the assumptions were described and owned. They saw the personal relevance to their lives; clients did as well. They saw the scope that comes from targeting human language as it is actually used. They realized that psychological flexibility principles could be scaled to groups and organizations. A vast playing field opened up – and top-quality practitioners and researchers ran into that field and began developing things of substance.

The most impressive feature of this research journey is its breadth in terms of topic area. There are at least five published studies in each of the following areas (in descending order of frequency, from "pain" with 22 studies): pain, depression, work stress and performance, social anxiety disorder, smoking, weight loss, exercise and sport, education and training, stigma, generalized anxiety disorder, mixed anxiety disorders, psychosis, substance abuse and adjustment to cancer. ACT deals with the interface between human language and cognition and direct contingency processes. Anywhere that a human mind goes, ACT can follow. Anyone reading this book cannot help but see the possibilities.

It is a bit surprising how well ACT has worked given that breadth and the fact that there has not been much time to fit these principles to the needs of specific populations. The most recent meta-analysis of the ACT literature (A-Tjak et al., 2015) found that ACT was superior to waitlist (Hedges' $g = 0.82$), to psychological placebo (Hedges' $g = 0.51$) and to the standard treatment as usual (Hedges' $g = 0.64$). ACT was also superior on secondary outcomes (Hedges' $g = 0.30$), life satisfaction/quality measures (Hedges' $g = 0.37$) and process measures (Hedges' $g = 0.56$) compared to control conditions.

All of the recent meta-analyses have similar findings (e.g. Hayes, Luoma, Bond, Masuda, & Lillis, 2006; Ost, 2008; Powers, Zum Vörde Sive Vörding, & Emmelkamp, 2009; Ruiz, 2010, 2012; Bluett, Homan, Morrison, Levin, & Twohig, 2014; Ost, 2014; A-Tjak et al., 2015) and some meta-analyses have found superiority for ACT over traditional CBT methods (e.g. Ruiz, 2012). Even the most severe scientific critics of ACT (e.g. Ost, 2014) now list it as having some degree of empirical support in a very wide range of areas. As researchers settle into specific areas and tweak the methods needed, it is likely that we will see additional progress.

The journey ahead

So, is the journey from here predictable? Should the CBS community take the obvious steps like applying what we know to more problem areas, working on dissemination and training, and trying to increase the efficiency of ACT applications? Sure we should (and will), but not at the expense of areas that are higher risk than that.

There are many, many areas of research need (see Hayes, Barnes-Holmes, & Wilson, 2012), but let me mention four broad areas that seem particularly important.

RFT and ACT

As I have tried to state very clearly in this foreword, the ACT research journey has always been about understanding human language and cognition as it is actually used. That is why RFT is so important. I do not think ACT can advance much farther than advances seen in RFT. As I noted above, ACT did not really become a viable research program until RFT matured enough to be a focus of empirical work. ACT as a mere collection of technological elements is a minor step forward. As a window into a contextualistic approach to the issues raised by human language and cognition, it has a chance of transforming the discipline. I am not arguing that ACT is fully based on RFT – ACT has pulled along RFT as much as vice versa and the two are not fully integrated in many areas. My point is that a viable back-and-forth relationship is needed (what I have called a reticulated approach) in which the entire community takes responsibility for the entire agenda. This is different than the traditional bottom-up approach in behavioural psychology. RFT is too important for it to be left to someone else. Practitioners dare not leave this important area to basic psychologists without active assistance, support and cooperation.

In research I believe that this means we need to begin to examine RFT processes inside psychotherapy, using language analysis, implicit measures and component studies. We need to build other applied wings of RFT in education, social persuasion, stigma reduction and language development, among other areas. We need laboratory studies of psychological flexibility processes and extensions of RFT ideas directly into clinical processes. We need to see if RFT can help us develop a new nosology, or needed research-domain criteria. Clinical researchers should model their ideas using RFT methods and RFT research should extend their ideas into the applied arena.

Psychological flexibility

The psychological flexibility model contains processes that can link directly to a new transdiagnostic approach to human suffering and human prosperity. We need more studies on mediation and moderation. We need more assessment development, especially outside of one-time self-report measures, into behavioural measures, implicit measures, transcript scoring, measures of in-session emotion and cognition, measures of flexibility processes in therapeutic relationship, experience sampling measures (including measures of context, not just action), biological measures and the like. We need component studies of psychological flexibility in all of its key areas. We need to take the psychological flexibility model into the entire range of evidence-based care and into human experience more generally. We have a model that is doing extraordinarily well. In the model of truth inside CBS, we test the pragmatic utility of models and concepts by pushing them to their limits and then drilling down into the exceptions we find. That spirit will carry the model far beyond its current confines.

CBS and evolution science

CBS is not an island – it embodies an evolutionary approach to human functioning. That was always Skinner's vision (Skinner, 1981) and it is time to make it real. I believe that CBS is destined to heal the historical breach between behavioural science and evolutionary science once and for all. That could have a truly profound impact on behavioural science as we know it.

It is very, very easy to explain ACT as a form of evolution science. Create healthy behavioural variation through acceptance and defusion; situate it in the present context through mindful attention to the now; select what works via values; and retain what works through committed action. Situated variation and selective retention: ACT is applied evolution science (Wilson, Hayes, Biglan, & Embry, 2014).

As ACT researchers take this idea seriously, we will see studies of psychological inflexibility as an endophenotype; studies of the epigenetic impact of ACT; studies on psychological flexibility and cooperation as resulting from multi-level selection; and studies linking ACT to cultural development or to the functioning of groups inside the framework of evolutionary thinking. Several of these projects are already under way. They will take ACT and CBS in unpredictable directions.

Prevention and social change

The purpose of CBS is to create a behavioural science more adequate to the challenge of the human condition. ACT is not just about psychotherapy. It is about how to empower people to make transformational changes. We do not yet know how to increase psychological flexibility in the absence of contact with pain. So far, a real empirical strength of ACT is its impact on multi-problem or treatment-resistant patients, but the flip side of that is that more technological work is needed to help ACT foster the CBS purpose writ large when dealing with people who are not yet struggling or who are just beginning that downward spiral. Large and well-done longitudinal studies have shown conclusively that psychological inflexibility not only predicts the development of psychological disorders, but also mediates the tendency for people with single disorders to become multi-problem patients (e.g. Spinhoven, Drost, de Rooij, van Hemert, & Penninx, 2014). That tells us that these processes are key, but not how to change them.

This knowledge is needed not just for prevention, but also for prosocial change. We know that ACT can impact on stigma and prejudice, or can help empower indigenous peoples to rise to social challenges. It is time to become more systematic, trying out new ideas for how to move flexibility processes at a social level, across the world and across the full range of human needs.

Where will ACT research be a decade from now?

This book is primarily focused on the last decade because that is the time period in which over 90% of the research literature on ACT has been developed. It is hard to know where this is going, but ACT methods and ideas are being assimilated into other approaches at an astonishing rate. There is no reason to get grabby or to be annoyed when the sources of influence are unstated or when false distinctions are proposed ("this new method is not ACT. ACT doesn't really ___*fill in the blank with superficially plausible but often ignorant statements* ___"). That is just how revolutions work. But becoming mainstream is not the goal of ACT. The community will need to dig into the even more difficult work ahead in order to move the field in a contextual direction. Frankly, I expect the exponential growth of the ACT community to slow a lot as people realize this.

No matter. ACT is here to foster a values-based journey. That is true in its research program as well as in work with a given client. If we can go to the edges of knowledge and push, we have a chance to open up new areas that will make a difference in the lives of those we serve. That is exactly what we should do in the years ahead. Whether it is easy or popular is not the issue. The issue is the prize we seek: a behavioural science more adequate to the challenges of the human condition.

Steven C. Hayes
University of Nevada

References

A-Tjak, J. G. L., Davis, M. L., Morina, N., Powers, M. B., Smits, J. A. J., & Emmelkamp, P. M. G. (2015). A meta-analysis of the efficacy of acceptance and commitment therapy for clinically relevant mental and physical health problems. *Psychotherapy and Psychosomatics, 84*, 30–36.

Bluett, E. J., Homan, K. J., Morrison, K. L., Levin, M. E., & Twohig, M. P. (2014). Acceptance and commitment therapy for anxiety and OCD spectrum disorders: An empirical review. *Journal of Anxiety Disorders, 28*(6), 612–624. doi: 10.1016/j.janxdis.2014.06.008

Gaudiano, B. A. (2009). Öst's (2008) methodological comparison of clinical trials of acceptance and commitment therapy versus cognitive behavior therapy: Matching apples with oranges? *Behaviour Research and Therapy, 47*(12), 1066–1070. doi: 10.1016/j.brat.2009.07.020

Hayes, S. C. (1984). Making sense of spirituality. *Behaviorism, 12*, 99–110.

Hayes, S. C., Barnes-Holmes, D., & Wilson, K. G. (2012). Contextual behavioral science: Creating a science more adequate to the challenge of the human condition. *Journal of Contextual Behavioral Science, 1*, 1–16. doi: 10.1016/j.jcbs.2012.09.004

Hayes, S. C., & Brownstein, A. J. (May 1985). *Verbal Behavior, Equivalence Classes, and Rules: New Definitions, Data, and Directions*. Invited address presented at the meeting of the Association for Behavior Analysis, Columbus, OH.

Hayes, S. C., Luoma, J., Bond, F., Masuda, A., & Lillis, J. (2006). Acceptance and commitment therapy: Model, processes, and outcomes. *Behaviour Research and Therapy, 44*, 1–25.

Hayes, S. C., Strosahl, K. D., Wilson, K. G., Bissett, R. T., Pistorello, J., Toarmino, ... & McCurry, S. M. (2004). Measuring experiential avoidance: A preliminary test of a working model. *The Psychological Record, 54*, 553–578.

Öst, L. (2008). Efficacy of the third wave of behavioral therapies: A systematic review and meta-analysis. *Behaviour Research and Therapy, 46*(3), 296–321. doi: 10.1016/j.brat.2007.12.005

Öst, L. (2014). The efficacy of acceptance and commitment therapy: An updated systematic review and meta-analysis. *Behaviour Research and Therapy, 61*, 105–121. doi: 10.1016/j.brat.2014.07.018

Powers, M. B., Zum Vörde Sive Vörding, M. B., & Emmelkamp, P. M. (2009). Acceptance and commitment therapy: A meta-analytic review. *Psychotherapy and Psychosomatics, 78*(2), 73–80. doi: 10.1159/000190790

Ruiz, F. J. (2010). A review of acceptance and commitment therapy (ACT) empirical evidence: Correlational, experimental psychopathology, component and outcome studies. *International Journal of Psychology and Psychological Therapy, 10*, 125–162.

Ruiz, F. J. (2012). Acceptance and commitment therapy versus traditional cognitive behavioral therapy: A systematic review and meta-analysis of current empirical evidence. *International Journal of Psychology & Psychological Therapy, 12*(3), 333–357.

Skinner, B. F. (1981). Selection by consequences. *Science, 213*, 501–504.

Spinhoven, P., Drost, J., de Rooij, M., van Hemert, A. M., & Penninx, B. W. (2014). A longitudinal study of experiential avoidance in emotional disorders. *Behavior Therapy, 45*, 840–850.

Wilson, D. S., Hayes, S. C., Biglan, T., & Embry, D. (2014). Evolving the future: Toward a science of intentional change. *Behavioural and Brain Sciences, 34*, 1–22. doi: 10.1017/S0140525X13001593

Zettle, R. D., & Hayes, S. C. (1982). Rule-governed behavior: A potential theoretical framework for cognitive-behavior therapy. In P. C. Kendall (Ed.), *Advances in cognitive-behavioral research and therapy* (pp. 73–118). New York: Academic.

Acknowledgements

There are a number of wonderful people that deserve recognition for their contribution to this book. First and foremost, Dr Steve Hayes, Dr Rob Zettle and Dr Kelly Wilson have given, despite ever-increasing workloads, their utmost support to this project in various ways; to them we are grateful. Sometimes, we feel that readers of ACT books might think that acknowledging these "founding fathers" is something that we "have" to do, but the truth is that these people are genuinely very special to us. Secondly, we would like to thank Dr Louise McHugh, former PhD supervisor to both authors, who has proven to be a constant source of inspiration and wisdom; we would not be who we are if it was not for you. Thirdly, the "profile researchers" kindly gave their time to inform us how they feel ACT research can improve in the coming years, and it is this aspect of the book that makes it most powerful. We will therefore spend the next ten years buying drinks for these new-found friends at conferences! Fourth, a good friend of ours, Dr Miles Thompson, in addition to providing ideas and support throughout the writing process, supplied us with a wonderful resource that ensured our references were correct (reciteworks.com), which as you can imagine, is quite crucial in a book about research. Fifth, a number of our students have proofread the manuscript for us, but special thanks must go to Geetanjali Basarkod. Sixth, the people at Palgrave Macmillan have been supportive and patient, in particular we would like to acknowledge the efforts of Nicola Jones, Libby Forrest and Eleanor Christie. Finally, ACT has a wonderful scientific and clinical community that is humbling in its generosity and support. The number of people who have helped out by sending small emails with crucial information is difficult to count. We really hope this is a resource that all of you will enjoy.

Prologue

There are a number of reasons one might pick up a book designed to describe the research published about acceptance and commitment therapy (ACT, said as the word "act" rather than the initials "A-C-T"). One is that you, the reader, are a psychology student being forced to engage with this material because it is part of your curriculum. We have all been there. Another reason is that you are a clinician, interested and perhaps trained in ACT, but plagued by the feeling that you should know more about the research behind it. A third reason is that you are an academic and would like to use this book as a time-saving device when writing grants or journal articles. A fourth reason is that you are someone in a field that is related but different from ACT and you are curious or critical of ACT. Whatever your reason, we welcome you.

Why undertake the intimidating task of describing the ACT research journey? The answer to this question is important, as it will let you know our original intentions (and biases). First, we felt that this book could be a valuable resource for the community of people interested in the ACT model. Instead of scouring Google Scholar for journal articles in a particular diagnostic area, everything is here for you in one place. Instead of trying to describe how much research ACT has accumulated to an interested colleague, now you can just hand them this book. In short, it is hoped that our endeavour will reduce the effort others have to make when investigating ACT research.

Second, there seem to be many ACT books and manuals being published these days, even for disorders in which there is little empirical evidence showing that ACT works. For this reason, it is important that we determine whether the amount of research conducted on ACT matches the hype surrounding it. For better or for worse, this book will allow the reader to see exactly how well supported the ACT model is. It is important to note that we are not doing this to "prove" that ACT is evidence-based. Instead, this book will allow us to see if we are getting ahead of the data, as recently implied by critics of ACT (Öst, 2014).

This leads us to the third reason: without this volume many are unlikely to discover the gaps in ACT research without an exhaustive literature search. The gaps will be obvious after you have read this book, and it is our hope that it will inspire people to run research in areas where it is lacking. Fourth, this book could function as a glue in the

ACT community; that is, it could bring together researchers around the world who have similar interests. It is important that these collaborations develop, as it is not solely the celebrated profile researchers that will move ACT forward in the coming years. Relatedly, this book could provide people from different backgrounds with a common place from which to strike up a relationship. For example, the words, "Hey, I read your paper on ..." is a great ice-breaker with researchers at conferences; give it a try! Fifth, running research is a time-consuming, slow and often frustrating process. The most important reason why we have taken on this task is to salute the researchers that have put ACT on the map in the last three decades.

The current volume is divided into three parts. The purpose of Part I is to situate psychotherapy within the wider context of the world and then to situate ACT within the wider context of psychotherapy. Knowing these things has implications for how you might want to read the book. Specifically, if you have a history with psychotherapy, you may want to skip the first two chapters, and if you know about the development of ACT, then you may want to miss out Part I altogether. Having said that, we feel that these chapters set the scene for what comes later.

In Part II, ACT research across diagnostic categories is presented. This part was tricky to write, as not only is a book about research unlikely to be a page-turner, but it also has the tendency to seem like a list. Although both of those issues are somewhat unavoidable, we have tried to spice up the book via the inclusion of "profile researcher" sections. These sections detail the academic biographies of the most prolific ACT researchers and include their thoughts as to how ACT research can improve in the coming years. Finally, Part III is the conclusion, where the research in this book will be broken down into statistics and where the future directions of ACT research will be summarized.

As we have tried to create a coherent whole that can be read in one go, it is likely we will have delusions in the coming months about readers working their way through the entire book, chapter by chapter, and enjoying every second of it. However, in reality, we have no doubt that this book will function best as a reference resource; that is, if you want to know the ACT research for "insert disorder", then you know you can look at *The Research Journey of ACT* and find a chapter about it. For this reason, you will probably dip in and out when the situation calls for it.

There are a few final things you need to know. Firstly, we have tried to include every ACT research study ever conducted (up to the end of 2014), but there is no doubt that we have missed some out. Indeed, every time Dr Eric Morris uploaded a new article to his Twitter account, we usually lost sleep due to the horrifying realization that we would never find all of the empirical ACT investigations. This has been made especially difficult by the recent creation of the *Journal for Contextual Behavioral Science (JCBS)*, which seems to be a conveyor belt of good ACT research. It has been made even more difficult by the publication of ACT research in languages other than English. We apologize profusely for not getting everything in here, especially to those researchers whose valuable work we have not found. Secondly, being in contact with the present moment is a crucial part of the ACT model. However, there are also a number of other mindfulness-based approaches in psychotherapy. Despite the fact that research evidence supporting those other approaches indirectly supports the ACT model, in this volume, only studies that have ACT at their heart will be included. Thirdly, this book is designed to be accessible to people without a background in research. Therefore, you will not find effect sizes, detailed statistics or lots of jargon.

ACT has been delivered in various ways with various populations: it has been delivered in brief format and in full-length format, it has been taken apart to its individual components and it has been compared to a plethora of control groups, it has been applied all over the world and it has been used with people of all ages. We hope the current volume will help you to learn about this incredible variety and progress, in what is essentially a history of ACT research.

Part I

Theoretical and Historical Background

1
The Need

If you have been to any ACT trainings or have read any ACT books, you may be familiar with the phrase "the ubiquity of human suffering". This sentiment suggests that the reason mental health issues are so widespread is that suffering is simply an inevitable artefact of being human. It lies in stark contrast to the mainstream notion of "healthy normality", which is the idea that it is normal to be psychologically healthy, meaning that if you are not happy, then you are not normal. Many people may not realize that the ubiquity of suffering actually takes centre stage in the ACT model because it provides the space for acceptance; that is, if suffering is normal and common, then maybe acceptance, rather than avoidance, is the way to manage it. Of course, if a major premise of the ACT model is that human suffering is widespread, this would be evidenced by high prevalence rates of mental health disorders.

The World Health Organisation (WHO; Kessler & Üstün, 2008) aimed to determine the likelihood of mental health problems in 17 participating countries (Belgium, Colombia, France, Germany, Israel, Italy, Japan, Lebanon, Mexico, the Netherlands, New Zealand, Nigeria, the People's Republic of China, South Africa, Spain, Ukraine and the USA). In these studies, people were required to complete a structured interview that screened for diagnostic criteria according to the fourth edition of the *Diagnostic and Statistical Manual of Mental Health Disorders* (*DSM-IV*; American Psychiatric Association, 1994), both during the past year of the person's life and during their lifetime. The results were surprising: between 12% (Nigeria) and 47.4% (USA) of people had experienced a mental health disorder in their lifetime. This means, if you live in the USA, that every second person you meet will, at some point, experience enough mental health troubles to warrant a psychiatric diagnosis. The figures for 12-month prevalence were just as startling, with as many as every fourth person reaching the criteria for diagnosis.

These figures provide evidence that there is a need for psychotherapy in helping to manage the growing burden of mental health issues, but this burden is not limited only to those actually suffering. Mental illness is considered the most costly health problem in the Western world (Bloom et al., 2011). In 2010, the direct cost of mental illness (i.e. diagnosis, treatment and care costs) was reported to be 823 billion USD globally. Indirect costs (i.e. housing issues, loss of income, research and sick pay) were 1624 billion USD. Those figures are expected to increase to 1995 billion and 4051 billion USD, respectively, by the year 2030. Additionally, the cost in lost output (i.e. the depletion of a country's gross domestic product [GDP] due to people being less able to work or manage capital) associated with mental illness is projected at 16.3 trillion USD between 2011 and 2030. Important as the economic burden of mental health is, many of us work within this profession because we want to be able to improve lives at ground level. Therefore, whereas the financial relief that psychotherapy could provide may not totally resonate with us, seeing people suffer does. And, as the aforementioned research suggests, people do indeed suffer. Perhaps this cannot better be illustrated than via statistics about the ultimate act of self-destruction: suicide. According to the WHO (Kessler & Üstün, 2008), suicide, which can often be attributed to mental health issues, is the second leading cause of death among 15–29-year-olds globally; over 800,000 people succeed in suicide yearly and there are many more who fail in suicide attempts. Furthermore, Chiles and Strosahl (1995) put the prevalence rate of serious suicidal ideation over the course of a lifetime at almost 50%. That includes attempted suicide (10%) and suicidal ideation with (20%) or without (20%) a specific plan.

You will find these sorts of chapters in many books about psychotherapy. Often, the words about mental health issues and suicide roll from our tongues and we probably do not fully process the information. But the figures tell a grim story; mental health issues are not something that happen in a far off land, rather they happen all around us. Think about this when you next see your co-workers, your friends, or your family. With ever-growing rates of mental illness, it seems as though suffering is indeed ubiquitous and a part of life. Consequently, many people need help in managing their unwanted thoughts and feelings. With huge concern arising over psycho-pharmaceutical drugs (Whitaker, 2011), the development of psychotherapies has been crucial in the battle to treat mental illness, and finding evidence-based approaches is currently being emphasized the world over. We will now turn our attention to the evidence-based psychotherapeutic models of the middle to late 20th century in an effort to illuminate the roots from which ACT emerged.

2
The Three Waves

The first wave: Behaviour therapy

While the dominant psychoanalytical model of the early 20th century developed mostly from the clinical interactions of Freud and his patients, behaviour therapy emerged from the experimental psychology of John Watson. Watson had come into contact with the work of Ivan Pavlov and, although he was initially of the opinion that Pavlov's results were more physiological than psychological, he came to employ similar experimental conditions with his work in the USA. Watson viewed psychology as "a purely directive experimental branch of natural science" (Watson, 1913, p. 158) in reaction to the psychoanalytical models of the time. His manifest states that psychology should look at covert behaviour, and not bother itself with introspection and the experience of consciousness (Watson, 1913). The predominant interpretation of Watson's manifest, which has been debated over time (Barrett, 2012), was that he refused to allow any sort of information not available to the outside observer to be used in psychology. Watson's importance for behaviour therapy, beyond a first formulation of behaviourism, is in his experiment with "Little Albert" (Watson & Rayner, 1920), a nine-month-old child who was experimentally conditioned to fear a white rat. Watson, who was interested in the mechanisms by which emotional reactions developed, had observed that children seemed to startle at loud noises as a natural reaction. Together with graduate student Rosalie Rayner, Watson conditioned Albert to fear a white rat by striking a suspended metal bar with a hammer whenever Albert touched the rat. Experimentally, the *unconditioned stimulus* (the noise) occasions an *unconditioned response* (fear). Since this was performed in the presence of the *neutral stimulus* (the rat), the rat eventually becomes the *conditioned stimulus* for fear, which is then called a *conditioned response*. This means that after conditioning, the white rat itself was enough to cause Albert to become distressed and fearful.

Although the Little Albert experiment has been criticized both for ethical concerns (American Psychological Association, 2002) and for methodological flaws (Harris, 1979), it had clear implications about the development of psychopathology, namely that it could be explained by principles of classical conditioning. Of course, if this is the case, then clinical efforts needed to be developed to help clients re-learn unhelpful associations. Mary Cover Jones (sometimes known as the Grandmother of Behaviourism) was the first to do this. Upon attending one of Watson's lectures, she went on to design the first desensitization experiment. "The Case of Peter" (Jones, 1960) involved a three-year-old boy, who after having been conditioned to fear a rabbit, successfully had the fear reduced by gradually moving closer to the rabbit in the presence of candy. Although groundbreaking, the study garnered little interest until Joseph Wolpe directed attention to the work. Wolpe, who was both an experimental psychiatrist and a clinician, used the basic ideas of Cover Jones to develop the method of systematic desensitization. In Wolpe's method, the client is first taken through a progressive relaxation phase to inhibit an anxious response. Second, a hierarchy of feared stimuli is produced in collaboration with the client. Third, the client practices relaxation in the presence of feared stimuli from the hierarchy, starting with the least feared stimulus and moving to the most feared stimulus. To help in this work, Wolpe (1973) constructed the Subjective Units of Distress Scale (SUDS) that is used throughout the world in exposure treatments. The SUDS is a 0–10 scale of distress that involves, in one form or another, asking the client the following question: "On a scale from 0 to 10, 0 being the least distressed you have ever been to 10 being the most distressed you have ever been, how would you rate your current experience?" The measure can be employed in creating the hierarchy by putting stimuli on the hierarchy in ascending order of SUDS ratings. Additionally, in the exposure phase of treatment, clients are also often asked to report their current SUDS level so that it may be tracked.

Systematic desensitization is based on the classical conditioning paradigm and was successful in the treatment of post-traumatic stress patients in the South African army. However, many psychological problems were not treatable through these techniques. Agoraphobia (the fear of small spaces) was one such issue that seemed to benefit from a slightly different approach. Agras, Leitenberg and Barlow (1968) added social reinforcement to the treatment by praising the client upon approaching the feared situation. This use of reinforcement was of course based on the experimental analysis of behaviour by B. F. Skinner, who formulated the operant paradigm in psychology, whereby a behaviour changes in accordance with its consequences (Skinner, 1938). This addition of social reinforcement is one of the success stories in the history of clinical psychology (Barlow, 2004).

The work of Watson, Cover Jones, Wolpe and Skinner all contributed to the development of behaviour therapy, whereby interventions based on the principles of operant and classical conditioning are designed to alter problematic behaviour. However, although behaviourism was the dominant force in psychology in the 1950s, the tide was turning. From the late 1950s, a new interdisciplinary field grew out of neuroscience, linguistics, computer science, anthropology and psychology. It came to be named cognitive science (Miller, 2003) and this approach would eclipse behaviourism as the dominant approach. This eclipse emerged due to the inability of behaviourism to account for language and cognition. Although Skinner developed an extrapolated account in *Verbal Behavior* (1957), it did not lend itself easily to the development of a research paradigm. The fledgling cognitive studies (the Harvard name for cognitive science pre-1977) criticized Skinner's account on both linguistic and meta-theoretical grounds (e.g. Chomsky, 1991). Consequently, in psychotherapy, a so-called cognitive revolution occurred through the development of cognitive therapy (CT), which has its own explanation for the advent of psychological disorders (Ramnerö, 2012).

The second wave: Cognitive therapy

Albert Ellis, who was originally a psychoanalyst, developed rational-emotive behaviour therapy (REBT) in 1955 (Ellis & Ellis, 2011). REBT is an active form of psychotherapy, where irrational, negative beliefs are to be restructured so that the client can see their irrationality, self-defeatism and rigidity. Ellis' focus on irrational cognition caused uproar in psychoanalytic circles and it would be another few decades before the cognitive approach became fully accepted (A. Ellis, 2010). When the change did happen in the 1970s, it was due to the work of Aaron T. Beck, who had also become disillusioned with the psychoanalytical approach. His clients seemed to have dysfunctional and unrealistic negative beliefs about themselves and rapid, difficult to control, negative thoughts. When he explored and challenged these thoughts and beliefs with his clients, they seemed to improve (e.g. Beck, 2011). This led

Beck to develop CT, which views negative cognitions as being related to negative emotions and actions. It therefore uses a variety of means, such as cognitive restructuring, to reduce the frequency and intensity of such cognitions, or to change them into more desirable forms, as a way to reduce negative emotions or undesired actions (Masuda, Hayes, Sackett, & Twohig, 2004). Eventually, the Association for the Advancement of Behaviour Therapy (AABT) recognized the impact of CT and renamed itself the Association for Behavioural and Cognitive Therapies (ABCT). According to some, this was not an easy transition; Hayes (2008) recounted Joseph Wolpe saying that cognitions were accounted for already and that cognitive models brought nothing new to the table. Nevertheless, over time the "old" behaviour therapists and the "new" cognitive therapists coined a new approach: cognitive behaviour therapy, or CBT (Hayes, 2004).

This combination seemed to be useful; behaviour therapy, which specialized in behaviour change, now had a complementary approach that targeted cognition. However, even though CBT encompasses a large treatment package, including a number of behavioural techniques, the hallmark mechanism of change is still the modification of maladaptive cognitions or cognitive restructuring (Beck, 1979; Longmore & Worrell, 2007). Judith Beck (2011) explains cognitive restructuring as a method of teaching clients to challenge the absolute truth of maladaptive cognitions. This is approached by training the client to note evidence for and against the thought, to identify thinking errors and to find or develop alternative cognitions that better reflect the full range of their actual experience. Cognitive restructuring, which often takes the format of guided discovery, is thought to teach clients to respond to their dysfunctional thoughts in a more constructive manner, ultimately alleviating their psychological disorder.

CBT has dominated psychotherapy over the past 30 years and part of its success can be attributed to the scores of outcome studies conducted on its effectiveness. The current state of CBT evidence shows it to be the most efficacious treatment for many different disorders, including anxiety and depression disorders, as well as personality disorders and eating disorders (http://www.div12.org/PsychologicalTreatments/treatments.html). CBT even outdoes medical treatments for depression and anxiety (e.g. Butler, Chapman, Forman, & Beck, 2006). Although it is far beyond the remit of the current volume to describe the amount of research behind CBT, a quick search of the literature will substantiate the claim that CBT is the most successful therapeutic approach on the planet.

The aforementioned outcome data made the alliance between the cognitive and behavioural interventions of CBT relatively solid. Still, a number of researchers were curious to see what it was that really made the biggest difference in clients' lives: the behavioural components or the cognitive components. In 1996, Jacobson and colleagues found that adding cognitive components in the treatment of depression made no difference in outcome compared to just doing behavioural interventions (Jacobson et al., 1996). A few years later, Borkovec, Newman, Pincus and Lytle (2002) made a similar discovery for generalized anxiety disorder (GAD). This made people question the validity and effectiveness of cognitive restructuring for these diagnoses. It was this line of thinking (in combination with the fact that CBT is not always effective for every disorder) that opened up the field for new approaches in the treatment of psychopathology. Some have named this changing tide *the third wave*.

The third wave

Hayes (2004) includes a number of recent therapeutic models in the third wave, for example, behaviour activation (Kanter, Busch, & Rusch, 2009), mindfulness-based stress reduction (MBSR; Kabat-Zinn & Hanh, 2009), mindfulness-based cognitive therapy (MBCT; Segal, Williams, & Teasdale, 2012), dialectical behaviour therapy (DBT; Linehan et al., 1999) and acceptance and commitment therapy (ACT; Hayes, Strosahl, & Wilson, 1999). According to Hayes (2004), what makes a therapy third wave is the focus on altering the context and function of negative cognitions and emotions instead of challenging or changing the content and frequency of them. Across these new approaches, one common ingredient seems to be a vehicle for achieving this: mindfulness.

Mindfulness is a fairly recent phenomenon in Western medical and mental health approaches. What is called "mindfulness" today, originated in ancient Hindu, Daoist and Buddhist traditions that recognized the benefits of these practices for hundreds, if not thousands of years (Baer, 2005). Today, mindfulness is described in a number of ways. John Kabat-Zinn developed MBSR and defines mindfulness as "paying attention in a particular way: on purpose, in the present moment, and nonjudgmentally" (Kabat-Zinn & Hanh, 2009, p. 4). Marsha Linehan, who developed DBT, defines it as "the intentional process of observing, describing, and participating in reality nonjudgmentally, in the moment, and with effectiveness" (Robins, Schmidt, & Linehan, 2011, p. 37). Although there is broad agreement across most definitions of mindfulness, contention certainly arises when discussions begin about how mindfulness works (e.g. Fletcher, Hayes, & Schoendorff, 2010). What is not debated, however, is the amount of research evidence that mindfulness-based interventions have accumulated in the past decade. Indeed, a recent meta-analysis indicated that mindfulness is effective for treating many common psychological disorders, including anxiety, depression and stress, with small to moderate effect sizes (Khoury et al., 2013).

Although mindfulness connects many of the aforementioned therapies, it is possible that the term "third wave" may not. Recently, some advocates of these approaches have indicated that they do not identify themselves as third wave therapies, but instead conceptualize themselves as an extension of second wave CBT. Indeed, this led David and Hofmann (2013) to suggest that there is, in fact, only one-third wave therapy, and that is ACT.

What is acceptance and commitment therapy?

At its heart, ACT is designed to increase psychological flexibility (PF). Although when one first reads those words they can seem like complicated jargon, the definition is straightforward: "Psychological flexibility is the ability to contact the present moment more fully as a conscious human being, and to change or persist in behaviour when doing so serves valued ends" (Hayes, Luoma, Bond, Masuda, & Lillis, 2006, p. 7). In other words, when unwanted thoughts and feelings emerge, many people will try their best to avoid or suppress them. Often this means acting in ways that conflict with valued living. For example, imagine someone who avoids going to a job interview because they want to avoid feeling incompetent or anxious. The job of the ACT therapist is therefore to discover in what ways the client avoids unwanted thoughts and feelings, and then to increase their PF, in the service of helping them move towards the things that are important to them.

Within the ACT model, the attempted avoidance of unwanted thoughts and feelings is called *experiential avoidance*. Experiential avoidance is the definitional negative of PF, and according to ACT, virtually every problem that human beings face is related to or exaggerated by experiential avoidance. Indeed ACT has sometimes been labelled a treatment for an *experiential avoidance disorder* that we all have to some degree. Although the decision was made to present each disorder separately in this book for ease of access, the ACT model is actually transdiagnostic. In other words, treatments can be developed that target the reduction of experiential avoidance and can be applied to any disorder, regardless of the varying symptoms between diagnoses.

If the transdiagnostic nature of experiential avoidance were robust, then one would expect people presenting with psychological disorders to record high scores on measures of experiential avoidance. The most common measures are the first and second edition of the Acceptance and Action Questionnaire (AAQ & AAQ-2; Hayes et al., 2004; Bond et al., 2011). These Likert-type questionnaires, which aim to determine where a participant lies on the continuum between PF and experiential avoidance, have been linked to a large number of mental health problems. For example, Ruiz (2010) found 20 correlational studies of experiential avoidance and a standard depression measure (Table 2.1), such as the

Table 2.1 Correlational studies of experiential avoidance and depression with author (year), type of depression measure, n and r, first presented in Ruiz (2010)

Citation	Depression measure	n	r
Andrew & Dulin (2007)	GDS-dep.	208	0.37
Barraca (2004)	BDI	114	0.74
Boelen & Reijntjes (2008)	SCL-90 dep.	402	0.63
Boelen & Reijntjes (2008)	SCL-90 dep.	99	0.56
Boelen & Reijntjes (2008)	SCL-90 dep.	60	0.66
Bond & Bunce (2000)	BDI	97	0.66
Chapman & Cellucci (2007)	BDI-II	74	0.49
Dykstra & Follette (1998)	BDI	41	0.72
Forsyth, Parker, & Finlay (2003)	BDI	94	0.57
Gold, Marx, & Lexington (2007)	BDI-II	145	0.65
Gold, Dickstein, Marx, & Lexington (2009)	BDI	72	0.77
Kashdan & Breen (2007)	BDI-II	144	0.59
Langer, Ruiz, Cangas, & Luciano (2009)	BDI	123	0.45
McCracken & Zhao-O'Brien (2010)	BC-MCDI	144	0.69
Pistorello (1998)	BDI-II	51	0.60
Plumb, Orsillo, & Luterek (2004)	BDI	37	0.50
Polusny, Rosenthal, Aban, & Follette (2004)	BDI	304	0.51
Roemer, Salters, Raffa, & Orsillo (2005)	DAAS-dep.	19	0.40
Santanello & Gardner (2007)	BDI-II	125	0.52
Strosahl, Hayes, Bergan, & Romano (1998)	BDI	419	0.36
Tull, Gratz, Salters, & Roemer (2004)	BSI dep.	160	0.55
Tull & Gratz (2008)	DASS-21	391	0.55
Weighted mean		3323	0.55

Table 2.2 Correlational studies of experiential avoidance and anxiety with author (year), type of anxiety measure, *n* and *r*, as presented in Ruiz (2010)

Citation	Anxiety measure	*n*	*r*
Andrew & Dulin (2007)	GAL-anxiety	208	0.43
Barraca (2004)	sTAL	114	0.76
Boelen & Reijntjes (2008)	SCL-90 anxiety	60	0.57
Boelen & Reijntjes (2008)	STAI	99	0.59
Forsyth, Parker, & Finlay (2003)	ASI	94	0.71
Greco, Lambert, & Baer (2008)	MASC	513	0.58
Karekla, Forsyth, & Kelly (2004)	STAI	54	0.16
Kashdan, Barrios, Forsyth, & Steger (2006)	ASI	382	0.37
Kashdan, Barrios, Forsyth, & Steger (2006)	STAI	382	0.65
Langer, Ruiz, Cangas, & Luciano (2009)	ASI	132	0.46
Roemer, Salters, Raffa, & Orsillo (2005)	DAAS-anxiety	19	0.47
Stewart, Zvolensky, & Eifert (2002)	ASI	205	0.52
Strosahl, Hayes, Bergan, & Romano (1998)	BAI	419	0.58
Toarmino, Pistorello, & Hayes (1997)	BAI	202	0.35
Tull, Gratz, Salters, & Roemer (2004)	BSI anxiety	160	0.53
Weighted mean		3043	0.52

Beck Depression Inventory, second edition (BDI-II: Beck, Steer, & Brown, 1996). In these 20 studies, with a total participant count of 3323 people, correlations between experiential avoidance and depression were found to range between $r = 0.37$ and $r = 0.77$.

Ruiz (2010) also found 14 studies exploring the relationship between experiential avoidance and standard measures of anxiety (Table 2.2). With a total of 3043 participants, correlations were found ranging from $r = 0.16$ to $r = 0.76$. Since the ranges are quite broad and participant counts vary from the different studies, a weighted correlation was constructed from the studies, resulting in $r = 0.55$ for depression and $r = 0.52$ for anxiety.

Thus far, these tables show that people with high levels of experiential avoidance also tend to present with high levels of depression and anxiety. However, research has been conducted that links experiential avoidance to almost every psychological disorder that exists. Indeed, if you find yourself with some spare time, then search for "experiential avoidance and correlations" on Google Scholar and you will get about 3250 hits. The sheer amount of this research means that it is outside the scope of this volume to describe it further.

If experiential avoidance underpins all psychological disorders, then reducing experiential avoidance in order to facilitate valued action can be thought of as *the* target in any ACT-based intervention. The most

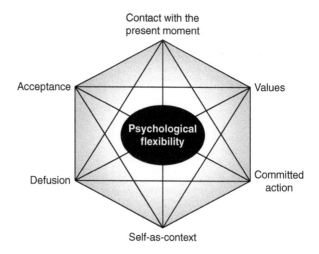

Figure 2.1   The Hexaflex or psychological flexibility model

common ACT model, the Hexaflex, includes six core processes that interact to increase PF (see Figure 2.1): (1) *Contact with the present moment* (sometimes called *self-as-process*) involves attending to perceptions, thoughts and emotions every moment in a fluid and flexible way. (2) *Acceptance* is the ability to embrace any inner experience in order to pursue meaningful living. (3) *Defusion* means being able to see all thoughts simply as thoughts, rather than seeing thoughts as having literal truth that can control one's behaviour. (4) *Self-as-context* is perhaps the most challenging process to a novice, as it is the full experiential realization that you are not just what you call "I", but the unique perspective throughout the time that you have had that experience. Any stories that you fill your "I" with are not really you, but thoughts about you. (5) *Values* refer to verbally constructed, broad life domains that are chosen by the individual as being meaningful to work towards. (6) *Committed action* means acting in accordance with your self-chosen values, and returning to those actions and values when psychological inflexibility pulls you away from them. ACT defines mindfulness as the first four of these processes: contact with the present moment, acceptance, defusion and self-as-context, while values and committed action fall under the rubric of behaviour activation (Wilson & DuFrene, 2009).

It should be noted that the Hexaflex is not the only model for ACT or PF. Indeed, Polk and Schoendorff (2015) presented another prominent

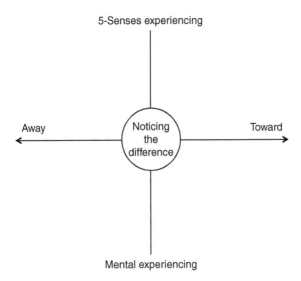

Figure 2.2   The matrix, an alternative ACT conceptualization model

approach in the form of a matrix. As you will see in Figure 2.2, the 2 × 2 matrix is divided by two intersecting lines wherein clinical work can be conceptualized. The horizontal line is seen as the "skin" of the individual, and at the top of the matrix, something akin to "5 senses" is written, meaning that the top part of the matrix deals with events in a physical, non-mental world. At the bottom is written "inside", or something alluding to the mental world of the client. The bottom part thus concerns private events. The vertical line is a functional division between left ("moving away from") and right ("moving toward"), where moving away from what the client is struggling with and moving towards what the client would value are contrasted. The client and the therapist then collaborate in sorting things the client does into the four quadrants, separating out functional actions from dysfunctional control strategies.

In FACT (Focused ACT), a brief intervention adaptation of the model (Strosahl et al., 2012), there is likewise a trinity of analysis and intervention processes illustrated by pillars of openness, awareness and engagement. Openness means being open to private experiences (thoughts and feelings) rather than fighting them needlessly, corresponding to the Hexaflex processes of defusion and acceptance. Awareness means being aware both of the present moment and being able to take perspective of your self; similar to the contact with the present moment and self-as-context processes of the Hexaflex. Engagement is being involved in values-driven activities, as in values and committed action in the Hexaflex (Strosahl et al., 2012).

No matter how ACT is conceptualized, the underlying principles remain the same; reduce avoidance and increase PF so that clients can move in valued directions. After reading these pages, you may have come to the same conclusion about ACT that many people do when they first encounter the approach; that it is very simple. What many do not realize is that ACT was decades in the making and arose out of a philosophical and theoretical premise. As we now hope to illustrate.

3
The History of ACT

Zettle (2005) divides the development of ACT into three periods: (1) formative, where an early version of ACT was created; (2) transitional, where, unsatisfied with current accounts of language, Hayes and colleagues established relational frame theory (RFT; Hayes, Barnes-Holmes, & Roche, 2001) as an updated behaviour analytic alternative; and (3) a dissemination and investigative period where ACT was further developed as an evidence-based treatment model.

The formative period started in 1976 when Rob Zettle became the first graduate student of Steven Hayes, a newly appointed faculty member at the University of North Carolina at Greensboro. Zettle and Hayes agreed on the importance of human language (including private use of language i.e. thinking) and rule-governed behaviour in the development of psychological problems. They also shared dissatisfaction with the cognitive and mechanistic models for language processes (Zettle, 2005). Trained in behaviour analysis, they first tried to use Skinner's notion of verbal behaviour in their analysis of language (Skinner, 1957). At this point, it is important to clarify a common misunderstanding regarding Skinner's *radical* behaviourism; that it is uninterested in cognition. That is true for the metaphysical or *methodological* behaviourism of Watson, but not of Skinner's radical behaviourism. Skinner notes, "my toothache is just as physical as my typewriter" (Skinner, 1984, p. 552) to illustrate that allowance could be made for the analysis of "private events" that are only observable to the individual experiencing them (i.e. thoughts, emotions, memories and bodily sensations). In doing so, however, cognition is judged to be a behaviour that could be influenced in the same way as overt behaviour; that is, the radical behaviourist position maintains that only events that one is able to manipulate directly (antecedents and consequences) are valid in an analysis with the goal of prediction and influence of a behaviour. Therefore, as "private events" are behaviours themselves, they too can be influenced by altering the antecedents and consequences surrounding them, but cannot be causes of behaviour themselves in the analysis. Even though cognitions are not deemed sufficient as causes to overt behaviour or action, as they are behaviours themselves, they can be seen to have a behaviour–behaviour-controlling effect on the overt behaviour of a person. Thus, not causing, but controlling (Hayes & Brownstein, 1986).

As confusing at this may seem, it is philosophically sound within the radical behaviourist paradigm. By extending the definition of behaviour to include private (covert) events that are observable by the individual experiencing them, behaviour analysts reduced the risk of stopping their analysis before reaching the goal of "prediction and control" that is fundamental in behaviourism. Thus, while one behaviour can result in another behaviour, it does so because it itself was caused by certain outside events. Mentalistic causes, on the other hand, are causes that are not directly observable. So while the thought "I'm just awful at everything" can in some ways be seen as influencing one to give up prematurely, the construct of confidence cannot, as it is outside the observable world of the individual. What remains then is to explain the contextual variables that give rise to both overt and covert behaviours, and even more importantly, those that support a controlling relationship between the two behaviours. Because it is plausible that the socio-verbal environment we humans have around ourselves is such a context, and therapy is an example of a particular type of socio-verbal context, it should be possible to create a specific socio-verbal context inside therapy wherein this behaviour-behaviour control is reduced. That is, to create a context where the thought "I'm just awful at everything" is not a cause for inaction, but just an event among other events at that time, like the smell of your apartment, the sound of cars outside or the weight of your clothes on your body.

In developing this particular verbal context, or treatment model, as we might recognize it, the team elaborated upon Skinner's model for rule-governance (Skinner, 1966, 1969). This elaborated model eventually came to be important in the development of RFT, but we will come to that later. It's still 1982, and the development of the treatment takes a name based on a component in the new cognitive therapy proposed by Beck (1979): *comprehensive distancing* (CD). Distancing is important in the cognitive model as it enables a person to view their thoughts from a distance, thereby allowing them to evaluate them much as one would if another person spoke them. Zettle and Hayes (1982, p. 107) write:

Beck has emphasized the necessity of clients being able to "distance" themselves from their beliefs, or stated somewhat differently, being able to observe their own verbal behaviour from the perspective of a listener. Over time, self-rules are often not viewed critically by the person formulating them. The usual listener behaviours in a public interaction (e.g., examining the credibility of the statement and the speaker; recognizing that reality and descriptions of it may not always be in harmony; and so on) may be gradually suspended for self-rules. This has several destructive effects. For example, augmenting functions may occur automatically – in a sense, the person-as-listener may become needlessly emotionally invested in a particular view of things . . . Distancing allows self-rules to be viewed as behaviour of an organism – not as literal reality or as the organism itself.

CD was the precursor to ACT. As such, it has many of the components found in ACT: the emphasis on deliteralizing language; aspects of self-work, included after 1985; and defusion via the inclusion of exercises and metaphors. It lacked values clarification and committed action, at least as they appear in ACT today, relying instead on a homework approach similar to behaviour activation (e.g. Jacobson et al., 1996). So in fact, this proto-ACT was based on rule-governance of behaviours. However, Skinner's account for rule-governed behaviour was not judged to be functional (Hayes, 2014, personal communication); it lacked a functional account for what a "rule" was.

The transitional period (the mid-1980s to the first ACT book in 1999) saw a refinement of the therapeutic model as well as development of RFT. During this period, a number of different names were tried for the model; CD was thought of as being too narrow and too similar to cognitive therapy. Between 1986 and 1991, "a contextual approach to psychotherapy", "a contextual approach to therapeutic change" as well as "contextual therapy" (Zettle, 2005) were used in parallel to "comprehensive distancing". In 1991, the first paper using "acceptance and commitment therapy" was presented at the conference of the AABT in New York (Wilson, Khorakiwala, & Hayes, 1991).

Describing the history of RFT is beyond the scope of this volume, as is a comprehensive account of its clinical relevance. If you wish to learn more about RFT, Niklas Törneke's (2010) *Learning RFT* is a good place to start. For more advanced readers, both the original RFT book (Hayes, Barnes-Holmes, & Roche, 2001) and the latest edited research review (Dymond & Roche, 2013) are among the most comprehensive resources. However, it is important we dedicate some space to the influence of RFT, as its development moved the community of researchers into a post-Skinnerian account for language and cognition, and cemented ACT as separate from the therapies that preceded it.

Beyond the influence of Skinnerian radical behaviourism, Steven Hayes ran his lab together with Aaron Brownstein. Brownstein brought *stimulus equivalence,* a phenomenon attributed to Sidman (1971), into the development of RFT. Sidman had been able to show that a person with developmental difficulties who had been taught to match spoken words (i.e. the sound "cat") to text (i.e. the word "cat") and spoken words to pictures (i.e. of a cat) would spontaneously and reliably, with high experimental control, match text and picture. This phenomenon, which describes that if we are taught A = B and B = C then we can also match A = C without direct reinforcement of this behaviour, is called "derived stimulus relations" and it is something that goes beyond ordinary operant principles in the behaviour analysis that is based on animal research.

RFT began with studying stimulus equivalence, but moved fairly quickly into looking at other forms of relating. By this time, Hayes' lab had moved to the University of Nevada at Reno and was collaborating with Dermot Barnes (and later Barnes-Holmes when he married Yvonne Barnes-Holmes, née Holmes) at the National University of Ireland at Maynooth. Incorporating all manner of relations between phenomenon, coordination, difference, comparison, hierarchy and later, perspective (called *deictic* framing in RFT), RFT researchers expanded on stimulus equivalence and operant psychology until it could be termed "a coherent post-Skinnerian account for language and cognition" (Hayes, Barnes-Holmes, & Roche, 2001). In RFT, relational framing is seen as a generalized operant. A generalized operant is an operant which has become automatic to the organism, but like when we learn to walk or ride a bicycle, the constituent parts of the behaviour need not be separately reinforced. These parts in a *relational frame* (which should be seen as a discriminate section of analysis and not as a reified thing that resides somewhere metaphysically) are mutual entailment, combinatorial entailment and transformation of stimulus functions. Mutual entailment can perhaps be seen most clearly in how humans learn the equivalence between objects and their names. For example, a newborn baby will orient its gaze towards light. An attentive adult will name the object (e.g. "lamp") and eventually the child may be able to name the object "lamp". Further, when asked "where is the lamp?" orienting behaviour of the child to the lamp will be reinforced. Throughout thousands of such experiences of object–name/name–object pairings, the generalized operant of mutual entailment becomes firmly established. We know that if A = B, it follows that B = A. Similarly trained is combinatorial entailment (A = C), of which an example is given in Sidman's study (1971) above. The difference in RFT is that these forms of responding follow any relation, rather than just equivalence. For example, if Nic is younger than Andreas, and Steve is older than Andreas, we can derive that Steve is older than Nic (as well as Andreas being younger than Steve, Andreas being older than Nic and Nic being younger than Steve).

Transformation of stimulus function then explains that if we think that age gives wisdom, and we know something about the wisdom of Andreas (a function of the stimulus "Andreas"), this will transform inside this relational frame to both Nic and Steve, respectively; that is, Nic is the least wise. Transformation of stimulus functions explains that once a relation is formed, our relationship to the stimulus is changed. Consider the above example but imagine we change the context by saying that "youth gives vitality". Suddenly, other stimulus functions transform; that is, Nic shows most vitality.

This simple concept explains the generativity in human language that Skinner could never account for; that is, combinations of previously learned relations derive into new relations. These principles can also explain the availability of negative emotional reactions, because thinking of a negative event by mutual entailment will bring an emotional reaction. This easily gives rise to self-rules (Hayes, Barnes-Holmes, & Roche, 2001, chapter 7) about not thinking about the negative event. However, trying to protect oneself by not thinking about a negative event is futile, as has been shown by many researchers to date (e.g. Wegner & Gold, 1995; Hooper, Saunders, & McHugh, 2010; Hooper, Stewart, Duffy, Freegard, & McHugh, 2012). Also, rule-governed behaviour had been shown to make behaviour insensitive to direct contingencies, which is a probable account of why so many people stay loyal to unworkable coping strategies.

The development of RFT and its relationship to the developing ACT model is shown in the differences between the original CD model and the account in the 1999 book *Acceptance and Commitment Therapy: An Experiential Approach to Behaviour Change* (Hayes, Strosahl, & Wilson, 1999). Because RFT emphasized that language processes were both dysfunctional and functional, using values was introduced as a guide to behavioural homework and goal formulation. "Values" was defined at this point as "verbally constructed life consequences" (Hayes Strosahl, & Wilson, 1999, p. 207), and the idea was that while using the distancing techniques of defusion, contact with the present moment, acceptance and SAC to improve dysfunctional verbal control, there are often direct consequences of behaviour that are dysfunctional too. In order to harness this possibility for functional effects of language, ACT included values clarification and committed action.

The dissemination and investigation period (2000–present), according to Zettle (2005), has begun and is ongoing, now that the fully developed ACT model is being tested in the treatment of mental health issues. Indeed, one could describe Part II of this book as a description of the dissemination and investigative period thus far.

4
Contextual Behavioural Science

Another crucial feature of ACT is that it belongs to a wider scientific field that terms itself contextual behavioural science (CBS; Hayes, Barnes-Holmes, & Wilson, 2012). CBS has grown around the community that developed ACT and its close relative RFT. ACT and RFT are historically linked and have been co-developed for many years (Zettle, 2005; Hayes, Barnes-Holmes, & Wilson, 2012). The relationship between these models has been defined as reticulated, meaning that they influence and enhance each other while remaining autonomous models in their own right (Hayes, Barnes-Holmes, & Wilson, 2012). The strength of the reticulated relationship with RFT, from the perspective of ACT, is that RFT has generated both basic and applied data with 174 published articles between 1986 and 2010 (Dymond, May, Munnelly, & Hoon, 2010). The strength of the reticulated relationship with ACT, from RFT's perspective, is that ACT can be seen as a way of talking about these phenomena in a way that is easier in a clinical or everyday setting, without resorting to too much jargon.

In the reticulated model of CBS, there is an assumed philosophy of science for RFT and ACT: functional contextualism (Hayes, Strosahl, & Wilson, 1999). This is commonly framed in comparative opposition to other psychotherapies, for example CBT, which most closely embodies critical rationalism (Hofmann & Asmundson, 2008). Functional contextualism is often explained according to the *worldviews* of Stephen Pepper (1942). Pepper argued that worldviews or *world hypotheses* can be defined by their underlying root metaphor and truth criterion. In this analysis, functional contextualism is a form of contextualism (Hayes, Hayes, & Reese, 1988). Pepper defines contextualism as having a root metaphor of *the act in context*; that is, the unit of analysis is the act situated historically and situationally in a context from which it is inseparable. This is similar to the three-term contingency in traditional applied behaviour analysis (ABA). Without the behaviour, there is nothing that an antecedent precedes, and without the antecedent, there is no behaviour. Similarly, as the antecedent signals the availability of the consequence, there is no consequence without any of the others. Thus, all three terms are dependent on the other two and can never be identified independently. Contextualism also has a *pragmatic* truth criterion, which can be simplified as "successful working". A pragmatic truth criterion is not Machiavellian in that "the end justifies the means", but the end, or the goal, is what the analysis or means is measured against. The truth-value in an analysis or hypothesis, according to contextualism, is judged by how effectively it facilitates reaching a stated goal. This makes it important to have a goal set before you analyse. The goal of functional contextualism is "prediction and influence, with precision, scope, and depth, of whole organisms interacting in and with a context considered historically and situationally" (Hayes, 1993).

In "prediction and influence with precision, scope and depth", influence means that a behaviour needs to be explained in terms of contextual phenomena whose manipulation can be shown to move behaviour in predicted and desired directions (Ruiz, 2010). This is often mistaken for some physically manipulable phenomenon, but thanks to the reticulated relationship with RFT, this shows up in a focus on the verbal (as defined by RFT) context (including thoughts, memories and feelings) of the psychological struggle. ACT views thinking the same way it views any behaviour. That is, functionally, as acts taking place in and with a specific context (Hayes, Strosahl, & Wilson, 2011). Precision means that fewer analytical concepts should be used to explain phenomena; for example, defusion is called defusion regardless of whether it is used in the treatment of eating disorders or psychosis. Scope means theoretical concepts can be applied to a breadth of phenomena, just like ACT has been applied to many different areas, from occupational health services and productivity to addiction. Finally, depth means that concepts should be coherent with regards to data from other levels of analysis, such as biological or sociological studies.

Functional contextualism is fundamentally a-ontological, meaning it neither assumes that there exists a reality outside the analysis, nor that there is not one. This is because the goal is what the analysis is being evaluated against, not how it corresponds to an outside reality. One interesting and clinically helpful way in which this shows up is that the therapist does not need to argue over realism with the client. The client chooses the values that function as the goal in ACT; the therapist facilitates but does not control that choice. In a defusion exercise, the therapist might simply ask the client to consider if their thought is "helpful" in moving them towards those values, not how realistic or truthful they are; hence, it is a-ontological. Steps that make up committed actions in those valued directions are likewise evaluated in terms of how well they move the client towards their values (Hayes, Strosahl, & Wilson, 2011).

It is timely to note at this point that clinicians do not need to fully understand the importance of functional contextualism or RFT in order to do ACT. However, we would encourage any reader to take the time to learn these philosophical and theoretical underpinnings, as many ACT clinicians describe how knowing these things has improved their practice.

5
The Importance of Empirical Research

In order help people in need find effective treatment, and to aid service providers/policy makers in selecting treatments, many of the major psychological associations of the West have accepted some form of evidence-based practice policy for their members. For example, the American Psychological Association, the American Psychiatric Association, the Cochrane Reviews and the National Institute for Health and Clinical Excellence (NICE) all have guidelines as to what constitutes "evidence-based". This development has walked hand in hand with third-party financers of care, such as governmental bodies or health insurance firms, demanding that treatments are empirically supported. In fact, similar movements are happening in related disciplines, such as social work and education.

Although the idea of evidence-based practice is a step in the right direction, the story is not straightforward. One problem is that evidence-based practice is defined somewhat differently in different systems, which means an approach can be listed as an empirically supported treatment (EST) according to one authority, but not according to another (David & Montgomery, 2011). This has resulted in numerous debates about the evidence base of various approaches in the treatment of psychopathology. A second problem is that evidence-based practice is usually defined solely on outcome studies, without taking the underlying theory or mechanisms of change into account. This means that unscientific theories may become evidence-based treatments, as they are likely to tap into processes that contribute to therapeutic success (David & Montgomery, 2011). Although not yet part of the evidence-based practice definitions, the use of mediation and moderation analyses will increase in the coming years; that is, more evidence will begin to emerge not just showing that a treatment works, but how and why it works (Kazdin, 2007).

As you will read later in this volume, ACT is now considered evidence-based by a number of authorities, mainly due to the increasing amount of outcome studies displaying its effectiveness. However, hopefully this book will allow you to appreciate the great depth and breadth of ACT research, over and above the impressive number of RCTs. To help the newer members of the psychological research community navigate their way through research terminology, we have included a brief glossary below.

Baseline	Pre-intervention level of a dependent variable. For example, what the participant scored on a depression inventory before the experiment began.
Case study	A study of only a few particular clients. Case studies usually have richer content, which may be more applicable in a therapy setting. However, they can be limited in their generalizability.
Clinical significance	Defined by Jacobson and Truax as "the extent to which therapy moves someone outside the range of the dysfunctional population or within the range of the functional population" (1991, p. 12).
Component research	The study of the individual parts of a treatment package.
Correlational research	Research looking at the relationship between two variables. For example, the relationship between psychopathology and experiential avoidance. NB: correlation is not causation and does not imply which variable is more dependent on the other.
Dependent variable (DV)	The variable that is impacted upon by the independent variable (IV), for example, depression score (DV) impacted on by a brief ACT treatment (IV).
Effect sizes	A type of analysis that estimates the magnitude of the effect of a treatment. Differs from significant tests in that they are less sensitive to sample size. Often the data used in a meta-analysis.
Follow-up	Repeating outcome measures at a specified time after the end of treatment so as to find out if the results are lasting.
High end-state functioning	A subclinical or normative score on a clear majority of indices of the disorder measured (e.g. normal range on six out of eight measures of depression).
Intent to treat analysis	Analysis that uses the baseline data from participants as post-intervention data for non-completers.

(Continued)

Mediational analysis	Analyses how a mediator, that is a third variable, explains how or why the IV affects the DV (e.g. changes in experiential avoidance may mediate depression scores).
Moderating variables	Moderating variables are variables that are neither dependent nor independent but that affect the strength or direction of a relationship between the independent and dependent variable in a study (e.g. baseline scores of experiential avoidance may moderate the effectiveness of treatment).
Multiple baseline design	Research design that introduces the intervention after increasing lengths of baseline for different participants, used to ensure that effects seen are not caused by time passing or external variables that may be shared with other participants.
Open trial	A type of study where both the participant and researcher know if the participant is getting the active treatment or control. Other types are single-blind studies, where only the researcher knows which condition a participant is in, and double blind, where neither participant nor researcher knows if the participant is in the active or control condition.
Preliminary trial/Pilot study	Smaller scale studies conducted at the beginning of a research stream. These are usually conducted prior to large-scale investigations.
RCT	The current gold standard of empirical intervention research, the *randomized controlled trial* is a type of study using, at least, one active condition and one control condition and wherein participants are randomized to the different conditions.
Reliable change	Indicates that changes seen from initial scores to follow-up are unlikely to have occurred due to chance.
Treatment as usual (TAU)	Common control condition that is usually less controlled and consists of the normal treatment for that population. As such, it may include highly efficacious treatments.
Waitlist control group	Common control condition in which the participants receive no intervention during the study period, but are offered the intervention once the study period is over.

Part II
Empirical Research

6
Depression

In order for any therapy to be taken seriously by clinicians throughout the world, it is pivotal that the therapy be useful in treating the most severe mental health problems. Although later in this volume much effort has been made to explore the variety of areas in which ACT has been applied, arguably it is most important to display its utility in treating the core problems of depression, anxiety disorders and serious mental illnesses. The next three chapters will aim to introduce you to the research published in these areas.

Depression is a good place to start this empirical journey for two reasons. First, depression is the major mental health problem in the Western world with a high prevalence rate (Gotlib & Hammen, 2009) and substantial economic implications (Cuijpers et al., 2007). Second, given that this book is aiming to detail the journey of ACT research, not many would know that the first RCT in ACT involved patients with depression, making this the perfect place to begin.

Zettle and Hayes (1986) compared CT and CD in the treatment of depression. As mentioned earlier, CD was the early formulation of the ACT model. It involved three themes: challenging the control agenda, questioning the causal relationship between thoughts and behaviour, and developing the ability to distance oneself from one's thoughts. In each condition, six depressed women received 12 individual weekly sessions. Results indicated that although both groups improved, CD was most effective at reducing depression (assessed via outcome measures and interviewer-rated depression) at post-treatment and two-month follow-up. Most importantly, the researchers found that the improvements made in each condition occurred via different mechanisms, where those in the CD condition experienced greater reductions in believability. This classic paper underpins much of the

ACT rationale that was to develop in the following 20 years. For example, it was one of the first empirical articles to suggest that many clients enter therapy with reasons for their behaviour that point towards emotions ("I cannot go to the shopping centre because it makes me anxious"). According to the authors, statements like these have become accepted and reinforced by the verbal social community such that they exert control over behaviour. But from the viewpoint of a radical behaviourist, the behaviour of reason-giving cannot by itself cause subsequent behaviour (a behaviour–behaviour relationship), but is maintained via environmental contingencies (reinforcement of reason-giving behaviour). Therefore, instead of attempting to alter someone's feelings or thoughts, which is arguably difficult to achieve, it is possible to change one's relationship to them such that a therapist can encourage a client to experience anxiety and still make that trip to the shopping centre. Interestingly, from this early stage, the authors inadvertently pointed towards issues of measurement that you will see mentioned time and time again in this volume; the utility of most clinical interventions is measured by symptom reduction, yet ACT does not aim to reduce symptoms, but to lower the way in which negative thoughts and feelings exert influence over behaviour.

The take-home message from the Zettle and Hayes (1986) study was that CD decreased depression and reason-giving via lowering believability, without reducing the frequency of unwanted private events. Zettle and Rains (1989) later conducted a similar study when they compared the application (in group format) of CD, CT and CT without distancing (PCT: partial cognitive therapy) to depressed clients. Although results indicated that all three interventions significantly reduced depression, Zettle, Rains and Hayes (2011) later suggested that those in the CD group tended to record better scores on the depression outcome measure (the BDI), while those in the PCT group came in a close second. This is an interesting finding, as CD involved explicit distancing and PCT involved no distancing, yet both approaches worked, therefore suggesting that clinical improvement might have occurred via different pathways. This assertion was substantiated by the finding that dysfunctional attitudes were reduced in both CT groups but not in the CD group. In other words, although clinical improvement was made in the CD group, like Zettle and Hayes (1986), this did not happen due to altering the form or frequency of negative thoughts.

Given that these studies were published so early, it is not surprising that the authors did not run a formal mediational analysis to determine the mechanisms underlying clinical improvement. Luckily they did keep the data, so were able to publish a re-analysis of both papers 20 years later. Hayes et al. (2006) found that outcome differences between the CD and CT conditions in the Zettle and Hayes (1986) article were mediated by the believability of depressive thoughts and not the occurrence of these thoughts. Zettle et al. (2011) published a slightly more detailed re-analysis of the Zettle and Rains (1989) article. In the original paper, the results did not take into account participants who dropped out of therapy. The re-analysis therefore adjusted for the impact of missing data. Additionally, it ran a mediational analysis to determine the mechanisms of change. The intent-to-treat analysis indicated that CD produced greater reductions in depression, while the process analysis found that believability (cognitive defusion) mediated the outcome effects observed at follow-up. Importantly, the occurrence of depressive thoughts and levels of dysfunctional attitudes were not mediators.

These early research studies are hugely important. Historically, they set the ACT ball rolling, but empirically, these studies displayed that ACT has utility in treating depression and that clinically relevant change occurs via different pathways to those observed in cognitive-based approaches. This is important to bear in mind when reading ACT investigations of the other diagnoses presented in this volume. For information about one of the leading researchers in the CBS community, please see Dr Rob Zettle's researcher profile and his thoughts about the future for ACT research.

Researcher profile: Dr Rob Zettle

Dr Rob Zettle is currently Professor of Psychology at Wichita State University, where he has been on the faculty since his Doctorate in Clinical Psychology from the University of North Carolina at Greensboro in 1984. While at North Carolina, he became the first doctoral student of Steven Hayes before Dr Hayes relocated to the University of Nevada, Reno. Interestingly, Dr Zettle completed his clinical internship at Aaron Beck's Center for Cognitive Therapy at the University of Pennsylvania, hence the comparisons of ACT and CT in his early work. Depression, and to a lesser degree, anxiety disorders, has remained the primary focus of Dr Zettle's clinical research and practice, which culminated in *A Clinician's Guide to Using Acceptance & Commitment Therapy in the Treatment of Depression* (see Further Resources). Dr Zettle has also maintained a basic research program centring on analogue and laboratory-based studies of various processes that contribute to PF. He is also on the full or consulting editorial boards of four psychological journals and is one of four co-editors (along with Steven Hayes, Dermot Barnes-Holmes and Anthony Biglan) of the upcoming *Wiley Handbook of Contextual Behavioural Science.*

Ultimately, future research in ACT, in my view, must continue to focus on doing a better job of preventing and alleviating human suffering. Outcome research in ACT has a good track record so far, but we can and must do better. For example, if I consider my own clinical research, ACT for depression is at least comparable to cognitive therapy (CT) and, especially on some follow-up measures, could even be argued as being more efficacious. However, whatever edge may exist for ACT, it is not so large that I would feel comfortable in always recommending ACT over CT. There may well be some clients, for example, for whom ACT is the preferred treatment option, and others for whom CT is the better choice. This is, of course, an empirical question that can only be addressed by investigating possible moderating variables through treatment utility designs. To address this specific question and the larger issue of optimizing the impact of ACT more generally, and its treatment of depression, in particular, more work is needed in developing sensitive and ACT-consistent measures of outcome, mediating/process, and moderating variables. In other words, my concern is that efforts to make ACT more powerful may be limited by progress in measurement refinement and development.

Outcome measures

In some sense it can be argued that ACT has been playing the randomized clinical trial game at a disadvantage because most of the key outcome measures comparing it against CBT and other interventions focus on symptom reduction (e.g. BDI-II scores). More measures relating to quality of life, day-to-day functioning (work productivity/absenteeism), utilization of health services, etc. need to be developed, if necessary, and included in RCTs. ACT has held its own vs. traditional CBT in symptom reduction. Let's see how it fairs when quality of life/valued living measures are also routinely evaluated.

Mediating/process measures

Advances in process research are of necessity linked to progress in the development of more sensitive and ACT-consistent outcome measures. The focus should be on what processes "move" outcome variables that are of most relevance to ACT (increases in valued living) rather than on symptom reduction (reduced depression), which has been the case so far for the most part. These ACT-sensitive and consistent outcome measures ideally should be ones that can be administered and tracked on a session-by-session basis to permit the use of time-series analyses and single-subject designs examining the temporal relationship between changes in process and outcome measures. To do so, brief state measures of ACT-relevant processes that can be efficiently administered will need to be developed insofar as most process measures in ACT (e.g. AAQ-II) appear to be self-reports of dispositional variables. Ideally, at least some of these micro-level process measures would also be more behavioural in nature (perhaps based on codings of in-session client verbal and nonverbal behaviour) and less dependent on self-report and susceptible to demand characteristics.

Moderating variables

Because many of the purported process measures developed by ACT researchers appear to be more dispositional than state-like, less work may need to be undertaken in developing ACT-consistent instruments assessing moderating variables that may be related to treatment responsivity than is the case with outcome and process measures. Rather, the challenge appears to be consistently using such measures in undertaking a coherent program of treatment utility research to determine what measures can potentially be used in making therapeutic decisions that optimize outcome. For example, pre-treatment levels of client psychological flexibility may have implications in choosing whether ACT or some other option should be the treatment of choice. Even if ACT is selected, do pre-treatment AAQ-II scores moderate therapeutic outcome, and if so, what adjustments could accordingly be made in treatment delivery? The rather modest body of research that has examined possible moderating relationships involving ACT, in particular, and psychotherapy, more broadly, suggests that a "strengths-based" rather than "remediational" model may more common. If so, those with relatively lower pre-treatment, rather than higher levels, of psychological inflexibility may be better candidates for ACT. This seemingly counterintuitive finding – the more effective treatment is the one that builds on existing strengths and not the option that seeks to remediate weaknesses – if anything, underscores the need for more moderating and treatment utility research by ACT investigators.

Although a couple of important conceptual articles were published highlighting the potential importance of acceptance-based methods in the management of depression (Dougher & Hackbert, 1994; Kanter, Baruch, & Gaynor, 2006), it was not until 2007 that further research was conducted to investigate the utility of ACT in this area. Forman, Herbert, Moitra, Yeomans and Geller (2007) conducted an RCT comparing ACT with CT in the treatment of both depression and anxiety. Results indicated that both treatment groups made significant improvements. However, no differences were found between the groups in any of the tested domains, some of which included outcomes measures of depression and anxiety, clinician-assessed functioning and quality of life. Process analyses once again suggested that the outcomes were mediated by different mechanisms. The CT group experienced increases in observing and describing one's experiences, while the ACT group recorded reductions in experiential avoidance.

This article is a wonderful contribution to the literature. Firstly, the introduction brilliantly makes the argument that altering cognition does not necessarily mediate clinical improvement, thereby setting the stage for the investigation of ACT and its processes. Secondly, the research controlled for many potential confounding variables: it measured therapist allegiance, employed novice therapists who took part in both conditions – and these therapists had similar training for both CT and ACT –, it took measurements of therapist treatment adherence, and measured therapist and client expectations and efficacy ratings for treatment. However, the authors suggest that two major improvements could be made: the inclusion of a waitlist control group and post-treatment follow-up tests. Forman et al. (2012) revisited the clients included in their earlier study 1.5 years later and found that those in the CT group were more likely to have maintained their gains than those in the ACT group. Although the authors suggest that the counterintuitive nature of ACT may make it more difficult to apply long term and that ACT may be more useful with clients who suffer from severe depression, the results do raise the possibility that the influence of ACT treatment becomes weaker with time.

Around the same period as Forman et al. (2007) published their research, Lappalainen et al. (2007) compared ACT with CBT in the treatment of participants presenting mostly with mood disorders. In RCT format, their study required 14 trainee therapists to treat one client within each model, which meant that 28 participants took part in the study. Results indicated that although both groups improved, those exposed to the ACT model showed better symptom improvement in general mental health, depression and social functioning. In terms of processes of change, acceptance mediated outcome in the ACT group. The authors note that the primary aim of the study was to determine if therapists with as little as six hours training (plus supervision) in ACT could cause clinical improvement in clients. The results showed that this was the case, even though the trainee students felt less knowledgeable about ACT and fearful when using it. Although not its primary aim, the study did involve comparing the efficacy of CBT and ACT, and running the study in this format overcame a number of therapist-related issues that can often affect research of this kind. In other words, therapist allegiance and experience with each model were not factors that could have affected outcome, instead the content of both models were compared on their own merit, and ACT showed promising results.

Following the 20-year hiatus between the original classic studies of Zettle and the impressive contributions of Forman et al. (2007) and Lappalainen et al. (2007), there was somewhat of an explosion of research investigating the utility of ACT for depression between 2009 and 2014, especially after findings suggested that experiential avoidance may be linked to the development of psychopathologies such as depression (Fledderus, Bohlmeijer, & Pieterse, 2010; Gird & Zettle, 2010). Hayes, Boyd and Sewell (2011) published an open trial that compared ACT versus TAU in a depressed adolescent population in a psychiatric setting. Participants received 15–20 hours of each approach in individual session format. Results suggested that those in the ACT group recorded a greater reduction in depressive symptoms at post-treatment and follow-up, although the follow-up data is tentative due to the low number of participants. The results of the study prompted Livheim et al. (2014) to conduct a further investigation using ACT with adolescents. The researchers found that an eight-session ACT program functioned to decrease depressive symptomology and increase PF in an Australian school setting. Interestingly, in the same article, the eight-session protocol was applied in RCT format to reduce levels of stress in an adolescent sample in Sweden, an example of the transdiagnostic nature of ACT.

In addition to the work conducted with adolescents, Bohlmeijer, Fledderus, Rokx and Pieterse (2011) conducted an RCT to determine if ACT could be useful to adults suffering from mild to moderate distress. In other words, ACT was used as an early intervention strategy with those in the initial stages of depression. Early intervention studies could be crucial, as catching the disorder at a premature stage could function to reduce the development of clinical depression (Hosman, Jane-Llopis, & Saxena, 2005). Results indicated that eight two-hour weekly group sessions of ACT significantly reduced depression compared to the waitlist control group. In fact, in many cases, participants moved below the cut-off score for depression on the outcome measure and these effects were maintained at three-month follow-up. The researchers additionally found that reductions in experiential avoidance mediated reductions in depressive symptomology.

In a similar study, Fledderus, Bohlmeijer, Pieterse and Schreurs (2012) also applied the ACT model to those with mild or moderate depression. However, instead of administering ACT in individual or group format, clients were aided via a self-help program. This study is important because many clients suffering with the initial stages of depression may prefer to avoid face-to-face counselling. This RCT employed three groups. The first group were given a self-help program based on the ACT book *Living to the Full* (Bohlmeijer & Hulsbergen, 2008), the second group were given the same self-help book and extensive email support, and the third group was a waitlist control group. Results showed that those in the ACT groups experienced a significant reduction in depressive symptoms at post-intervention and three-month follow-up. The ACT groups also showed improved scores on anxiety, fatigue and quality of life measures. Interestingly, there were no differences between the ACT group with minimal support and the ACT group with extensive email support, suggesting that ACT-based self-help interventions can be rolled out with minimal therapist cost. Overall, the findings of this study are valuable because they display that self-help tools are useful in reducing the risk of developing clinical depression. In terms of process, the authors found that experiential avoidance decreased and mindfulness increased in the ACT groups across treatment. However, Fledderus, Bohlmeijer, Fox, Schreurs and Spinhoven (2013) later ran a formal mediational analysis and found that PF mediated the reported outcomes.

In the past few months, Bohlmeijer, Lamers and Fledderus (2015) have published a wonderful paper in which they returned to the data of their 2012 self-help intervention study and re-analysed it in terms of whether the ACT intervention could increase "flourishing" in its participants. Although a mentally healthy person would be defined as someone without a mental illness, flourishing refers to people with positive levels of well-being. Results indicated that those in the ACT conditions reported significantly greater increases in flourishing when compared to those in the waitlist control group. As the explicit aim of ACT is to enable people to live a meaningful life, research assessing flourishing, rather than the absence of mental illness, may increase in the coming years.

Carlbring et al. (2013) conducted another study where ACT was delivered unconventionally. In RCT format, the researchers administered Behavioural Activation (BA) plus ACT to depressed patients over the internet. The package was an interactive eight-week protocol in which the participants were exposed to BA and ACT in seven modules. Participants additionally had a supplementary CD-ROM with mindfulness and acceptance instructions. Although there was minimal contact between the participant and a supporting therapist, participants were encouraged to contact their therapist once a week for about 15 minutes of feedback and support. Results indicated that compared to the waitlist control group, those who received the internet protocol experienced significant reductions in depression, such that in the treated group, 25% of participants fell below a score of ten on the BDI-II (a score indicating remission). The figure was only 5% for the waitlist control group. What is most interesting about this research, as we move forward in a technological world, is that the effect sizes found for the internet-delivered protocol were similar to those seen for face-to-face psychotherapy in the depression literature. This finding, which mirrors earlier work in which a self-help book alone had the same effect as a self-help book with therapist support (Fledderus, Bohlmeijer, Pieterse, & Schreurs, 2012), has intriguing implications for the need for clinical and counselling psychologists. In the discussion, the authors rightly suggest that future research should attempt to measure the processes powering clinical improvement; that is, it was impossible to know if BA or ACT was most helpful in reducing depression.

Lappalainen et al. (2013, 2014) recently published two studies that further assess the utility of ACT in unconventional format. In the first study, the researchers gave an ACT-based intervention, which was delivered to men with mood problems, via a combination of technologies, ranging from a smartphone App to a website and telephone counselling. Results indicated that compared to the waitlist control group, the participants who received the intervention reported decreased depression and increased self-rated health and working ability. The researchers point out that adherence to the variety of technologies used in the study was high, which suggests that technology is one way in which access to psychological therapies can be improved. In the second study, the researchers built on this idea of a technological approach to therapy by directly comparing an internet-delivered ACT protocol with face-to-face ACT. Results indicated that although both approaches lowered depressive symptomology and improved general well-being after treatment and at 18-month follow-up, the minor differences between the groups actually favoured the internet-delivered protocol.

Three more studies of note have been conducted in the past few years. Firstly, Peterson and Zettle (2009) found that clients who presented with co-morbid depression and alcoholism recorded significant reductions in levels of depression following exposure to a 12-week ACT program. In this study, although the TAU group experienced similar reductions in depression, it was found that ACT required a shorter treatment phase and a smaller dose of individual therapy, which has practical and economic implications. The study also found that lower levels of experiential avoidance in the ACT group correlated to the successful treatment outcomes. Secondly, Folke, Parling and Melin (2012) conducted a preliminary study investigating the utility of ACT in treating unemployed individuals on long-term sick leave for depression. Using a small sample, results indicated – from pre-treatment to 18-month follow-up – that participants who received one individual session and five group sessions of ACT recorded significant improvements on measures of depression, general health and quality of life, compared to a control group. However, no differences emerged between the groups with regards to sick leave and employment status, which is a shame given ACT's emphasis on behaviour. Thirdly, an RCT published in the *Zahedan Journal of Research in Medical Sciences* showed that ACT and CT both improved depressive symptomology (Tamannaeifar, Gharraee, Birashk, & Habibi, 2014). Although no quality of life measure or long-term follow-up was included, research of this kind is exciting, as it shows that ACT may be useful with people of various cultures. Indeed, this is not the only non-Western ACT investigation described in this volume.

Overall, the evidence that ACT is useful in treating depression is growing at a startling rate, with the majority of research conducted within the past five years. During this time, a variety of approaches have been employed: open trials, feasibility studies, RCTs, studies in which depression is co-morbid with other issues, interventions that have been delivered in different formats and interventions that have been conducted with a range of sample sizes across the world. The evidence consistently suggests that ACT is useful. However, there is no doubt that more research evidence investigating ACT's utility in treating this particularly important and prevalent disorder is being conducted as these words are typed onto this page. For further information about the type of research that is likely being conducted, see Dr Raimo Lappalainen's researcher profile below.

Researcher profile: Dr Raimo Lappalainen

Dr Raimo Lappalainen, PhD, is Professor in Clinical Psychology and Psychotherapy at the Department of Psychology, University of Jyväskylä, Finland. He has acted as the vice head and the head of the Department of Psychology between the years 2008–2013. Raimo is a licensed psychotherapist and he has over 25 years of experience of CBTs, with expertise especially in third wave CBT and ACT. Raimo is author of more than 100 scientific articles and books. His main research interests are the development of brief psychological interventions based on ACT, especially for depression, including web- and mobile-based interventions for depression, well-being and wellness management.

An overall observation that I have made during the 15 years I have been working with ACT is that the principles and methods of ACT are highly effective and well-accepted among clients. Our research group has run several ACT interventions for depression but also developed and tested ACT interventions for weight management, stress, student well-being, sleep disorders, sports, physical inactivity and persons using sign language.

Although the scientific evidence has grown rapidly, there is still work to do to investigate the methods and effects of this approach. Even though there are many critical voices pointing out weaknesses of the quality of ACT research, it is probably wise to continue doing research in a broad scale. When looking back and taking into account all the research evidence produced internationally during a relatively short period of time, some of the criticisms may feel unfair. Interestingly, there is an increasing number of scientific and evidence-based observations coming from other, non-ACT-based, fields such as research concerning eating and weight management, supporting the ACT model and its processes – whatever those may be called in future. Perhaps we need to look more into this evidence.

One of the challenges of the ACT approach is how the main ideas and methods are described, presented and applied. Although the main point of contextual psychology is very basic, e.g. the inter-action between the environment, actions, thoughts and emotional reactions, it may sometimes be difficult to convince beginners who start using these methods (such as the "milk, milk" exercise). Maybe we need to work more to solve this gap between science and common language.

On the basis of our data and experiences a large amount of clients benefit from brief ACT-based interventions. However, a small minor-ity of clients reporting mild to moderate depression symptoms (around 10–20%) do not benefit from these brief ACT face-to-face and web interventions. Some of the things that characterize this group of clients seem to be that they do not believe or rely on the intervention methods right from the beginning. They do listen to the therapist and study the materials provided during the intervention, but they do not apply or use the methods/exercises in their everyday life. Some of them show great interest for understanding their problems, but they do not take any actions for change. Overall, the evidence for acceptance and values-based interventions for depression disorders is increasing, and we need to understand more of those clients not benefitting from these interventions.

The six core processes in the ACT model need to be clarified and probably reformulated. For example, there are indications that it matters in which way mindfulness skills are trained or applied. Thus, within the concept of mindfulness, there are different skills or ways of behaving that may have different effects on the out-come (for example, depression symptoms). Increased knowledge of the processes associated with depression (and other psycholog-ical problems) is crucial for developing more precise intervention methods.

There are probably several ways to do this. As an example, new types of process measures need to be developed, sophisticated statistical procedures are needed to differentiate different dimensions of psy-chological flexibility, and single case and laboratory studies should also be used. Perhaps we need to look more towards RFT and for the existing "basic" research (not necessarily laboratory research) to develop further assessment tools for understanding better the crucial processes of psychological change.

It is clear that web- and mobile-delivered psychological interven-tions are effective in facilitating well-being. Interventions based on principles derived from contextual psychology provide a very rich and flexible source of methods for these interventions. In fact, ACT interventions seem to be very suitable for developing technology-based interventions. As an example, it is relatively easy to produce audio recordings using metaphors. The point is that contextual psychology provides a scientific base for developing "mini-interventions" to be used in web and mobile interventions. This is a field that we need to look more closely into.

7
Anxiety Disorders

According to the National Institute of Mental Health (NIMH) website, anxiety disorders can be characterized as any prolonged feelings of fearfulness and uncertainty that manifest themselves more intensely than the brief discomfort caused by stressful events. The NIMH suggests that 18% of adults in the USA will suffer from an anxiety disorder in a given year. Given this high prevalence rate, any research investigating ways to improve the lives of those suffering is worthwhile. Although somewhat late to the game, in the past ten years researchers have begun to investigate the utility of ACT in treating many psychological issues that fall under the umbrella of anxiety disorders. These include obsessive compulsive disorder (OCD), generalised anxiety disorder (GAD), social anxiety disorder (SAD), post-traumatic stress disorder (PTSD) and panic disorder (PD).

Obsessive compulsive disorder (OCD)

Exposure with ritual prevention (ERP) and exposure with ritual prevention plus cognitive therapy (ERP-CT) represent two of the more popular and empirically supported treatments of OCD. As ERP involves exposing the client to the exact stimulus that causes them anxiety while preventing the compulsive behaviours that often provide a sense of relief, it is unsurprising that issues have arisen with the approach. First, the dropout rate is around 25% (Abramowitz, Taylor, & McKay, 2009), second, 5%–22% of participants refuse to take part once they have been informed of what ERP involves (Foa et al., 2005) and third, practitioners seem reluctant to use it (Olatunji, Deacon, & Abramowitz, 2009). Given that these issues have been reported in previous exposure research (Levitt, Brown, Orsillo, & Barlow, 2004), ACT may be useful in increasing exposure in OCD while avoiding the high dropout and overt refusal rates (Twohig et al., 2010). Interestingly, from an early stage, ACT was acknowledged to be an exposure-based approach: "it gives people an opportunity to practice experiencing anxiety without also struggling with anxiety" (Hayes, 1987, p. 365). However, whereas in ERP, response flexibility is gained through potentially aversive formal exposure exercises, exposure is facilitated in ACT through the development of PF.

Over the past decade, ACT has accrued evidence displaying that it is useful in the treatment of three OCD-related disorders: skin picking (Twohig, Hayes, & Masuda, 2006b), Tourette syndrome (Franklin, Best, Wilson, Loew, & Compton, 2011) and trichotillomania (Twohig & Woods, 2004; Woods, Wetterneck, & Flessner, 2006; Flessner, Busch, Heideman, & Woods, 2008; Crosby, Dehlin, Mitchell, & Twohig, 2012; Fine et al., 2012). However, it was not until 2006 that ACT would be applied to OCD itself. In this study, Twohig, Hayes and Masuda (2006a) achieved impressive findings with four participants in a multiple baseline design. Results showed that ACT moved OCD severity from the clinical to non-clinical range with the gains maintained at three-month follow-up. In the following years, two further case studies were published, one showing ACT to be useful in treating an adult with OCD (Twohig & Whittal, 2009) and a second showing the utility of ACT in treating a young learning-disabled person experiencing obsessive thoughts (Brown & Hooper, 2009). Additionally, a process analysis found PF to be an important mechanism of change in the treatment of OCD (Twohig, Whittal, Cox, & Gunter, 2010). Encouraged by some of these investigations, Twohig et al. (2010) ran the seminal investigation in this area and later published the first RCT of ACT for OCD.

In their study, 41 participants received eight sessions of ACT, while 38 participants received eight sessions of progressive relaxation treatment (PRT). PRT was chosen as it had been used in past research as a credible control condition (Fals-Stewart, Marks, & Schafer, 1993). Although formal exposure interventions are consistent with the ACT model, any element of exposure was removed from the eight-week protocol in order to ensure that uniquely ACT processes were powering the results. Findings indicated that those in the ACT condition not only experienced a significant reduction in OCD severity compared to the PRT condition, but they maintained these gains at three-month follow-up. Interestingly, those in the ACT condition who presented with mild depression also recorded significant improvement on the depression inventory and the quality of life measure. Finally, analysis of the process measures suggested that constructs important in ACT (PF and defusion) showed greater improvement in the ACT condition.

There are three points worth mentioning about this research. First, participants received only eight one-hour sessions of ACT, which can be contrasted with the average of 25 hours that ERP usually requires (Abramowitz, Taylor, & McKay, 2009). This suggests that ACT may be more efficient in producing clinically relevant change than an empirically supported approach like ERP. Second, the authors make particular effort to provide a detailed description of the ACT protocol that they employed. This would be helpful to any clinician or researcher in the area as it provides a template of how to use ACT with this population. Third, although this version of ACT for anxiety explicitly removed any exposure components, ACT can and will use exposure in treatment (as exemplified in a conceptual paper by Tolin, 2009).

Since the seminal investigation, two studies employing a multiple-baseline across participants design have been conducted on those suffering from OCD. Dehlin, Morrison and Twohig (2013) displayed that ACT was useful in treating scrupulosity-based OCD, while Armstrong, Morrison and Twohig (2013) found a 40% mean reduction in self-reported compulsions in a small sample of adolescents. Furthermore, a case study was recently published in the *Iranian Journal of Psychiatry* displaying that ACT reduced OCD symptom severity through increases in PF (Vakili & Gharraee, 2014); another example of ACT's cross-cultural appeal. Finally, research has also targeted the relationship between individual components of ACT and OCD; Wetterneck, Lee, Smith and Hart (2013) found that following one's values was a significant predictor of reduced OCD severity.

Although these results are promising, it is important to note that research investigating ACT in the treatment of OCD is still in its infancy. For a detailed description of the ACT approach to OCD, see the recent review papers by Bluett, Homan, Morrison, Levin and Twohig (2014) and Twohig, Morrison and Bluett (2014). And for information about the leading researcher in this area, please see Dr Michael Twohig's researcher profile below.

Researcher profile: Dr Michael Twohig

Michael P. Twohig, PhD, is Associate Professor of Psychology at Utah State University in Logan, UT. He completed his undergraduate and master's work at the University of Wisconsin-Milwaukee (UWM) where he focused on behaviour analysis with humans and non-humans. While many people influenced him at UWM, Doug Woods had a major impact on Mike and his career. He then went on to the University of Nevada to work with Steven Hayes and researched ACT. After one year doing CBT for anxiety disorders at the University of British Columbia Hospital, he started at Utah State University and has been there since. He runs a research team that focuses on basic and very applied behavioural work, including ACT. He has been successful and influential, with many publications including books, federal and foundation grants, and he speaks nationally and internationally on ACT and related topics.

I am truly interested in helping those who struggle psychologically. This can include those with psychological disorders, but it also includes those who are just trying to have fun days but their minds get in their way. This functional way of thinking certainly comes from my training in behaviour analysis. Thus, while I may do a lot of work on particular diagnosable disorders such as OCD or trichotillomania, I am more interested in the processes involved in these disorders than the disorders themselves. I find the ways people get caught in their thoughts amazing; while it can be frustrating, I like helping people find motivation in tasks they find really aversive; and, I am intrigued by the way a harmless stimulus can bring on such fear for certain people. That is why I consider myself a behavioural researcher more than an "OCD" researcher.

I have a great group of graduate students and our future will involve engaging in research across the whole spectrum of behaviour analysis and contextual behavioural science. We will write about philosophy; study the parameters of basic behavioural principles such as extinction; research how language works using relational frame theory; test components of ACT; develop measures to guide our work; and, we will do a lot of treatment studies. Our work will be more diverse than many know about with studies currently running on anxiety, substance dependence, cultural issues, stigma, eating disorders, as well as work on parenting and the fidelity of treatments. This is one of the reasons I have always loved the behavioural way of looking at things: if it involves human actions we probably have something to say about it!

Generalized anxiety disorder (GAD)

Clients presenting with GAD exhibit tension, chronic and persistent worry, significant distress and psychosocial impairment (Kessler, Walters, & Wittchen, 2004). Additionally, due to its chronicity, research suggests that sufferers do not improve without treatment (Yonkers, Warshaw, Massion, & Keller, 1996). However, when clients with GAD do receive psychological support, it is statistically one of the least success-fully treated anxiety disorders (Brown, Barlow, & Liebowitz, 1994). Even CBT has only achieved modest results with this population (Waters & Craske, 2005), suggesting that there is room to develop other treat-ment approaches. In response to this need, Susan Orsillo and Lizabeth Roemer have published a number of interesting investigations in which acceptance-based behaviour therapy (ABBT) has been used to treat GAD.

Although ABBT is an integration of various mindfulness and acceptance-based approaches, including dialectical behaviour ther-apy (DBT), mindfulness-based cognitive therapy (MBCT), traditional behaviour therapy and ACT, the protocol used by these researchers includes substantial overlap with the ACT model. For example, much of this body of work stems from a conceptual article and a correlational study in which experiential avoidance was linked to the development and maintenance of GAD (Roemer & Orsillo, 2002; Roemer, Salters, Raffa, & Orsillo, 2005). As described in an earlier chapter, experien-tial avoidance is an integral principle within the ACT model; therefore, the use of any method that aims to reduce experiential avoidance is entirely ACT consistent. More evidence for the overlap between the two approaches can be seen in the first empirical investigation of ABBT for GAD. Orsillo, Roemer and Barlow (2003) employed ten sessions with their clients. At least seven of those sessions were explicitly ACT, while the other three sessions were also ACT consistent. The results showed that ABBT improved quality of life and psychosocial functioning, with all four clients making significant life changes throughout the course of therapy. This piece of research was the first study in a line of care-fully designed investigations that nicely illuminate how to adhere to the scientific method.

Following the initial case study, Roemer and Orsillo (2007) conducted a small open trial in which 16 participants with GAD were individ-ually given four 90-minute and twelve 60-minute sessions of ABBT. Results indicated that participants showed reduced severity of GAD symptoms, anxiety, depression and experiential avoidance. They also displayed significant improvement in quality of life at post-treatment and three-month follow-up. Given these positive results, the researchers later published the seminal study in RCT format. Roemer, Orsillo and Salters-Pedneault (2008) allocated 15 participants to receive the same ABBT protocol from their open trial, while 16 participants were entered into a waitlist control group and were later offered the treatment package. Utilizing an intent-to treat analysis, results revealed large treatment effects on GAD symptoms and depression. Medium effects were found for symptoms of anxiety and quality of life. These gains were observed from post-treatment to nine-month follow-up. Incredibly, 78% of treated participants no longer met the criteria for GAD post-treatment and 77% achieved high end-state functioning (i.e. they recorded scores on outcome measures that were within normative ranges). These proportions either stayed constant or increased across post-treatment and follow-up. At the time, the researchers found that the important psychological processes of experiential avoidance and mindfulness also changed throughout the course of therapy, however a further process analysis of the data conducted by Hayes, Orsillo and Roemer (2010) found that participants receiving ABBT experienced increases in acceptance and engagement of valued activities, and that these changes were related to decreases in worry and increases in end-state functioning and quality of life.

This line of research is engaging, methodical and meticulous. In the articles described above, the authors thoroughly detail the theoretical rationale for why ABBT might work with GAD and go on to test these hypotheses, conducting appropriate analyses and describing their approach in detail. It is, therefore, no surprise that recent investigations have followed their lead. Wetherell et al. (2011) investigated the utility of an ACT-only package in treating GAD. In their study, 21 clients, all of whom were of an older age, either received 12 weekly individual sessions of ACT or CBT. Results indicated that although participants in both treatment groups recorded lower levels of depressive symptoms and worry at post-treatment, no difference emerged between ACT and CBT. In the discussion, the authors go on to raise some interesting points that should provide the basis for future research. Firstly, the effect sizes in their study were much lower than typical effect sizes seen in comparable ACT research. They suggest that with older participants, perhaps a treatment protocol that focuses on values and committed action would be most beneficial. Secondly, they detail that these results were found even though novice therapists administered ACT, suggesting that ACT is relatively easy to learn and therefore easy to disseminate.

Two recent RCTs have added to the research evidence of ACT for GAD. Firstly, Hayes-Skelton, Roemer and Orsillo (2013) conducted the largest scale investigation in the area. The researchers compared 16 sessions of ABBT ($n = 40$) with the active comparison condition of applied relaxation ($n = 41$), which is an empirically supported treatment for GAD. Results indicated that both groups recorded improvements across outcome measures at post-treatment and follow-up, but no differences emerged between the groups. Secondly, Avdagic, Morrissey and Boschen (2014) assigned 51 participants to receive a group-based six-week intervention in either ACT or CBT. The results mirrored those from Wetherell et al. (2011) and Hayes-Skelton et al. (2013). Namely, participants in both groups recorded significant treatment gains that were maintained at three-month follow-up, but few differences emerged between the two approaches. Having said that, one difference that did emerge is very interesting. At post-treatment, 78.9% of participants in the ACT condition reported reliable change in worrying symptoms, compared to 47.4% in the CBT condition. However, at follow-up, both groups recorded equal amounts of reliable change (60%), suggesting that the CBT condition had improved between post-treatment and follow-up, whereas the ACT condition had worsened. This finding has implications for the utility of ACT when the client is no longer in contact with the therapist and resembles the results from the Forman et al. (2012) study described in the chapter about depression.

Nevertheless, Hayes-Skelton et al. (2013) suggested that their results show ACT to be a viable option in the treatment of GAD. Indeed, when you combine their study with the other research investigations presented in this chapter, the case becomes stronger. However, the combined number of participants who have taken part in these studies is relatively low, meaning that more will have to be done in the future. How that research might look is described below in the combined researcher profile of Dr Susan Orsillo and Dr Lizabeth Roemer.

Researcher profile: Dr Susan Orsillo and Dr Lizabeth Roemer

Dr Susan Orsillo is Professor of Psychology at Suffolk University in Boston, MA. Author of over 100 journal articles and book chapters, and co-editor of two books, her current research is focused on both exploring the role of emotional response styles, most notably experiential avoidance, in maintaining psychological difficulties and developing prevention and treatment programs that integrate acceptance and mindfulness with evidence-based behavioural approaches. Dr Lizabeth Roemer is Professor of Psychology at the University of Massachusetts Boston in Boston, MA. She has also published over 100 journal articles and book chapters, and co-edited two books on the role of emotion regulation, mindfulness and experiential avoidance in a range of clinical presentations, and the use of acceptance-based behavioural therapies and behaviour therapy more generally. Together, with the support from the NIMH, Drs Roemer and Orsillo have developed an acceptance-based behavioural therapy for generalized anxiety and co-morbid disorders, and have examined its efficacy and mediators and moderators of change. They are currently examining adaptations of this approach across varied contexts. They are co-authors of *Mindfulness-and Acceptance-Based Behavioural Therapies in Practice* and *The Mindful Way through Anxiety*. Drs Orsillo and Roemer regularly conduct training workshops around the country and throughout the world, and their work has been featured in *Elle Magazine, Oprah.com, the Shambhala Sun, Women's World Magazine, FIRST for Women Magazine* and on the Audrey Chapman Show. More information about their work, including guided mindfulness exercises, is available at http://mindfulwaythroughanxiety book.com.

The field has made great strides in developing acceptance-based behavioural therapies, like ACT, that help clients make clinically significant and meaningful changes in their lives. Although more research on common and unique mediators of outcome, as well as the temporal course of change in ABBTs and other CBTs is clearly warranted, we have made some good progress identifying the core mechanisms of change. One important next step will be identifying methods by which clinicians can be trained in flexibly adapting ABBTs to fit the idiographic needs of particular clients in unique settings that are informed by this research. Using our growing knowledge of the most powerful mechanisms of change underlying ABBTs to develop efficacious case formulation-based training models is the best way for us to increase the dissemination and implementation of these potentially powerful forms of therapy.

Along these same lines, more research is needed on how best to adapt ABBTs (again through emphasis on targeting mechanisms of change efficiently) so they can be used in varied contexts, such as primary care, school and university settings, and community settings for health promotion, reducing the barriers of stigma and accessibility that diminish use of psychotherapy in many communities. Finally, continued research on cultural considerations in ABBTs (e.g. Fuchs, Lee, Roemer, & Orsillo, 2013; Sobczak & West, 2013) and ways to use ABBTs to address the psychological impact of racism and other forms of discrimination (e.g. Graham, West, & Roemer, 2013; West, Graham, & Roemer, 2013 *see under Stigma for reference*) will be essential contributions to the literature.

Social anxiety disorder (SAD)

Research investigating ACT for social anxiety tends to fall into two categories: ACT for public-speaking anxiety and ACT for generalized social anxiety. Block and Wulfert (2000) published the first study about the use of ACT with public-speaking anxiety. The researchers randomly assigned students with phobic anxiety to receive four 1.5-hour sessions of ACT or CBT (a waitlist control group condition was also included). As the participant numbers were low (three or four in each condition), formal statistical analyses were not possible. However, trends in the data suggested that those in the ACT and CBT groups both experienced reductions in phobia/fear and increases in willingness. The CBT condition showed a slightly greater reduction in anxiety while the ACT condition showed a slightly greater increase in willingness. By highlighting the low power of the study and its reliance on self-report, these authors paved the way for further research in this area: more participants and a behavioural measure of public speaking.

Over a decade after Block and Wulfert (2000) published this initial study, England et al. (2012) incorporated these recommendations by comparing six two-hour group sessions of ACT-based exposure ($n = 21$) to standard habituation-based exposure ($n = 24$) in the treatment of public-speaking anxiety. Results firstly indicated that participants felt the ACT protocol to be as credible and acceptable as standard habituation-based exposure. Furthermore, the ACT condition was found to be more effective in helping participants to achieve diagnostic remission by six-week follow-up. In both conditions, improvements were seen in self-reported confidence in public speaking and social skills on a behavioural-speaking task, as assessed by an independent observer. The results from these two studies suggest that ACT has some utility with helping clients manage public-speaking anxiety. However, there is much room for more research of this kind.

Traditionally, CBT has fared well in the treatment of generalized social anxiety. However, researchers have recently become concerned that some clients who receive CBT make minimal improvement (Hofmann & Bögels, 2006) and experience continued dissatisfaction with life (Eng, Coles, Heimberg, & Safren, 2005). Given these developments, effort has been made to investigate the utility of acceptance-based approaches with this population. As with all other disorders in this book, social anxiety is thought to be maintained by experiential avoidance that takes one away from valued activity (Herbert & Cardaciotto, 2005). For example, imagine a client values having intimate relationships but avoids going on first dates due to social anxiety. In this situation, the person is moving away from their value in the service of avoiding unwanted thoughts and feelings. This role of experiential avoidance in social anxiety disorder has been supported by some interesting research from Todd Kashdan's lab. For example, Kashdan et al. (2013) measured experiential avoidance associated with social anxiety in real-time every-day interactions, by use of a handheld device. The results suggested experiential avoidance in social situations is what distinguishes people with SAD from those without SAD, more so than social anxiety itself. In a similar study, Kashdan et al. (2014) found that those who engaged in experiential avoidance, in an experimentally manipulated intimate situation, were more likely to experience social anxiety for the remainder of that interaction. ACT directly targets experiential avoidance by training the client to be psychologically flexible enough to move in valued directions in spite of negative private content.

Three preliminary studies have been conducted that display noteworthy results. Ossman, Wilson, Storaasli and McNeill (2006) gave participants ($n = 12$) ten two-hour sessions of ACT in group format. Results showed that throughout treatment, participants gradually scored higher on a questionnaire that measured how effective they felt at pursuing valued social relationships. Interestingly, participants recorded a marked increase on this measure at three-month follow-up, suggesting that the effects were maintained long after the intervention. Additionally, participants showed lower levels of experiential avoidance and social phobia following treatment. Dalrymple and Herbert (2007) later conducted a similar experiment where 19 participants completed a 12-week program, except they received individual one-hour sessions that combined exposure therapy with ACT. Results found that from pre-treatment to three-month follow-up, significant improvements occurred in social anxiety symptoms and quality of life. The authors were quick to point out that although it is a bonus that social anxiety symptoms were reduced, this is not of utmost importance in ACT treatment. Indeed, what was most encouraging about the results of this study is that, following the intervention, the participants reported avoiding social situations less, despite still experiencing anxiety. Finally, the researchers observed that the psychologically important process of experiential avoidance significantly decreased across the course of the study. Kocovski, Fleming and Rector (2009) conducted a third preliminary study when they recruited 29 participants to complete 12 two-hour group sessions in which they received a combination of ACT and exposure. The researchers firstly found that the participants felt the ACT approach to be acceptable.

They also found that the participants in the study recorded reductions in social anxiety, depression and rumination. All of the gains were maintained at three-month follow-up. Finally, the authors found that the important processes of acceptance and mindfulness were mediators of clinically significant treatment change.

The major problem with the aforementioned research in this area is that they did not include a control condition. In an effort to address this problem, Kocovski, Fleming, Hawley, Huta and Antony (2013) ran the first RCT in the area. Participants received 12 weekly two-hour sessions of group ACT ($n = 53$), group CBT ($n = 53$) or were assigned to a waitlist control group ($n = 31$). Results indicated that post-treatment, both the ACT group and the CBT group showed a reduction in social anxiety symptoms compared to the control group; these gains were maintained at three-month follow-up. The amount of change was meaningful for both groups with around 40% of treatment completers reaching the criteria for clinically significant change. No difference emerged between the two active groups, suggesting that ACT may be just as effective as CBT in treating SAD. However, the results were not perfect in terms of the psychologically active processes measured throughout therapy. For example, participants in the CBT group did not record greater cognitive reappraisal than the ACT or control groups, the CBT group recorded similar gains in acceptance and mindfulness as the ACT group and the ACT group did not record greater improvement in valued living compared to the CBT group, none of which would be predicted. The authors suggest that these results may have occurred due to the overlaps between the ACT and CBT protocols. In the discussion, the authors provide two important pieces of information that may be helpful for other researchers in this area; firstly, they describe how smaller effect sizes are generally found for group-delivered versus individual-delivered psychotherapy. Secondly, they point out that their study relied wholly on self-report and that, in the future, behavioural measures of improvements would better reflect the predictions an ACT therapist would make for clients.

In the last year, two further investigations have been published. Firstly, Dalrymple et al. (2014) published a pilot study in which participants presenting with depression and co-morbid SAD were treated with acceptance-based behavioural treatment. Participants ($n = 38$) were given 16 sessions of ACT integrated with behaviour activation. Results showed significant reductions in depression and SAD severity over the course of treatment and moderate effect sizes were found for quality of life measures. For those of you who are interested, this is another article that nicely outlines a caveat in ACT research: although symptom reduction is the major way in which therapeutic utility is measured, symptom reduction is not the aim of the ACT model. Instead, ACT is geared towards engagement with life, and for this reason it is important that research employs quality of life measures. The authors also raise the importance of mediational analyses in clinical research to ensure that mechanisms of change are noted. They mention that Behavioural Activation and PF were related to clinical change in their clients, but in order to run formal mediational analyses, a control group would be needed.

Secondly, Craske et al. (2014) published an RCT in which ACT ($n = 29$) was compared with CBT ($n = 33$) and a waitlist control group ($n = 25$) in the treatment of social phobia. Participants in the active conditions received 12 weekly one-hour individual sessions and assessment was taken at pre-treatment, post-treatment, six-month and 12-month follow-up. Results indicated that both ACT and CBT outperformed the waitlist control group in terms of self-reported social anxiety, clinician-rated social anxiety and distress during a public-speaking task. No difference emerged between the ACT and the CBT group. In fact, the similarities between the two treatments across many of the outcome and adherence measures were somewhat uncanny. The authors did make the effort to measure moderating factors at baseline in order to determine which participants would do best with which approach. Interestingly, those with higher levels of experiential avoidance fared better in the CBT group than in the ACT group. Of further interest is that the authors suggest that those in the CBT group may have become more psychologically flexible than those in the ACT group. This is a very interesting suggestion and a wonderful indicator of why process analyses are crucial to empirical clinical research; because although the topography of treatment approaches may seem vastly different, they may be working by the same processes.

Niles et al. (2014) later published a mediational analysis using some of the data from the Craske et al. (2014) study and found that both ACT and CBT resulted in lower levels of experiential avoidance across treatment, but that greater reductions in experiential avoidance were recorded in the ACT condition. Interestingly, negative cognitions decreased in both conditions across treatment, but this happened more quickly in the ACT group. The authors, when mapping the gains made by participants against the content covered in each session, suggested that defusion in the ACT condition and behavioural exposure in the CBT condition had the most effect on reducing experiential avoidance and negative cognition. Finally, reductions in experiential avoidance mediated successful outcome, but only in the ACT group.

Overall, these results are exploratory and, as multiple authors have suggested, more will have to be done to measure the psychological processes responsible for clinically relevant improvement in studies of this kind. However, as a start, the results of the aforementioned studies investigating the use of ACT with socially anxious individuals are encouraging and no doubt they will inspire researchers to conduct further investigations. For example, only recently a study conducted in Iran, although low in participants, showed that those assigned to receive 12 sessions of ACT reported reduced social anxiety at post-intervention (Yadegari, Hashemiyan, & Abolmaali, 2014). For further information about how this research area needs to develop in the coming years, see Dr Nancy Kocovski's researcher profile below.

Researcher profile: Dr Nancy Kocovski

Nancy Kocovski, PhD, is Associate Professor of Psychology at Wilfrid Laurier University in Waterloo, Ontario, Canada, where she teaches in the area of clinical psychology and maintains an active research program focused on social anxiety, mindfulness and acceptance-based treatments, and CBT. She received her doctoral degree from York University in Toronto and completed a postdoctoral research fellowship at the Anxiety Disorders Clinic, Centre for Addiction and Mental Health in Toronto, funded by the Social Sciences and Humanities Research Council (SSHRC) of Canada. She has received funding for her work on social anxiety and mindfulness/acceptance from an Ontario Mental Health Foundation New Investigator Fellowship and an Ontario Ministry of Research and Innovation Early Researcher Award. This funding enabled Dr Kocovski and her colleagues to complete an RCT for SAD, comparing an ACT-based group with a traditional CBT group and a waitlist control group. The ACT-based protocol was revised and published as a self-help book (Fleming & Kocovski, 2013), the *Mindfulness and Acceptance Workbook for Social Anxiety and Shyness*, in order to offer this approach to the public. Dr Kocovski also works as a clinical psychologist in private practice at CBT Associates of Toronto and lives in Unionville, Ontario, Canada, with her husband and three children.

> We now have evidence for the efficacy of ACT for social anxiety, with outcomes that are comparable to traditional CBT. We are now focused on mechanisms of change, which thus far have been more similar than different for ACT compared to traditional CBT. Our hope is that

we can focus more strongly on such mechanisms to improve outcomes. We have developed a measure to assess acceptance specific to social anxiety; however, moving beyond self-report is an important future goal. We are also seeking to identify moderators of treatment outcome. Some of these questions are best answered through randomized controlled trials sufficiently powered to test for mediators and moderators. However, some questions can also be brought to the lab and tested by experimentally inducing anxiety and manipulating key hypothesized mechanisms and determining the effects on various outcomes. We are focused on such lab-based approaches to understanding how we can improve psychological flexibility among those who struggle with social anxiety. Finally, given that only about a third of those who meet criteria for social anxiety disorder actually seek treatment, methods other than the delivery of traditional psychotherapy are important. We are hopeful that our self-help book is one avenue people can take and are planning to actively evaluate its efficacy. Dissemination requires much more research attention moving forward.

Post-traumatic stress disorder (PTSD) and panic disorder (PD)

PTSD, which can be characterized as the severe stress, fear, horror and powerlessness associated with a traumatic event, has a lifetime prevalence of around 8% (American Psychiatric Association, 2000). Much research has found that avoidance of unwanted thoughts may be a causal and maintaining factor in PTSD (Orsillo & Batten, 2005), therefore treatment approaches typically involve the opposite of avoidance – exposure. Despite evidence existing in favour of exposure-based approaches with PTSD, it has not always been conclusive across all outcome measures (Rothbaum, Meadows, Resick, & Foy, 2000). Additionally, many therapists and clients avoid exposure-based approaches in PTSD because they guarantee that one will be exposed to the exact painful memories that one has spent so much time avoiding, and such a suggestion puts a question mark over how acceptable and disseminable the treatment approach is (Kazdin, 1998).

Much like for OCD, researchers felt that ACT could be used for PTSD to increase exposure while avoiding therapist and client dropout. Orsillo and Batten (2005) thoroughly describe the theoretical ideas underpinning ACT's potential usefulness in this area and how the approach might be administered to a client. However, despite describing the application of ACT via a composite case study, the paper is somewhat conceptual in nature, rather than empirical. Although Batten and Hayes (2005) wrote a similar article when they described the positive effects of ACT when applied to a client presenting with co-morbid PTSD and substance abuse, Twohig (2009) published a more recent article that is well worth reading. In case-study format, a client who had not responded to cognitive challenging and exposure was given 21 sessions of ACT (the content of these sessions is described in detail in the article). Results indicated significant reductions in PTSD severity, depression and anxiety. Process measures showed that PF improved as PTSD severity decreased, while a reduction of trauma-related thoughts and beliefs decreased by sessions 16–21. Interestingly, the authors point out that the client had experienced a significant drop in PTSD severity before any changes in the frequency of trauma-related thoughts and beliefs had occurred, suggesting that unwanted thought frequency does not have to change in order for PTSD severity to decrease.

Recent small-scale investigations have found that ACT can improve parenting in veterans suffering from PTSD (Casselman & Pemberton, 2015) and reduce symptomology among adolescents presenting with PTSD (Woidneck, Morrison, & Twohig, 2013). Additionally, Ojserkis et al. (2014) turned back the CBS clock with the finding that a brief Comprehensive Distancing (CD) intervention can reduce negative emotions surrounding moral disgust, shame and guilt in individuals with PTSD symptoms. Despite these studies, large-scale controlled investigations are lacking. What it most surprising about this is that ACT has long held strong ties with associations dedicated to the rehabilitation of veterans. We would therefore expect the emergence of more evidence with this population in the coming years. For a wonderful conceptual paper of how ACT might be useful in treating PTSD, and the way in which ACT and exposure can fit together, see the article "Using Acceptance and Commitment Therapy to Guide Exposure-Based Interventions for Posttraumatic Stress Disorder" by Thompson, Luoma and LeJeune (2013).

PD, which can be characterized by recurring severe panic attacks, is associated with marked reductions in quality of life (Keller et al., 1994) and has a lifetime prevalence of around 3% (Kessler et al., 1994). Much like for PTSD, large trials investigating the ACT approach for PD are lacking. Instead, a couple of brief intervention studies, a case study and a small-scale pilot study populate this area. Based on the finding that participants with high levels of experiential avoidance are more likely to react anxiously to a panic-inducing procedure (Feldner, Zvolensky, Eifert, & Spira, 2003), Eifert and Heffner (2003) gave participants a brief acceptance intervention before asking them to complete a carbon dioxide (CO_2) challenge; that is, a challenge in which participants are required to breathe in CO_2-enriched air. Results showed that those in the acceptance condition were less behaviourally avoidant, reported less intense fear, fewer cognitive symptoms and fewer catastrophic thoughts, in comparison to an avoidance and control condition. Levitt, Brown, Orsillo and Barlow (2004) conducted a similar study and found that participants who received a brief acceptance intervention were significantly less anxious, less avoidant and more willing to undergo a second CO_2 challenge than those in a suppression and control group.

Although the results of lab studies are interesting, López (2000) published the first attempt at using a full ACT protocol to treat a client suffering from PD with agoraphobia. After 12 sessions, the client had recovered and was discharged from therapy. However, the authors acknowledge that their use of retrospective measures could be improved and that as they have no follow-up data, there is no way to know if the ACT protocol had long-term effects. Meuret, Twohig, Rosenfield, Hayes and Craske (2012) arguably conducted the most important study in the area thus far. The researchers gave 11 clients presenting with PD (with and without agoraphobia) four sessions of ACT that heavily focused on acceptance, defusion and values-based action, followed by six sessions of traditional exposure therapy. Results indicated that clients experienced large reductions in panic-symptom severity during the ACT sessions and continued improvements were seen during the exposure phase of treatment. Participants also recorded significant reductions in anxiety sensitivity and maladaptive thoughts, and increases in mindfulness. Analysis of transcripts suggested that the clients used their newly learned ACT rationale to aid them with their panic.

This study thoroughly details the content of the ACT sessions and even provides video clips and transcripts throughout the article. In the discussion, the authors suggest their results indicate that ACT is a feasible and likely effective intervention for PD. However, they do acknowledge that without an exposure-only control condition, it is difficult to determine just how effective ACT is. For further details of the role that acceptance could play in the treatment of PD, see the conceptual article by Meuret, Wolitzky-Taylor, Twohig and Craske (2012).

General anxiety research

This section includes anxiety research that does not fit nicely into any of the previous sections. Interestingly, some of the historically and theoretically most important ACT studies in the area of anxiety disorders will be found here.

One classic study published by Zettle (2003) gave students with math anxiety either six weeks of ACT or systematic desensitization. Results displayed that although decreases in trait anxiety were only recorded by those in the systematic desensitization group, both groups displayed reductions in self-reported measures of test and math anxiety that were maintained at two-month follow-up. Crucially, the author included a behavioural measure by asking participants to complete a math test at pre- and post-intervention. However, no improvement was recorded on math performance in either condition. These results are explored in great detail in the discussion section of the paper that paved the way for future research.

For example, Brown et al. (2011) later published a study that further explored the use of ACT in this domain. These authors conducted a pilot RCT comparing CT with ABBT in the management of test anxiety. The authors note that test anxiety is a serious issue within college populations as it can severely impair performance (Rothman, 2004). Additionally, it is relatively common with the prevalence of functionally impairing test anxiety at around 20%–35% (Zeidner, 1998). In their study, Brown et al. (2011) randomly assigned students with test anxiety to receive either a two-hour CT or two-hour ABBT group workshop. In order to determine the efficacy of each workshop, the authors took a behavioural measure of test performance in addition to a number of self-report process measures. Results indicated that while the CT workshop worsened subsequent exam performance (assessed via mid-term and final exam marks), the ABBT group recorded better performance. Additionally, although both groups experienced reductions in test anxiety, the ABBT group recorded greater reductions. From an ACT perspective, the authors raise an interesting issue in the discussion; although cognitive restructuring techniques served to decrease anxiety in the short term, they did not improve performance. This is important because it contradicts the common-sense notion that one has to get rid of anxiety before one can perform optimally. ACT would hold that one can both have anxiety and perform well. However, like a lot of ACT research, the major problem with this investigation is the low number of participants.

Although research has recently been conducted in which ACT was successfully applied to a client with post-stroke anxiety (Graham, Gillanders, Stuart, & Gouick, 2014) and some strong investigations have shown the importance of ACT and PF in treating health anxiety (Eilenberg, Kronstrand, Fink, & Frostholm, 2013; Hoffmann, Halsboe,

Eilenberg, Jensen, & Frostholm, 2014), the remainder of ACT anxiety research tends to involve applying ACT to clients with mixed anxiety disorders. In other words, any person presenting with a diagnosis of any anxiety disorder qualifies for treatment. It is important to remember, at this point, that ACT is transdiagnostic; that is, it sees experiential avoidance as underlying all disorders. Therefore, any ACT protocol should be useful with any disorder, regardless of how topographically different those disorders may seem.

Eifert et al. (2009) conducted the first study in which participants of varying anxiety diagnoses were given the same 12-week ACT protocol. Using a case-study format, they found increases in quality of life and decreases in traditional anxiety and distress. All participants reported maintaining or improving on their post-treatment level of functioning at six-month follow-up. Importantly, increases in the psychological constructs of acceptance and mindfulness and decreases in experiential avoidance were reported. Codd, Twohig, Crosby and Enno (2011) ran a similar case-study investigation and reported positive results. Participants showed clinical improvements in their specific anxiety disorders that were maintained at eight-month (or more) follow-up. Interestingly, and in line with some of the research already described, throughout treatment, the participants reported less avoidant behaviour without experiencing lower anxiety; that is, the participants managed to control their behaviour more effectively in the face of difficult emotions and thoughts, suggesting that the participants had changed the way that they responded to anxiety.

Although case studies often provide the initial investigation into the utility of a therapy for a given disorder, the seminal study for mixed anxiety disorders was conducted by Arch et al. (2012), where they compared ACT with the gold-standard treatment for anxiety disorders, CBT. In the introduction, the authors note that despite experiencing considerable success (Tolin, 2010), some people who receive CBT for anxiety disorders do not respond to the treatment (Barlow, Gorman, Shear, & Woods, 2000), relapse following successful treatment, seek additional treatment (Brown & Barlow, 1995) and remain vulnerable to developing anxiety and mood disorders across the lifespan (Craske, 2003). Given the recent empirical advances that mindfulness-based therapies had been making, Arch et al. (2012) conducted an RCT to determine whether ACT could be useful in this area.

Of 143 participants, 57 were randomly allocated to receive 12 sessions of ACT and 71 received 12 sessions of CBT. The researchers, in a thorough analysis, measured participants at pre-treatment, post-treatment, six-month follow-up and 12-month follow-up on a number of questionnaires that assessed both symptoms of anxiety and quality of life. They also took treatment-credibility, treatment-adherence and therapist-competence measures. Results showed that both ACT and CBT recorded significantly improved clinical severity ratings. In other words, clinical diagnoses via interview at post-treatment found marked improvement in the participants who received ACT and CBT. Additionally, both groups of participants showed significant improvement in PF and self-reported quality of life. These gains were maintained or improved upon at both follow-up points.

Group differences also emerged; ACT participants recorded significantly lower clinical severity ratings than the CBT condition at 12-month follow-up, in other words ACT reduced anxiety symptoms better than CBT. However, at 12-month follow-up, CBT participants reported significantly higher quality of life than ACT participants. As the authors note, given that valued living is the focus of ACT, and that symptom reduction is the focus of CBT, one would expect these results to be reversed. Finally, consistent with ACT principles, participants in the ACT condition recorded significantly higher PF at 12-month follow-up. In the discussion, the authors raise several issues with the research that would need to be addressed in other RCTs of this kind. Firstly, participants in the CBT condition received face-to-face therapy sessions while those in the ACT condition mostly had Skype sessions. Secondly, the authors suggest it would be important to make more effort to determine the reason for high attrition rates, in order to assess whether people dropped out due to their dissatisfaction with the treatment. Thirdly, they encourage the use of a TAU comparison condition to gauge the efficacy of both treatments.

The authors conclude the article by stating that ACT is most certainly a viable treatment for anxiety disorders. They also point to a brilliant conceptual paper by Arch and Craske (2008) that highlights the way in which ACT and CBT may have similar underlying processes and that it is therefore no surprise that they might perform similarly on outcome studies. Arch et al. (2012) further point out that it is only via the use of mediational analyses that it will be possible to see the psychologically important constructs affecting clinically relevant improvement. In order to explore this, Arch, Wolitzky-Taylor, Eifert and Craske (2012) used some of the data from Arch, Elfert et al.'s (2012) RCT to run a mediational analysis comparing changes in cognitive defusion and anxiety sensitivity in participants who were allocated to receive either ACT or CBT. Results suggested that cognitive defusion (and not anxiety sensitivity) represents an important source of therapeutic change, as it mediated post-treatment ratings of worry, depression, behavioural avoidance and quality of life. Interestingly, it did this in both the ACT and CBT groups. In other words, the participants in the CBT group, despite having a protocol that does not explicitly target fusion, recorded lower cognitive defusion scores at post-treatment and these scores significantly mediated worry. Subsequently, Swain, Hancock, Hainsworth and Bowman (2014) found similar results when assessing mechanisms of change within a population of anxious adolescents. Specifically, increases in defusion and acceptance were found in both the ACT and CBT groups. In the discussion section of both articles, the authors nicely argue that present-day CBT and ACT may have similar underlying pathways.

In addition to mediational analyses, researchers are beginning to test under what circumstances various therapies work best; that is, they look to see if clients with certain baseline characteristics are likely to benefit from treatment. For example, Wolitzky-Taylor, Arch, Rosenfield and Craske (2012) found that clients with co-morbid mood disorders show greater improvement with ACT when compared to CBT. Additionally, in a recent study, Davies, Niles, Pittig, Arch and Craske (2015) found that ACT outperforms CBT on people who score high on behavioural avoidance pre-experimentally. However, moderation analyses are still uncommon in the psychotherapy literature. In the coming years we hope to see an increase in both analyses of moderation and mediation, as researchers seek to target the contextual factors that make interventions more powerful and the active mechanisms of change that cause clinically relevant improvement. For further details on how the area can move forward, see Dr Kristy Dalrymple's researcher profile below.

Researcher profile: Dr Kristy Dalrymple

Kristy L. Dalrymple, PhD, is Director of Adult Psychology at Rhode Island Hospital and the Miriam Hospital, and Associate Director of the Outpatient Psychiatry Practice at Rhode Island Hospital. She is also Assistant Professor (Research) in the Department of Psychiatry and Human Behaviour at the Warren Alpert Medical School of Brown University in Providence, Rhode Island. She received her doctorate from Drexel University in Philadelphia, Pennsylvania, and completed a clinical research postdoctoral fellowship in the Clinical Psychology Training Consortium at Brown University. Her primary research interests include developing novel psychosocial treatments for depression and anxiety, particularly acceptance-based treatments, and the assessment and treatment of individuals in routine practice settings (including outpatient and partial hospital settings). Her research on developing acceptance-based treatments for co-morbid depression and social anxiety has been funded by a Young Investigator Award from the Brain and Behaviour Research Foundation, as well as a career-development award from the NIMH. Dr Dalrymple has published over 70 articles and book chapters on topics including social anxiety, depression, acceptance-based treatments for mood and anxiety disorders, mindfulness, clinical characteristics of individuals experiencing depression and social anxiety in routine practice settings, and co-morbid obesity and psychological problems. Dr Dalrymple currently serves as an Associate Editor for the *Journal of Contextual Behavioural Science*.

Important strides have been made in examining the efficacy of ACT for anxiety problems, with studies indicating that ACT is at least as efficacious as other manualized treatments for a variety of anxiety problems (see Bluett et al., 2014 *under OCD in the reference section,* for a review). Preliminary work on mediation has found that PF, cognitive defusion and anxiety sensitivity may be potential mediators of treatment effects in ACT (Bluett et al., 2014). Preliminary data on moderators also show that individuals with co-morbid mood disorders at baseline experience greater improvement with ACT compared to CBT (Wolitzky-Taylor, Arch, Rosenfield, & Craske, 2012). The number of RCTs for anxiety problems is increasing, although many of the early studies in this area were open trials or utilized waitlist control group conditions. The temptation may be to call for additional studies that compare ACT to traditional CBT or other active treatments to examine differential efficacy; to some degree, more of these studies may be useful, but certain modifications that are more consistent with the ACT philosophy may be required. One potential modification is the determination of the primary dependent variables of interest. Based on the traditional medical model of testing treatment efficacy, symptom-related variables (e.g. reduction in anxiety symptoms) have been considered the gold standard. Unfortunately, this is inconsistent with what is considered to be most important in ACT: helping people to live more fulfilling and meaningful lives. More appropriate primary outcome variables from an ACT standpoint would be quality of life and functioning. Therefore, it is understandable that ACT may not outperform traditional CBT when symptom reduction is the primary outcome of interest, given that traditional CBT emphasizes outcomes less consistent with the aims of the ACT model. Another potential modification would be changing the time frame of evaluating outcomes. Most studies have focused exclusively on short-term or acute results. However, what is of most interest, especially from an ACT framework, is to what degree these changes in quality of life and functioning can be maintained over longer periods of time.

There are other important areas in which to expand ACT for anxiety research. One distinctive feature of ACT research has been a greater focus on mechanisms of change earlier in the treatment development process, and this type of work should be continued. Given that both ACT and CBT target behaviour change, there may be more similarities than differences when it comes to outcomes. However, it may be a different story when it comes to mediators of change. As noted above, work has already begun in this area, and it will be important to continue this work to fine-tune our knowledge about changes in targeted mechanisms and how that relates to changes in outcome variables (either generally from pre- to post-treatment, by examining session-by-session changes, or by using innovations such as ecological momentary assessment to gather even more precise data between sessions).

In general, one of the largest challenges we face in our field is to improve the use of evidence-based treatment in community and routine practice settings. ACT is no exception to that, and there may be particular ways in which ACT principles can be studied and used to increase the utilization of evidence-based practices for anxiety. As an example, a recent study by Meyer, Farrell, Kemp, Blakey and Deacon (2014) examined factors related to therapists excluding patients from exposure therapy to treat anxiety. They found that therapists' own fears of anxiety reactions (anxiety sensitivity) were significantly associated with a greater likelihood of excluding clients from exposure therapy. Additional research could be done in this area to examine further the role of experiential avoidance experienced by therapists and how this impacts their decision on whether to use exposure-based therapy with their clients. If results from these studies continue to support a relationship in which high experiential avoidance experienced by therapists results in reduced use of exposure-based treatment, perhaps brief protocols could be developed to reduce experiential avoidance in therapists and thus facilitate their use of exposure treatments with their clients.

8

Serious Mental Illnesses

The previous chapters illustrate that ACT has been successfully applied to the problematic issues of depression and anxiety. However, not many disorders can match borderline personality disorder (BPD) or psychotic disorders in terms of the severe dysfunction they cause across multiple domains (Knapp, Mangalore, & Simon, 2004; Gunderson, 2009).

Borderline personality disorder

BPD (also called emotionally unstable personality disorder, emotional intensity disorder or borderline type) is distinguished by a pattern of unstable interpersonal relationships, self-image and emotion that perseveres over different settings. Relationships are often characterized by altering between intense emotional closeness, idealization and devaluation. These problems tend to be continuously present from adolescence or early adulthood. Although the instabilities persevere over different settings, the individual is very sensitive to changes in their environment, real or imagined, and abandonment is frantically resisted by persons with BPD. That BPD is a personality disorder means that these problems are present over broad ranges of functioning, are extremely difficult to change and deviate from the norm in the person's culture. BPD is associated with increased risk of suicide, self-harm and risky behaviour. The ACT analysis of BPD is that these symptoms generally are explained by experiential avoidance (Chapman, Specht, & Cellucci, 2005). This indicates that it is not the intense negative emotions that are the problem but rather the counter-effective actions that the person takes in order to avoid experiencing these emotions, such as self-harm and drug or alcohol abuse (Strosahl, 2004; Chapman, Gratz, & Brown, 2006). Actually, BPD symptom severity is even more strongly related to experiential avoidance than it is to emotion dysregulation or distress tolerance difficulties (Iverson, Follette, Pistorello, & Fruzzetti, 2012), thus implying that ACT could be a good fit for BPD treatment.

Gratz and Gunderson (2006) conducted an RCT to determine if a combination of ACT and DBT would be useful in the treatment of deliberate self-harm among women diagnosed with BPD. DBT is a mindfulness-based treatment that was developed primarily for BPD and, thus far, has a large evidence base in this domain. Using a 14-week protocol, 22 participants recorded improvements on a number of outcome measures in comparison to the waitlist control group ($n = 10$). These outcomes included positive effects on self-harm, emotion dysregulation, experiential avoidance, BPD-specific symptoms, depression, anxiety and stress. Many of these effects reached clinical, in addition to statistical, significance. The authors recommend that future studies should involve larger scale controlled trials, the inclusion of follow-up data and a process analysis. Six years later, Morton, Snowdon, Gopold and Guymer (2012) conducted another small-scale RCT, but this time, ACT in combination with TAU was used to treat 21 participants with BPD. Following 12 two-hour sessions, those in the ACT group reported statistically and clinically significant improvements in self-rated BPD symptoms that were maintained at 13-week follow-up, when compared to TAU alone. PF improved throughout treatment and mediated the reduction of BPD symptoms. This article is a thorough exploration of ACT for BPD that should be consulted by anyone looking to run research in the area. It includes a number of outcome measures, several process measures and a detailed analysis. It also makes important suggestions for future research and includes brief videos of treatment. The authors conclude, given the low number of dropouts, that ACT is an acceptable and potentially effective approach for treating BPD, such that larger controlled trials are now needed.

Psychosis

Schizophrenia is a chronic and debilitating disorder (Pratt & Mueser, 2002) characterized by positive symptoms (hallucinations, delusions), negative symptoms (social anhedonia, flat affect) and cognitive symptoms (poor executive functioning, poor working memory and attention). Psychosis, rather than being a disorder itself, refers to the breaks with reality that sufferers from the "psychotic disorders" (schizophrenia, schitzo-affective and delusional disorder) might display. These breaks with reality are most likely to manifest themselves via positive symptoms, and given that the experience of positive symptoms is one of the best predictors of re-hospitalization (Tarrier, Barrowclough, & Bamrah, 1991), much has been done to assess the utility of psychological approaches in treating psychosis. Results have found that compared to TAU, CBT performs quite well (Gaudiano, 2005). However, as mindfulness-based therapies became more popular at the beginning of the 21st century, researchers hypothesized that ACT might be particularly useful in this area (Bach & Hayes, 2002; Gaudiano & Herbert, 2006a).

Although a number of clinical case studies have been published that lend support to the utility of ACT in treating psychosis (Garcia & Perez, 2001; Pankey & Hayes, 2003; García Montes, Luciano Soriano, Hernández López, & Zaldívar Basurto, 2004; Veiga-Martinez, Perez, & Garcia, 2008; Bloy, Oliver, & Morris, 2011), Bach and Hayes (2002) conducted the seminal investigation and published the first RCT in the area. In the introduction of the article, the authors describe how previous psychosocial interventions designed to help those with positive symptoms of schizophrenia may serve to exacerbate the disorder. Specifically, they argued that by trying to change the content or frequency of these symptoms via the control-based strategy of avoidance, they may in fact become more frequent and more intrusive. Therefore, ACT, which would involve asking clients presenting with psychosis to defuse from such thoughts and to control their behaviour in a value-driven manner, may provide a novel and promising psychosocial intervention.

The core rationale behind defusion is that when we are able to take a step away from our thoughts, we are then in a better position to choose whether acting on those thoughts would move us towards our values. A necessary side effect of viewing our thoughts in a functional, rather than literal manner, is that our thoughts become less believable. Believability is important because if we find a certain thought less believable, then its ability to affect our behaviour is weakened. For this reason, much ACT research employs believability measures to assess whether the client has, in fact, become less fused with problematic cognition. Bach and Hayes (2002) measured the effect of their ACT protocol in two ways. Firstly, they took a believability measure to ensure that, at post-treatment, clients presenting with psychosis were in a position to step away from unhelpful delusions and hallucinations. Secondly, they made an assessment of behaviour by measuring the likelihood of re-hospitalization following treatment.

To that end, 40 participants were randomly assigned to receive four sessions of ACT plus TAU and 40 participants were assigned to receive

TAU alone. The ACT condition involved four 45–50-minute individual sessions in which the patient was exposed to defusion, acceptance and values. The TAU condition involved medication, attendance of a psycho-educational group and individual therapy sessions once a week. Results indicated that those participants assigned to the ACT plus TAU condition stayed out of hospital in the four months following treatment for an average of 22 days longer than the participants in the TAU condition. Further analysis found that ACT patients were re-hospitalized at a significantly lower rate (20%) than the TAU patients (40%). Finally, analysis of the believability measure suggested that those in the ACT condition were significantly more defused from their hallucinations and delusions. The authors left the article with one strong point: although the results from such a brief ACT intervention are remarkable, they may be short-lived. Patients in the ACT group experienced a re-hospitalization rate of only 7% in the two months following the intervention compared with 30% in the TAU condition. However, in the final two months, both groups experienced similar re-hospitalization rates. In other words, lengthier treatment interventions may be needed in order to ensure long-term gains. In an effort to further explore this hypothesis, Bach, Hayes and Gallop (2012) returned to the data of Bach and Hayes (2002) and found that those participants in the ACT conditions did maintain reduced re-hospitalization, not just at four-month follow-up but also at one-year post-discharge. This suggests that just a four-session ACT protocol had enough power to significantly alter a patient's life for one year following treatment. These results also contribute to ongoing debates about the long-term utility of ACT previously mentioned in this volume.

Following the seminal study, Gaudiano and Herbert (2006a) replicated the Bach and Hayes (2002) study and found remarkably similar results: lower re-hospitalization rates and lower believability scores in those patients assigned to the ACT condition. It is important to add that although the ACT group recorded lower re-hospitalization rates than the control group, this difference did not reach the level of statistical significance. Nevertheless, the ACT group did record short-term improvements in affective symptoms, social impairment and distress associated with hallucinations. Gaudiano and Herbert (2006b) later ran a mediational analysis with the data from their first study and found that changes in believability were responsible for reductions in symptom frequency and hallucination-related distress. This result was later supported by further formal mediational analyses (Gaudiano, Herbert, & Hayes, 2010). Subsequently, Bach, Gaudiano, Hayes and Herbert (2013) also conducted a mediational analysis with the combined data sets from Bach and Hayes (2002) and Gaudiano and Herbert (2006a). The research showed that reductions in the re-hospitalization rate at four-month follow-up were mediated by symptom believability but not symptom-related distress. The take-home message of these mediational analyses is that believability had a significant impact on the outcomes of these studies, in terms of the reductions reported in both distress and re-hospitalization.

Since the research efforts of Bach and Gaudiano, others have success-fully linked ACT concepts with psychosis. For example, those suffering from schizophrenia and social anhedonia tend to have deficits in per-spective taking skills (Villatte et al., 2008, 2010, 2011; Vilardaga, Estevez, Levin, & Hayes, 2012). Clients with schizophrenia trained in perspec-tive taking score better on theory-of-mind tasks that underpin adaptive social behaviour (O'Neill & Weil, 2014). Increased PF and mindfulness may buffer against delusional ideation and auditory hallucinations (Oliver, McLachlan, Jose, & Peters, 2012; Oliver, O'Connor, Jose, McLachlan, & Peters, 2012; Morris, Garety, & Peters, 2014). ACT may be useful in reducing command hallucinations in those suffering from psy-chosis (Shawyer et al., 2012). And a qualitative analysis conducted with psychosis patients found that they deemed ACT to be useful, with mind-fulness, defusion, acceptance and values being described as the most helpful therapy components (Bacon, Farhall, & Fossey, 2014).

However, two of the more notable research studies involve the use of ACT in treating sufferers of psychosis who also present with depres-sion. White et al. (2011) conducted a blind RCT for emotion dysfunction in psychosis. Although CBT is useful in treating the positive and nega-tive symptoms of psychosis, the evidence is less clear about the ways in which CBT can additionally alleviate the depression, anxiety and hope-lessness that can follow an acute episode of psychosis (Wykes, Steel, Everitt, & Tarrier, 2008). Therefore, the researchers assigned participants either to receive ten weeks of TAU or ten weeks of ACT plus TAU. ACT was administered in a one-on-one format and was based on the work of Polk, Hambright and Webster (2009). Results indicated that those in the ACT condition had significantly fewer crisis contacts (i.e. the amount of times they contacted their service provider in a state of crisis) over the course of the study and a significantly greater proportion of them moved from depressed to not being depressed at four-month follow-up. Finally, the ACT group showed less negative symptoms of psychosis and greater increases in mindfulness skills.

In a somewhat similar study, Gaudiano, Nowlan, Brown, Epstein-Lubow and Miller (2013) aimed to determine the utility of an acceptance-based depression and psychosis treatment (ADAPT) for major depression with psychotic features. They employed a combination of ACT and Behavioural Activation (BA) for 14 participants over a 20-week period. Importantly, this therapeutic work was conducted in conjunction with pharmacotherapy; that is, the patients were also receiving anti-depressants and/or anti-psychotic drugs. Results showed that the patients displayed large reductions in depressive and psychotic symptoms at both post-treatment and nine-month follow-up. Patients also achieved increases in psychosocial functioning and the important processes of acceptance, mindfulness and values improved throughout treatment.

Overall, the evidence for treating psychosis with ACT has grown at a steady rate since the seminal study of Bach and Hayes (2002). For details of what needs to be done in future in order to develop the potential displayed in this research, please see Dr Brandon Gaudiano's researcher profile below.

Researcher profile: Dr Brandon Gaudiano

Brandon A. Gaudiano, PhD, is a clinical psychologist in the Psychosocial Research Program at Butler Hospital and also is Assistant Professor (Research) in the Department of Psychiatry & Human Behaviour at the Warren Alpert Medical School of Brown University in Providence, Rhode Island. He obtained his doctorate from Drexel University in Philadelphia and completed a T32 postdoctoral fellowship funded by the National Institute of Health (NIH) at Brown University. Dr Gaudiano has published over 100 articles, chapters and commentaries on various topics including psychotherapy development and testing, evidence-based practices in psychology, psychotic and mood disorders, and mindfulness/acceptance therapies. His research on ACT and other novel psychosocial interventions for psychosis has been funded by the NIMH. He also received a Young Investigator Award from the Brain and Behaviour Research Foundation for his research on severe mental illness. He currently serves as the Associate Editor of the journal *Psychology of Consciousness: Theory, Research, and Practice*, is an editorial board member of *Clinical Psychology Review* and is Associate Editor of the Treatment and Prevention section of *Wiley's Encyclopaedia of Clinical Psychology*.

Dr Gaudiano is also Editor of the recent text *Incorporating Acceptance and Mindfulness into the Treatment of Psychosis: Current Trends and Future Directions* (Oxford University Press). In this book, Dr Gaudiano actually dedicates an entire chapter to the future directions of ACT research in the treatment of psychosis, which he kindly agreed to show us pre-publication. Rather than recreate that chapter in this book, here is a brief summary of his recommendations: future research efforts should focus on developing a formal theoretical model of psychosis, strengthening comparison conditions used in clinical trials, testing mediators and moderators of outcomes, modifying treatment for different phases of illness, improving dissemination and implementation efforts and utilizing new technologies to expand the reach of treatment.

9
Substance Abuse

Depression, anxiety, BPD and psychosis can be considered serious psychological disorders. However, although many people may not suffer from one of those issues in their lifetime, it is likely that at some point they will have to battle against cravings to engage in behaviours that have dire consequences for their health. Before moving on to smoking behaviour and eating behaviour, we start with arguably a more destructive psychological problem: substance abuse.

Abuse of heroin and other opioids has implications at a societal and individual level. For example, abuse of these substances is associated with higher rates of mortality, health care, law-enforcement costs and family distress (Becker, Sullivan, Tetrault, Desai, & Fiellin, 2008; Clausen, Waal, Thoresen, & Gossop, 2009). Methadone and buprenorphine maintenance are the most effective treatments at reducing heroin addiction and other opioid dependence. These treatments are also associated with decreases in criminal activity and improvement in social functioning (Stotts, Dodrill, & Kosten, 2009). Rather than detoxifying patients addicted to opioids, methadone and buprenorphine are opioids themselves. The idea behind them is to tone down the addiction to an opioid-based substance that is less harmful. However, given the potential disadvantages of such treatment (Corkery, Schifano, Ghodse, & Oyefeso, 2004), recent community-based treatment programs have leaned towards opioid detoxification over maintenance. The problem with this shift is that detoxification is associated with high dropout rates and illicit opioid use (Chutuape, Jasinski, Fingerhood, & Stitzer, 2001; Magura & Rosenblum, 2001). This means that more effective detoxification procedures are needed. In other words, there is space for the development of psychological interventions that support clients as they work their way through withdrawal. So far the evidence suggests that such interventions have been unsuccessful, with an average of 30% or less of patients attaining abstinence at the end of a detoxification program.

Recent research has suggested that experiential avoidance may be an important mechanism underlying the poor rates of abstinence achieved in typical detoxification programs, as it is likely that substance abuse is maintained by the need to escape from unwanted negative private events. This assertion was supported by findings that substance-abuse patients are less tolerant of distress than those who do not present with substance-abuse issues (Compton, Charuvastra, & Ling, 2001) and that opioid users present with greater fear of anxiety (Lejuez, Paulson, Daughters, Bornovalova, & Zvolensky, 2006). ACT may therefore be well positioned to help those in detoxification programs, as its emphasis on PF directly targets experiential avoidance. Clients undergoing ACT treatment for substance abuse would be expected to report increases in willingness to experience withdrawal symptoms, without the necessity to act on their need to reduce discomfort.

Hayes et al. (2004) conducted the first investigation applying ACT to methadone-maintained opiate addicts. However, instead of using ACT in a detoxification program, these researchers aimed to reduce the amount of illicit drugs that clients were taking while on methadone maintenance. Put more simply, ACT was being used to increase the impact of methadone treatment. To that end, in RCT format, participants were allocated to receive 16 weeks of methadone maintenance alone ($n = 38$), ACT plus methadone maintenance ($n = 44$) or a popular intensive 12-step facilitation (ITSF) plus methadone maintenance. Results indicated that those in the ACT and ITSF conditions showed lower drug use (self-reported and objectively assessed) at six-month follow-up. In other words, these conditions lowered illicit drug use in their patients. However, as with previous research presented in this volume, no differences emerged between the two active conditions. Although preliminary, this study laid the foundation for later research.

Unfortunately, it took eight years for the next investigation to arrive. Stotts et al. (2012) conducted a pilot RCT using ACT for methadone detoxification. The researchers randomly assigned female opioid-dependent patients to receive 24 individual therapy sessions of ACT ($n = 30$) or drug counselling ($n = 26$) in a six-month methadone dose-reduction program. Results indicated that although no differences were found in opioid use during counselling, therapy completion rates were higher among those allocated to the ACT condition. More importantly, 37% of ACT patients achieved successful detoxification at the end of treatment, compared to just 19% in the drug-counselling condition. This percentage is higher than comparable opioid-detoxification studies. Although the results of process analyses were not perfect, for example, all patients reported higher levels of avoidance as methadone dose regressed to zero, those in the ACT group did record lower levels of avoidance and inflexibility. The results of the study are again preliminary, however, in an area in which there are few empirically supported treatments, Stotts et al. (2012) provide evidence that ACT may be useful in helping patients to navigate their way through opioid detoxification.

In addition to the two studies that have investigated ACT for opioid abuse, Smout et al. (2010) conducted an RCT investigating the utility of ACT in treating patients addicted to the stimulant methamphetamine. Participants presenting with methamphetamine dependence were randomly allocated to receive 12 weekly 60-minute sessions of ACT ($n = 51$) or CBT ($n = 53$). As defined in the introduction of the article, CBT has been successfully applied to methamphetamine disorders on a number of occasions, suggesting that it would be a credible comparison condition. Results firstly showed no differences between the groups in treatment attendance, suggesting that participants found the ACT protocol to be acceptable. Secondly, patients from both groups recorded reductions in self-reported methamphetamine use, dependence severity and negative consequences of methamphetamine use. However, given that only the CBT group showed significant reductions in objectively assessed methamphetamine use, that the attrition rates for both groups were very high and that no mediational analysis was conducted to measure the mechanisms underlying positive outcomes, it is impossible to say with confidence that the ACT model heralds positive results in this area until further research has been conducted.

Using marijuana may not be as obviously detrimental as opioid or methamphetamine abuse, but the investigation of marijuana addiction is arguably more important given its higher prevalence in society (Substance Abuse and Mental Health Services Administration, 2005) and its potential consequences (Tapert, Aaron, Sedlar, & Brown, 2001; Pope & Yurgelun-Todd, 2004). Although ACT has been successfully applied in case-study format to a client presenting with addiction to marijuana (Batten & Hayes, 2005), the more notable article in this area was published by Twohig, Schoenberger and Hayes (2007). These researchers, using a multiple-baseline across participants design, gave three clients eight sessions of ACT. Results indicated reductions in marijuana dependence at post-treatment and three-month follow-up.

In line with good practice, these reductions were both self-reported and objectively assessed through oral swabs.

Although two large-scale RCTs have recently been published by a research group at the University of Oviedo, in which ACT outperformed CBT at follow-up in reducing drug use among incarcerated inmates (González-Menéndez, Fernández García, Rodríguez Lamelas, & Villagrá Lanza, 2013; Villagrá Lanza, Fernández García, Rodríguez Lamelas, & González Menéndez, 2014), only seven studies, in total, have investigated the utility of ACT with substance abuse. Given the amount of people presenting with substance-abuse disorders, this area will need more attention in the next decade.

10
Smoking Cessation

After reading the previous chapter, it could be argued that little controlled research has been conducted to investigate ACT's utility in treating substance abuse. The same criticism, however, cannot be levelled against the application of ACT to smoking cessation. In recent years, a plethora of research has been conducted in which the ACT model has shown great results in this area. Although we will come to the celebrated work of Dr Jonathan Bricker and colleagues in due course, it was an early study by Dr Liz Gifford that catalysed the research area.

Gifford et al. (2004) conducted an RCT in which participants received ACT or nicotine replacement therapy (NRT). NRT, which was chosen as a comparison condition in the study due to its widespread success in the treatment of smoking cessation, involved a 1.5-hour NRT education session and a supply of nicotine patches. Those in the ACT condition received seven 50-minute individual sessions and seven 90-minute group sessions. The protocol, as described in detail in the article, involved a thorough exploration of the ACT model, in combination with exposure and Behavioural Activation. Results indicated no differences between the two groups at post-treatment; however, at one-year follow-up, those in the ACT condition reported better smoking outcomes. Indeed, in the long-term, those in the ACT condition were almost twice as likely to quit smoking as those in the NRT condition. Interestingly, the authors also reported that inflexible and avoidant responses to negative affect (unwanted thoughts, feelings and cravings) predicted quit rates and that improvement in these areas mediated outcome. This study is famous within the ACT literature. It was the first RCT conducted in the area of smoking and it included an analysis of the processes underlying clinical improvement. In the introduction, it also clearly describes the negatively reinforcing value of succumbing to a smoking craving. ACT arose out of this rationale: avoidance is maintained as it provides short-term relief, even if that means moving away from one's values in the long term. PF involves experiencing discomfort in the service of long-term valued behaviours.

This initial study was followed by a small trial in which ACT was used to increase distress tolerance with early lapse smokers (smokers who had not been able to quit for more than 72 hours). Results showed that those in the ACT condition reported around 24 days of continued abstinence rather than the three days usually reported by this population (Brown et al., 2008). However, the next major investigation of ACT for smoking cessation was conducted in 2009. Hernandez-Lopez, Luciano, Bricker, Roales-Nieto and Montesinos (2009) compared seven 90-minute group sessions of ACT ($n = 43$) with seven 90-minute group sessions of CBT ($n = 38$). This was an important comparison to make given that CBT is the most popular psychological treatment for smoking cessation (Fiore et al., 2008). However, as CBT had been criticized for stagnant or declining abstinence rates (Irvin & Brandon, 2000), the development of new interventions was needed (Niaura & Abrams, 2002). Results firstly showed that the ACT intervention was feasible and acceptable to the participants. Additionally, intent-to-treat analyses showed that participants in the ACT condition had higher abstinence rates at post-treatment, three-month, six-month and 12-month follow-up. In fact, at 12-month follow-up, participants in the ACT condition, assessed via self-report and an objective smoking measure, were almost twice as likely to have abstained from smoking for a 30-day period as those in the CBT condition were. More interestingly, these results were stronger for participants that completed five or more of the seven sessions. The results of this study were impressive for three reasons: the ACT treatment was brief, ACT compared well to CBT and the results were based on an objective biochemical measure of smoking.

This study, in combination with those that preceded it, inspired later researchers to become involved in the area. One of these people was Dr Jonathan Bricker, who became interested in testing the utility of ACT for smoking cessation, not just in face-to-face format, but in delivery formats that may be further reaching. In their first study, Bricker, Mann, Marek, Liu and Peterson (2010) ran a feasibility study to determine if five sessions of telephone-delivered ACT could outperform the government's *Quitline* smoking-cessation program. *Quitline*, which tends to use CBT as its counselling approach, reports a 12% 30-day abstinence rate at 12-month follow-up (Stead, Perera, & Lancaster, 2013). Results firstly indicated that the majority of the 14 participants found ACT treatment to be acceptable and useful. At 20-day post-treatment, 43% had not smoked that day, and 29% had not smoked in the previous seven days. At 12-month follow-up, 29% had not smoked in the 30 days prior to the test or in the 12-month period following completion of the program. This is over double the rate reported in *Quitline* programs. Finally, participants showed significant improvements in the important processes of acceptance and commitment. The authors point out in the discussion that a well-powered RCT was now needed to further determine its efficacy.

Although further analysis of the recorded sessions used in the Bricker et al. (2010) study revealed that ACT could competently be delivered over the telephone (Schimmel-Bristow, Bricker, & Comstock, 2012), the recommended large-scale RCT was not published until four years later. As Dr Bricker once mentioned at a conference, science takes time. Bricker, Bush, Zbikowski, Mercer and Heffner (2014) conducted an RCT comparing telephone-delivered ACT plus NRT ($n = 59$) with a telephone-delivered CBT *Quitline* program plus NRT ($n = 62$). As with Bricker et al. (2010), the sample was diverse in terms of ethnicity, gender and education. Given that the researchers aimed to create a program that could be widely disseminated at small cost, the fact that the study only used uninsured *Quitline* callers is a huge advantage. The study also used the same protocol as Bricker et al. (2010): one 30-minute session followed by four 15-minute sessions. Results indicated that ACT participants completed more calls, found it more useful and would be more likely to recommend the treatment to their friends in comparison to those in the CBT condition. The primary outcome measure indicated that, at six-month post-randomization, ACT participants reported a 31% 30-day abstinence rate, in comparison to 22% in the CBT condition. But this study is more than a standard comparison of two treatments; it also investigated moderators that might make ACT more or less effective. At six-month follow-up, results indicated that the abstinence rate for participants depressed at baseline was 33% in the ACT group and 13% in the CBT group, abstinence rates for heavy smokers were 36% for the ACT group and 17% in the CBT group and abstinence rates for those who scored low on acceptance were 37% in the ACT group and 10% in the CBT group. Finally, those in the ACT group reported significantly higher acceptance of cravings and these higher levels of acceptance at three-month follow-up predicted quit rates at six-month follow-up. These results are somewhat remarkable and set the stage for the next ten years of research in this area. However, the authors suggest that larger sample sizes will allow complex mediational analyses in future investigations.

In between the Bricker et al. (2010, 2014) studies, there are three further investigations of note in this area. Gifford et al. (2011) ran a huge RCT in which 303 smokers were randomly assigned to receive bupropion alone (bupropion is a widely used smoking cessation drug) or bupropion plus a combination of ACT and functional analytic psychotherapy (FAP), delivered in group and individual sessions. Results found seven-day abstinence rates of 31.6% in the ACT group at one-year follow-up as assessed by a biochemical measure; this figure was 17.5% for the bupropion-alone group. Levels of acceptance increased in the ACT group and these levels mediated outcome. The results again provide robust evidence for the utility of ACT with these populations when delivered in a standard format.

Finally, two studies have recently been published in a further effort to increase accessibility of psychological interventions in the area of smoking cessation. Firstly, Bricker, Wyszynski, Comstock and Heffner (2013) compared a web-based ACT package with the USA National Standard for smoking-cessation interventions (*Smokefree.gov*). In RCT format, 222 participants were randomly assigned to receive one of the two interventions. The ACT package was a self-paced eight-part program named *WebQuit* that was based on the earlier work of Bricker et al. (2010). While the comparison intervention named *Smokefree.gov*, which is the most widely accessed website for smoking cessation, involved quit planning, skills training, advice on pharmacotherapy and social support for quitting. Results indicated that participants spent significantly longer on *WebQuit* than *Smokefree.gov* and were more satisfied with the site. At three-month follow-up, 23% of the ACT condition had quit smoking for at least 30 days, in comparison to 10% in the *Smokefree.gov* condition. This effect was mediated by increases in acceptance. Although these abstinence rates are not as impressive as those observed in face-to-face and telephone-based research, the low cost of web-based interventions makes further development and exploration of *WebQuit* an important pursuit. Secondly, Bricker et al. (2014) compared an ACT smartphone App (*SmartQuit*) with the National Cancer Institute's App for smoking cessation (*QuitGuide*). Results indicated that participants randomly assigned to the *SmartQuit* condition opened their App significantly more than those in the *QuitGuide* condition. Furthermore, quit rates were significantly higher in the *SmartQuit* condition (13%) than the *QuitGuide* condition (8%). Again this difference was more pronounced among participants who scored low in acceptance at baseline. In the paper, the authors suggest that with this pilot trial showing such promising results, the foundation had been laid for a full-scale efficacy trial.

What is important about this area of research is that it is very easy to measure the behavioural impact of the clinical intervention. As has been previously suggested, the outcome measures for other disorders usually require a reduction in symptomology; that is, a reduction in unwanted thoughts and feelings. But ACT does not make predictions for those things; ACT makes predictions for behaviour. For example, with a depressed person, each individual will have a different set of values that determine appropriate value-based behaviour. This makes it very difficult to measure valued action objectively in those sorts of populations. The smoking-behaviour literature does not have to deal with that problem, as clients who take part in these interventions either smoke, or they do not. Whether this is measured by self-report or a biochemical instrument, the behaviour is salient. And arguably, it is in this area, where the measurement of success is not clouded by reductions in symptomology, that ACT has found the most success. Nevertheless, despite these impressive results, there are ways to improve, as described below in the researcher profile of Dr Jonathan Bricker.

Researcher profile: Dr Jonathan Bricker

Jonathan Bricker, PhD, is founder and leader of the Tobacco & Health Behaviour Science Group. A licensed clinical psychologist, he is Associate Member (equivalent to Associate Professor) in the Division of Public Health Sciences at the Fred Hutchinson Cancer Research Center. He is also Associate Professor (Affiliate) in the Department of Psychology at the University of Washington. His expertise is in (1) developing and testing innovative interventions for health-behaviour change and in (2) understanding the long-term psychosocial predictors of health-behaviour change. He has been applying this expertise to smoking cessation and plans to expand to other key health behaviours. He has served as principal investigator or co-investigator on a variety of NIH research projects. Among his current research grants, he has a five-year $3.2 million NIH grant for the new *WebQuit* study of web-delivered ACT for adult smoking cessation and he also has a $3.2 million NIH grant for the PATH study comparing ACT with traditional CBT. He has published over 40 peer-reviewed research articles in major scientific journals. Currently, he serves as Senior Editor of the journal *Addiction* and Consulting Editor of *Psychology of Addictive Behaviours* – the highest impact substance-abuse journal. Dr Bricker received his PhD in Clinical Psychology from the University of Washington.

ACT is a treatment approach based on an innovative theory of language derived from contemporary principles of contextual behaviourism, under the general umbrella of contextual behavioural science (CBS). To date, there have been many single case, analog, single arm, and non-randomized trials supporting ACT's basic processes of change and clinical outcomes. More importantly, there are many randomized trials of ACT published in scientific journals for a wide variety of clinically important problems, including anxiety, depression, tinnitus, pain, and smoking cessation. Overall, these trials generally support the ACT model, though a good many are equivocal. The most important limitations of our current knowledge base from randomized trials are that the overwhelming majority are not definitive. Although there are several notable exceptions (e.g. pain management), small sample sizes, short term follow-up, outcome data attrition, and the lack of best standard comparison groups limit our ability to know a very important overall question: Is ACT a major advance in behavioural care over the current best treatments? Or, is it at least a comparable alternative to them? The questions matter. They matter for the community of clinicians, scholars, and scientists who are interested in ACT and contextual behavioural therapies in general. And they matter for the healthcare systems and patients who might benefit from and decide to adopt a new treatment.

The evidence base for ACT is at a critical turning point. The evidence is promising. But in order for it to be definitive, new questions need to be asked using major trial methodology. What we need now are more focused programs of research that zero in on the clinical problems that afflict many and are expensive from a societal perspective. The breadth of clinical ACT trials are a testament to its focus on theory-grounded core processes that impact seemingly unrelated clinical problems. And now the next phase is to bring into focus certain content areas which ACT is theoretically best suited to impact and which, if impacted, would lead to ground-breaking advances in clinical care. Some examples include smoking, substance use, obesity, depression, anxiety disorders, and psychosis. If it can be shown that ACT is definitively more effective than the best current standard behavioural interventions for those clinical problems, it would save billions in annual healthcare costs, vastly improve the quality of life for people who suffer with these problems, and prolong lives.

Making this change means shifting how the ACT/ACBS community thinks. For example, ACT and contextual behavioural approaches do not view clinical outcomes as the core metrics of success. There are deep principled reasons for that. But if the theory underlying ACT is correct, it should be the case that changes in core underlying processes will in turn impact clinical outcomes. So it's not enough to merely show that we changed the process. Moreover, our field has to get beyond trying to convince ourselves that ACT is helpful. We can't just talk amongst ourselves. We instead have to focus on showing the mainstream clinical and scientific communities whether or not ACT is effective. That is a higher bar. A higher bar that, if reached, will lead to broader adoption and population-level impact. That includes publishing our science in journals that are not specialized behavioural or even psychology journals. Broader science journals and those that focus on specific clinical outcomes reach non-ACT readers. We have to change our reference group.

For that same reason, cost-effectiveness should become a part of the scientific evidence base for ACT. In general, cost-effectiveness has not been a part of the aims of behavioural intervention studies. That needs to change. Governments, healthcare payers, and healthcare systems are important reference groups. They are increasingly relying on cost-effectiveness data to help guide them in the adoption of new treatments. For example, ACT might be more effective than a standard treatment but that needs to be weighed against the cost of training and supervising staff in the delivery of ACT. Cost-effectiveness analysis can quantify both the value of the added clinical benefit and the costs of implementing the new treatment.

The bulwark of needed ACT research is the gold standard of science: the fully powered randomized controlled trial. Randomization is the best method science has to control for measured and unmeasured factors that can confound treatment outcomes. Power. We need fully-powered trials so the confidence intervals around the outcomes are tight enough to see differences between treatment groups. Long-term outcomes. We need to see long-term outcomes for clinical interventions. Lots of promising interventions have shown initial promise, only to lose their initial impact by the time longer follow-ups have been conducted. If ACT is a ground-breaking model, it should be durable. Some ACT trials so far have suggested a possible "sleeper effect" or "delayed effect" in which ACT participants were doing no better immediately, but doing much better at follow-up. The theory is that ACT participants struggle with letting go of fusion and avoidance at first. It's disruptive change. Intriguing. But this is not a consistent finding, and so a larger body of long-term evidence would show whether there is a true unique sleeper or delayed effect. And we need to continue to keep formal mediation analysis as a mainstay of ACT treatment research. Did we move the process? And if we moved it, did that explain treatment outcome differences?

My team and I at the Fred Hutchinson Cancer Research Center in Seattle Washington are doing our part to address these needs. We have a research program that I call "The Wheel." On each spoke of the wheel is a modality of treatment delivery, starting from the most clinical intensive-low reach to the clinically least intensive-high reach. Specifically, our spokes are: individual face-to-face, group, telephone, website, and most recently, smartphone apps. Each spoke of the wheel reaches people who are choosing these modalities of treatment. We are going to platforms where treatments are delivered. Right now, the entire wheel is focused on testing ACT to stopping the most preventable cause of human suffering and premature death: cigarette smoking. Smoking kills 6 million per year worldwide and annually costs 300 billion dollars in healthcare/productivity in the USA alone. For each modality of delivery, we are conducting randomized trials comparing ACT to the current best standards of care (e.g., traditional cognitive behavioural therapy) to determine which is more effective for helping people quit smoking. While our main focus is the general population of smokers, we are also conducting trials that focus on important high-need populations: smokers with depression, bipolar disorder, and psychoses. Overall, we have multiple randomized trials forming an NIH-grant funded research program totalling over 10 million US dollars. Our goal is to determine whether ACT is more effective in each of these spokes of the wheel, each of these treatment modalities. We are looking at mediation, and at cost effectiveness. And if ACT is more effective, our next step will be to conduct research on methods to broadly disseminate this new model of treatment.

In sum, the ACT/ACBS community is a masterful incubator of new ideas, approaches, clinical wisdom and creativity. We are a community of compassionate thinkers who care deeply about alleviating human suffering. Such thinking has spawned RFT, ACT, The Matrix, FAP, and PROSOCIAL approaches. That is a blessing. And to build on them, the future needs focused, programmatic, and solid science to rigorously test these brilliant ideas.

11
Eating Behaviour

The area of eating behaviour has been given much attention by ACT researchers in the past decade. In the current chapter, this research will be described in three sections: the ACT research that has been conducted on clients presenting with eating disorders, the application of ACT to the area of weight loss and body dissatisfaction in sub-clinical populations, and the utility of brief ACT interventions as techniques for managing specific eating behaviour.

Anorexia nervosa (AN) and bulimia nervosa (BN) are among the most deadly mental health disorders (Birmingham, Su, Hlynsky, Goldner, & Goa, 2005) and are notoriously difficult to treat (Fairburn, 2008). For this reason, researchers have linked ACT to this domain in a variety of ways. For example, three conceptual papers explored ACT's potential utility in the treatment of eating disorders (Orsillo & Batten, 2002; Baer, Fischer, & Huss, 2005; Merwin et al., 2010). Two case studies displayed that ACT could be useful in the treatment of AN (Heffner, Sperry, Eifert, & Detweiler, 2002; Berman, Boutelle, & Crow, 2009). A recent case study showed its efficacy in treating binge eating disorder (Hill, Masuda, Melcher, Morgan, & Twohig, 2014). One case study displayed that ACT could be useful in reducing emotional eating episodes (Hill, Masuda, Moore, & Twohig, 2014). Finally, investigations have found that disordered eating cognition is related to low levels of PF (Masuda, Price, Anderson, & Wendell, 2010; Masuda & Latzman, 2012) and non-acceptance (Merwin, Zucker, Lacy, & Elliott, 2010).

However, Juarascio, Forman and Herbert (2010) conducted the first major investigation in the area. In RCT format, the researchers compared CT ($n = 28$) and ACT ($n = 27$) in the treatment of sub-clinical eating pathology, rather than AN or BN per se. Participants, who were a sub-sample within a larger scale RCT for depression and anxiety

(Forman, Herbert, Moitra, Yeomans, & Geller, 2007), received an average of 12 therapeutic sessions (for specific details of the intervention, see the original study presented earlier in this volume). Results indicated that whereas those in the CT group recorded minimal reductions in eating pathology at post-treatment, those in the ACT group recorded significantly greater reductions. As discussed by the authors, despite the fact that targeting those with sub-clinical eating pathology can work as an early intervention strategy, future research should be conducted with those presenting with clinical levels of eating pathology.

The first attempt at using ACT with a clinical population came three years later when acceptance-based separated family therapy (ASFT) was used to help adolescents with AN (Merwin, Zucker, & Timko, 2013). In a small-scale study, six adolescents with AN or sub-threshold AN were given 20 sessions of an ASFT protocol that was grounded in ACT. Results indicated acceptability and credibility of treatment was good and that five of the six adolescents restored weight to their ideal body mass index (BMI) during or post-treatment. As pointed out by the authors, preliminary research of this kind needed to be followed by controlled larger trials that include process measures.

Around the same time as this initial exploration, Juarascio et al. (2013a) published the seminal paper in the area. In RCT format, the researchers compared ACT group therapy plus TAU ($n = 52$) with TAU alone ($n = 53$) at a residential treatment facility for eating disorders. TAU involved structured meals, individual therapy sessions, therapist-run group sessions and evening groups that were designed to aid with leisure planning, coping skills and female bonding. Interestingly, the eight-session, twice-weekly ACT protocol, which is described in the article and in greater detail in a subsequent publication (Juarascio et al., 2013b), was combined with a TAU that was based on aspects of psychodynamic, interpersonal, feminist and cognitive-behavioural interventions. Results indicated that participants in the ACT group showed slightly greater reductions in eating pathology than those receiving TAU alone. They also trended towards improved shape concerns, weight concerns and PF at post-treatment. Finally, participants in the ACT group ate twice as much of a "forbidden" food at post-treatment in a food challenge and were significantly less likely to have been re-hospitalized at six-month follow-up. The authors take encouragement from the fact that a relatively low dose of ACT significantly reduced eating pathology compared to TAU alone, even though the TAU-alone group reported significant reductions itself. This result suggests that the exploration of a full ACT protocol is warranted. Interestingly, the mediational analysis revealed that willingness (and not defusion, acceptance, mindfulness and values) significantly mediated treatment outcome, begging the question as to whether a willingness-heavy ACT protocol might be most useful with this population.

Juarascio, Kerrigan et al. (2013) later re-analysed the data set from their RCT to determine what baseline characteristics of the participants moderated the utility of ACT. Results indicated that those with more severe eating symptomology at baseline showed greater improvements in eating pathology in the ACT condition than the TAU condition, thereby suggesting that acceptance-based methods may be more effective in treating those with severe eating disorders. The same authors also published another re-analysis in which they attempted to determine if any relationship existed between acceptance-related constructs and quality of life (Juarascio, Schumacher, Shaw, Forman, & Herbert, 2014). Results indicated that improvements in acceptance and defusion were related to positive changes in quality of life. However, it is important to note that this occurred in both treatments conditions; that is, the ACT condition did not appear to increase acceptance, defusion or quality of life more than the standard treatment program. This is a very interesting finding that may resonate with researchers from the other diagnostic areas already mentioned in this book; sometimes approaches other than ACT may improve processes that are important in ACT; that is, defusion, acceptance, mindfulness and values. For information about one of the leading researchers in this area along with her thoughts for future research, please see Dr Adrienne Juarascio's researcher profile below.

Researcher profile: Dr Adrienne Juarascio

Adrienne Juarascio, PhD, is Assistant Research Professor in the Department of Psychology at Drexel University and a licensed clinical psychologist. Dr Juarascio's primary line of research involves the development and evaluation of novel treatments for eating disorders. She has served as the primary investigator on over a dozen research studies, including a full-scale RCT of an acceptance-based behavioural treatment for eating pathology. She is currently the primary investigator for the CARE project, a study assessing an acceptance-based group treatment for binge eating disorder, the inhibitory control training study, a project assessing the utility of computerized neurocognitive training programs for binge eating disorder, and the MOTIVATE study, an open trial of a values-based intervention to improve motivation among patients receiving a residential treatment program for eating pathology. In addition to these projects, Dr Juarascio collaborates with other faculty in the Laboratory for Innovations in Health-Related Behaviour Change and the Program in Eating Disorders and Obesity Research, where she serves as a co-investigator or collaborator on numerous ongoing projects related to treatment development for eating and weight disorders.

I believe the future of ACT research will be focused on identifying how aspects of this treatment approach can be integrated into existing behavioural treatment approaches to enhance outcomes. In the field of eating disorders, cognitive behavioural treatments are only minimally effective for anorexia nervosa and although the response rates are better for bulimia nervosa and binge eating disorder, there is significant room for improvement. Ideally ACT researchers can assess how best to incorporate existing behavioural treatment approaches for eating pathology (e.g. normalization of eating, reduction of rigid dietary restraint, regular monitoring of weight) into ACT treatment paradigms and determine whether this combined approach might improve the efficacy of treatment.

Consistent with the recent movement at NIMH towards personalized medicine and an experimental therapeutic approach to intervention development, I think the next generation of ACT research will be even more strongly focused on identifying why and for whom treatments work. Although CBT for eating disorders can work effectively for many patients, certain diagnoses (e.g. anorexia nervosa) or subtypes of patients (e.g. patients with bulimia nervosa who are high in weight suppression) may be less likely to benefit from treatment. These patients may benefit from the additional components in an ACT-based approach such as a greater focus on values clarity or the development of more experiential acceptance to enhance treatment engagement and compliance. The next stage of research may benefit from identifying the individuals for whom standard treatments are ineffective and who might show greater results in an ACT-based treatment.

Similarly, identifying the primary mechanisms of action, or why ACT produces improvements in eating pathology, will be essential in developing more effective treatment approaches. By identifying the key behaviours that maintain pathology and ensuring our treatment approaches effectively engage these clinical targets, we can crystalize treatment packages into their most effective components. For example, our group is examining whether patients low in motivation to change might benefit from a greater emphasis on values clarification and strategies designed to promote engagement in values-guided behaviours. If improved values clarity and committed action serve as mechanisms of this treatment approach, we may be able to build these aspects into treatment programs for patients low in motivation to change.

It is evident that more RCTs comparing ACT to a gold-standard treatment, in which mechanisms of change are measured via formal mediational analyses, are needed in order to ensure that ACT is a viable treatment for eating disorders. However, the results thus far are very encouraging. What may provide secondary support for its utility in managing eating disorders is that ACT has been successfully applied to related issues. For example, in addition to the research in which ACT has successfully reduced body dissatisfaction (Pearson, Follette, & Hayes, 2012; Rafiee, Sedrpoushan, & Abedi, 2013), much evidence has displayed that ACT can be used to reduce obesity. And given the amount of people suffering with obesity (Ogden et al., 2006), it could be argued that research investigating ACT's efficacy in this area is as important as research investigating its utility in treating eating disorders. This claim can be substantiated by the suggestion that current treatments for obesity are not performing at an optimum level (Butryn, Webb, & Wadden, 2011).

Forman, Butryn, Hoffman and Herbert (2009) ran the first investigation into the utility of ACT as a behavioural intervention for weight loss. In open-trial format, 29 participants received 12 sessions of ABBT: a treatment approach that combined ACT with standard behavioural components. As with most open trials, the aim of the study was not simply to reduce weight, but to determine if the approach was feasible and acceptable. Results indicated that the participants found the approach to be acceptable, as implied by high ratings on measures of helpfulness and satisfaction. Behavioural measures indicated that treatment completers ($n = 19$) recorded a 6.6% weight loss at post-treatment and 9.6% at six-month follow-up. These results are equivalent or favourable when compared to other 12-week weight-loss approaches (Wadden & Butryn, 2003), suggesting that ABBT is an effective approach that warrants further investigation. The article also reported some other interesting results: (1) the effectiveness of the treatment was tied to the dose of therapy where more treatment was equal to greater weight loss, resembling earlier work presented in the smoking-cessation chapter

(Hernández-López et al., 2009); (2) participants reported large increases in weight-related quality of life; and (3) weight loss at post-intervention and follow-up was associated with hypothesized changes in various acceptance-related processes such as experiential avoidance and mindfulness. This article is worth reading, as it takes time to systematically argue that there is space for acceptance-based methods in the area of weight loss. It also thoroughly explores the way in which this research could be improved in future: controlled trials and better mediational analyses to understand the mechanisms of change.

Before describing how Forman et al. (2009) followed up their open trial with a large-scale RCT, four further investigations were published in which ACT has showed promising results in helping people manage weight. First, in RCT format, Tapper et al. (2009) gave 31 participants looking to lose weight four two-hour ACT workshops, while 31 control participants were asked to continue with their normal diets. Results indicated, when participants who reported not using the intervention were removed ($n = 7$), that at six-month follow-up, those in the ACT group reported significantly greater weight loss (2.32 kg per week) and significantly more physical-activity sessions (3.11 per week) than those in the control group. The authors note that although these figures are slightly less than those typically seen in CBT weight-loss interventions, the ACT intervention was very brief in comparison. Interestingly, qualitative analysis in this study suggested that the defusion element of the protocol was the most successful and active ACT component and should, therefore, be emphasized in future protocols.

Second, obese people who report difficulty with eating in response to emotions and thoughts tend to be less successful at losing weight and keeping it off (Butryn, Thomas, & Lowe, 2009). Niemeier, Leahey, Palm-Reed, Brown and Wing (2012) asked participants who reported high levels of internal disinhibition to complete a 24-week ACT-influenced acceptance-based behavioural intervention (ABBI). Results firstly found high completion rates and satisfaction scores, suggesting that the protocol was acceptable. Secondly, participants lost an average of 12 kg during treatment and 12.1 kg at three-month follow-up; these results are favourable when compared to those typically seen in behavioural treatment programs. Finally, decreases in internal disinhibition and experiential avoidance were found at post-treatment and three-month follow-up, and given that decreases in experiential avoidance were associated with increases in weight loss at post-treatment, the authors suggest that experiential avoidance may be a potential mechanism of action. As the results of this study outperform those observed by Forman et al. (2009), the authors suggest that ACT may be particularly useful with this population of emotional overeaters; a sub-group of individuals who typically struggle with weight-loss programs. However, they also recommend that future research include a control group and longer follow-up measures.

Third, following the finding that 20–30% of patients who receive bariatric surgery regain weight within 24 months (Powers, Rosemurgy, Boyd, & Perez, 1997), Weineland, Arvidsson, Kakoulidis and Dahl (2012) conducted an RCT to determine if participants who received six weeks of internet-based ACT (*n* = 39) would show improved scores on a number of weight-related outcomes, when compared to TAU. Results indicated that those in the ACT condition significantly improved on measures of eating-disordered behaviours, quality of life, acceptance of weight-related thoughts and body dissatisfaction. The authors correctly point out that although changes in those domains are likely to affect subsequent behaviour, future research should include objective measures to determine if the ACT protocol helped participants successfully manage their actual weight.

Fourth, Katterman, Goldstein, Butryn, Forman and Lowe (2014) recruited female college students, judged to be at risk of future weight gain, and randomized them to an intervention group (*n* = 29) or an assessment-only group (*n* = 29). Those assigned to the intervention group received eight sessions of behavioural and acceptance-based strategies that aimed to help the participants prevent weight gain. The aim of the study was to determine if the addition of the acceptance-based intervention could reduce the likelihood of weight gain at a one-year follow-up period. Results indicated that those assigned to the assessment-only group gained weight at one-year follow-up, a finding confirming that this particular sample of participants were indeed at risk of weight gain. Those in the acceptance condition reduced their weight by 1.57 kg at 16 weeks and maintained this reduction at one-year follow-up. Given that the results compare favourably to other weight-prevention programs, the authors conclude that an ACT protocol may have potential with this population.

Forman et al. (2013) conducted the most comprehensive investigation of ACT's utility in the treatment of weight loss. In RCT format, 128 participants were assigned to receive 40 weeks of ABBT or standard behaviour therapy (SBT). Results indicated, in addition to high acceptability scores, that those in the ABBT condition lost 13.17% of their body weight at post-treatment and 10.98% at six-month follow-up. This was significantly more than those in the SBT condition, who lost 7.54% at post-treatment and 4.83% at six-month follow-up. Further results revealed that ABBT was particularly successful for those more susceptible to eating cues, and mediational analyses suggest that acceptance was a mechanism of action. The conclusions of this study are quite clear: an ACT-influenced protocol results in significant weight loss at post-treatment and six-month follow-up. However, there are two comments raised in the discussion that warrant further investigation. Firstly, the aforementioned results only occurred when expert therapists delivered ABBT. The effects were minimized when the protocol was delivered by novice therapists, suggesting – contrary to some of the previous research presented in this book – that it may take some time to become an effective ACT therapist. Secondly, it would be helpful to include longer follow-up measures and measures that are not so reliant on self-report. For a thorough discussion of the potential utility of ACT in aiding weight control, see the recent conceptual paper by Forman and Butryn (2015).

The research conducted thus far is impressive. It is, therefore, unsurprising that book-length treatment manuals are emerging that aim to help everyday people better manage their weight (Ciarrochi, Bailey, & Harris, 2014; Lillis, Dahl, & Weineland, 2014). Indeed, these sorts of books might have advice about how to manage specific cravings and subsequent eating behaviour. Two of the foods that we tend to crave more than most are chocolate and sweets. Four investigations have investigated the utility of ACT in managing eating behaviour specific to these foods, with the seminal piece of research conducted by Forman, Hoffman et al. (2007). This creative study required participants to carry a box of Hershey's kisses with them for a 48-hour period but not to eat anything from the box. Before beginning the arduous task of carrying around the chocolate with them, participants were given interventions to help them manage their cravings. They were randomly assigned to receive a 30-minute control-based intervention where participants were trained to distract themselves from their cravings, or a 30-minute acceptance intervention where willingness and defusion were emphasized. A control group who received no intervention was also included. Results indicated, when focusing on those with the highest susceptibility to the presence of food, that participants in the acceptance group experienced lower cravings and recorded less consumption of Hershey's kisses than those in the other two groups, suggesting that acceptance may be the way to manage cravings to eat chocolate. Forman, Hoffman, Juarascio, Butryn and Herbert (2013) later conducted a similar study, except the participants had to carry sweets with them, and the comparison condition was a cognitive-reappraisal intervention. Again results indicated that those in the acceptance condition reported less cravings and reduced consumption, especially for those with a greater susceptibility to the presence of food.

Somewhat inspired by the Forman, Hoffman et al. (2007) study (and the first author's love of chocolate), Hooper, Sandoz, Ashton, Clarke and McHugh (2012) divided participants into acceptance, avoidance and no-intervention groups before asking them to reduce, but record, their chocolate consumption. No differences emerged between the groups throughout the seven-day experimental period, though trends in the data suggested that participants in the acceptance group reported eating less chocolate despite experiencing more cravings. However, upon returning to the lab, all participants were required to complete a "taste test". In the taste test, those in the acceptance group ate significantly less chocolate in comparison to the other groups, suggesting that acceptance removes the rebound effect typically observed following avoidance-based instructions.

In an extension of the aforementioned research, Jenkins and Tapper (2013) compared acceptance versus defusion (and a control group) in the management of eating behaviour when asking participants to carry a bag of chocolate with them for a five-day period. This research is important, as the previous studies in this genre tend to include interventions that combine acceptance with defusion, rather than study them in stand-alone format. Results indicated that those in the defusion group ate significantly less chocolate than those in the acceptance and control groups and that those in the acceptance group did not eat less than those in the control group. In other words, defusion may be the most active component in helping people control their eating behaviour. This is in line with previous research in the area (Tapper et al., 2009). Furthermore, as with Hooper et al. (2012), no post-experiment rebound effects were observed.

These small-scale analogue studies may seem playful and creative, but they are important; they concern specific eating habits that are common among everyday people; that is, excessive consumption of chocolate and sweets. Therefore, if brief interventions can move eating behaviour, then these could be rolled out to the general public with relative ease. A second reason why such research is important is because it allows a breakdown of the ACT model into its components, thereby allowing a deeper analysis of which components work best in which contexts. Overall, this research in combination with those investigations that use the ACT model to treat weight loss and eating disorders has progressed at a fast pace. And in a world where eating-related issues are becoming more and more common, one cannot underestimate the importance of such research. For more information about a prolific academic in the ACT community and his thoughts on the future directions for this area, please see Dr Evan Forman's researcher profile below.

Researcher profile: Dr Evan Forman

Evan M. Forman received his BA from Cornell University and his Doctorate in Clinical Psychology from the University of Rochester. He completed clinical internships and fellowships at Albert Einstein College of Medicine, Harvard Medical School and the University of Pennsylvania. He is currently Associate Professor of Psychology at Drexel University. He co-directs, with Dr Meghan Butryn, the Laboratory for Innovations in Health-Related Behaviour Change, and, with Dr James Herbert, the Acceptance-Based Behaviour Therapy Program. He also serves as Director of Graduate Studies including Drexel's PhD Program in Clinical Psychology (ranked #7 in the USA by the *Chronicle of Higher Education*), and is Past-President of the Philadelphia Behaviour Therapy Association. Recently, he was named the 2014 Chair of the Committee on Science and Practice for Division 12 of the American Psychological Association as well as Managing Editor of *PsychologicalTreatments.org*, which is a large-impact effort of APA Division 12 to name, categorize and disseminate empirically supported psychological treatments to clinicians, policy makers and the general public. He has been lead investigator of studies comparing the effectiveness and processes of traditional CT relative to the newer ABBTs, is the author of 75 scientific publications and book chapters as well as Co-editor of the book *Acceptance and Mindfulness in Cognitive Behaviour Therapy* (Wiley, 2011). He has presented or co-presented 125 papers at scientific conferences and has given invited talks nationally and internationally. He is an investigator on a number of NIH- and other-sponsored projects (total funding $7,045,271). Dr Forman is Primary Investigator of the National Institute of Diabetes and Digestive and Kidney Diseases (NIDDK)-sponsored Mind Your Health project that compares standard and acceptance-based cognitive-behavioural interventions for obesity. He was a winner of the 2013 Shire-Drexel Innovation Partnership Competition, which funded the development of *TakeControl*, a smartphone App for the treatment of binge eating disorder. Additionally, he is a Stein Fellow at Drexel University in support of his work investigating neurocognitive aspects of eating behaviour in collaboration with scientists at Ben Gurion University in

Israel. He has appeared in national and international media outlets such as *The Independent, The Daily Mail,* MSNBC, CBS Television, *Self Magazine, Good Housekeeping, Women's Health* and *Family Circle.*

While acceptance-based behavioral treatments (ABBTs) show considerable promise for improving weight loss and maintenance outcomes (especially for certain subgroups), gaps remain in the current literature. Broad areas of need include: replication of existing findings and design of targeted trials, further investigation of moderators of efficacy, better understanding of mechanisms of action, and further study of long-term weight loss maintenance.

Only one large-scale RCT of ABBT for obesity has been published at this time. While available data on the overall effectiveness ABBT for weight loss are robust, the comparative efficacy of ABBT relative to other treatments remains unclear. The specific strategies provided to enhance commitment in the face of persistent counter-forces (e.g., biology, environment, declining reinforcement of salient weight loss) offer hope that ABBT may have the ability to enhance long-term outcomes. However, additional research needs to determine the differential impact of ABBT versus SBT on weight loss maintenance in the longer-term (e.g., one-two years post-treatment).

There are intriguing theoretical and empirical grounds for hypothesizing that an individual's response to ABBT will differ based on baseline characteristics such as depressive symptoms, level of emotional eating, or responsivity to food cues. Replication of previous findings (e.g., that ABBT is more effective than SBT for those with higher responsivity to eating-related cues) has the potential to lead to improved treatments, tailored treatments and the ability to match treatments to individuals.

While ABBTs generally have strong evidence for their putative mechanisms of action, such evidence is sparse within the field of weight control. Assessment of ABBT's mechanisms, especially with more objective, non-self-report measurement tools, would allow us to examine whether active ingredients are distinct from that of SBT, and could potentially point the way towards paring down ABBT to its most essential parts, resulting in a more efficient and potent treatment.

A related crucial point is the under-development of the construct of acceptance of reduction in pleasure. Acceptance-based treatments were originally designed to improve the ability to accept aversive internal experiences (e.g., pain, depression, anxiety). However, modifying eating and physical activity behaviour appear to have less to do with the acceptance of aversive experience, and more with tolerance of a less pleasurable option. At this time we have no method available to test this notion.

In conclusion, the initial evidence for ABBTs for weight control is strong and continues to grow. Despite the promise of such interventions for improving weight outcomes, gaps remain in the literature. The presence of few controlled RCTs of ABBT, and lack of investigation of long-term outcomes, and moderators and mechanisms, limits the ability to derive strong conclusions about the effectiveness and efficacy of ABBT for obesity. Future investigations in these areas will result in significant advancement in the study of ABBT for weight control.

12
Pain

Recently, ACT has begun to impact the broader psychotherapeutic community. For example, the USA Government's Substance Abuse and Mental Health Administration Services (SAMHAS) now lists ACT as an empirically supported treatment in its National Registry of Evidence-Based Programs and Practices (NREPP). Also, the Society of Clinical Psychology (APA's Division 12) has formally recognized ACT as having modest research support in the areas of psychosis, depression, mixed anxiety disorders and OCD. However, there is one area that is unrivalled in its quantity of high-quality ACT research. Indeed, this evidence led the Society of Clinical Psychology to deem ACT as having "strong research support" for managing chronic pain. Although we will come to the efforts of well-known researchers such as Dr Lance McCracken, Dr Kevin Vowles and Dr Rikard Wicksell, we will first consider a number of laboratory-based studies in which parts of the ACT model have been used to increase pain tolerance.

Laboratory research

Most laboratory-based pain-management studies tend to employ a similar design: participants complete a pain-tolerance test, then they are given an intervention to help them manage pain and finally they complete the pain-tolerance test again to determine if the intervention had any effect on the amount of pain they were able to tolerate. Although the studies may differ in terms of moderating variables that are being measured, the length of the intervention or the therapeutic component being targeted, this general procedure is pretty consistent.

Hayes et al. (1999) conducted the seminal investigation of this kind. Participants in their study were assigned to receive a 90-minute acceptance-based intervention, a control-based intervention or an attention-placebo intervention. The acceptance-based intervention sought to disconnect the relationship between thought and behaviour. Specifically, it tried to teach participants to accept uncomfortable feelings so that they could behave more effectively. The control-based intervention, which was drawn from a coping skills and stress-inoculation approach, was designed to help participants control their thoughts so that subsequent pain could be reduced. Finally, the attention-placebo intervention aimed simply to draw participants' attention to the phenomenon of pain. The behavioural dependent variable in this study, as with much other research in this domain, was the use of a cold-pressor task. In other words, participants had to submerge their hand in ice-cold water for as long as they could tolerate it. Results indicated that those who received the acceptance rationale kept their hands submerged in the water for significantly longer than the other two groups. Additionally, no significant differences were found in the participants' subjective experience of pain. This finding actually contradicted the authors' hypotheses; they expected, as the control intervention targeted thoughts, that it would be more effective in altering the participants' thoughts of pain intensity, pain unpleasantness and pain sensation. However, those in the acceptance condition, who received an intervention that targeted behaviour, reported similar subjective experiences of pain as the control group, despite keeping their hands submerged for longer. Finally, the authors found that the acceptance rationale altered the believability of reason-giving; a result suggesting that, as with previous research (Zettle & Rains, 1989), defusion may be an important mechanism powering outcome.

This study is an important addition to the literature. It controls for a number of confounding variables in its experimental design, describes how reason-giving might be reinforced by our social environment and details that this research is useful because it may parallel pain in the clinical world. However, it is most important because it set the tone, not just for future laboratory-based studies of pain management, but also for research investigating how acceptance-based procedures might be helpful in the management of chronic pain.

Since this seminal piece of research, a number of studies have emerged that aimed to build on the results published by Hayes et al. (1999); Takahashi, Muto, Tada and Sugiyama (2002) found that an acceptance rationale, in combination with an acceptance exercise and background information on ACT, increased pain tolerance in a Japanese sample, when compared to thought suppression and placebo. Gutiérrez,

Luciano, Rodriguez and Fink (2004) aimed to strip the Hayes et al. (1999) protocol of its various components so that acceptance alone, in the form of a 20-minute intervention, was compared to a control-based intervention. Using a wonderful dependent variable that required the participants to continue to receive electric shocks in order to gain more points on a match-to-sample procedure, results indicated that those in the acceptance condition recorded greater pain tolerance and lower believability of pain-related thoughts, and that these results were more pronounced when the shocks were longer and more frequent (the authors called this a "high-pain context"). Finally, it seemed as though participants in the ACT group were able to continue with the pain task even when they had thoughts of experiencing "very much pain". This finding was not repeated in the control group. This suggests that participants who received the ACT rationale successfully understood that they could experience discomfort without acting to avoid it.

In the four years following the Gutiérrez et al. (2004) study, numerous laboratory-based investigations of pain were published. Keogh, Bond, Hanmer and Tilston (2005) found that compared to control, acceptance reduced subjective pain reports and that this effect was especially strong among women. Feldner et al. (2006) found that participants who recorded high levels of experiential avoidance recorded lower pain tolerance and endurance and recovered slower from a cold-pressor task. Kehoe, Barnes-Holmes, Barnes-Holmes, Cochrane and Stewart (2007) published a thorough paper in which various acceptance-based metaphors were superior to distraction in increasing pain tolerance. Masedo and Rosa Esteve (2007) found a 20-minute acceptance rationale to be superior to thought suppression and a spontaneous coping group (participants who were told to cope in whichever way they saw fit) in increasing pain tolerance on a cold-pressor task. McMullen et al. (2008) found that a full acceptance protocol, including experiential exercises and a metaphor, successfully increased pain tolerance. No increases in pain tolerance were found among participants assigned to the distraction and control groups. What is most interesting about this investigation is that those participants given an acceptance rationale without experiential exercises and metaphors showed no increases in pain tolerance, suggesting that a didactic intervention alone may not be too helpful. Finally, Paez-Blarrina et al. (2008) displayed the important motivating function that values can have in increasing pain tolerance.

After 2008, there was a six-year drought in laboratory-based pain research. However, two studies have been published recently that

continue this tradition. Forsyth and Hayes (2014) found that participants assigned to both an acceptance group and a mindfulness med-
itation group recorded significantly better tolerance on a cold-pressor
task than those assigned to a spontaneous coping group. This study is
important, as it is the first to compare acceptance and mindfulness in
the management of pain. The authors point out that future research
will need to determine if the gains made by these interventions occurred
via similar pathways. The second study was conducted by Carrasquillo
and Zettle (2014), who found that a 20-minute self-as-context (SAC)
intervention significantly increased pain tolerance on a cold-pressor
task, when compared to a control-based intervention and an attention-
placebo intervention. This research is not only the first to use SAC alone
in the context of pain, but it is also one of the first to investigate an
isolated SAC component in any area of ACT research.

Outcome research in chronic pain

The major problem with the aforementioned research is that the studies were conducted on ordinary people in an artificial laboratory setting
where pain was induced. In an effort to bridge the gap between the
non-clinical and clinical world, Vowles et al. (2007) published one of
the first RCTs for chronic pain when attempting to determine what
effect brief "pain-acceptance" and "pain-control" strategies would have
on those suffering with chronic lower back pain. To that end, they gave
sufferers a brief acceptance or control rationale before asking them to
do a physical-impairment index that required them to complete seven
behavioural exercises likely to cause them pain. Results indicated that
although pain ratings associated with the exercises did not improve in
any group, those in the acceptance group displayed significant improvements on the behavioural measure. This finding emphasizes that it is
possible to control one's behaviour even when pain is perceived as high.

Given the results of these laboratory-based pain studies, in which brief
acceptance interventions can increase pain tolerance in non-clinical and
clinical samples, researchers felt that exposure to the full ACT model
might improve the lives of those suffering from chronic pain. Although
an early case study displayed promise in the treatment of an adolescent
girl with generalized pain (Wicksell, Dahl, Magnusson, & Olsson, 2005),
it was an RCT and two pilot studies that catalysed the research in this
area. Dahl, Wilson and Nilsson (2004) conducted an early RCT when
they aimed to determine if ACT was comparable to medical treatment as
usual (MTAU) in preventing those with chronic pain and chronic stress

from taking sick leave. In a small-scale study, 11 participants received four 1-hour sessions of ACT in which values, defusion, exposure and commitment were targeted. Importantly, these participants also had free access to MTAU. Results indicated that at post-treatment and six-month follow-up, compared to MTAU alone, the ACT intervention successfully reduced sick leave and the amount of medical treatment that the patient received. However, no differences were found between the groups in terms of levels of pain, stress or quality of life.

What is most remarkable about the Dahl et al. (2004) study is that participants only received four hours of ACT. This begs the question about what may be possible if an extensive ACT protocol is employed. McCracken, Vowles and Eccleston (2005) conducted the first study in which a comprehensive acceptance-based regime was tested in the treatment of chronic pain. A three- or four-week ACT protocol was completed by 108 participants in a residential or hospital setting. This protocol, which encouraged willingness to have pain present without responding to it and engagement with daily activities regardless of pain, involved exposure to the ACT model five days a week in combination with other important components in the treatment of chronic pain, including relaxation training and habit-reversal training. We would encourage readers to scan the first two paragraphs of the discussion section of this paper, as the results are quite remarkable. Pain intensity and functioning improved significantly during the protocol and were maintained at three-month follow-up. The researchers reported significant improvement in depression, physical disability, psychosocial disability and hours of rest the patient had in a day due to pain. Results also indicated that patients significantly improved on a behavioural measure that required them to move from a sitting to a standing position as many times as possible in a minute. Finally, data indicated that patients visited a doctor for medical treatment less times following the intervention and were more likely to be in work. A process analysis that revealed significant increases in acceptance, as measured by improved scores recorded in activity engagement and pain willingness, prompted the authors to conclude that acceptance was the process by which treatment operated. This investigation sent out a clear message: ACT can help patients suffering with chronic pain.

Shortly after the McCracken et al. (2005) study, Wicksell, Melin and Olsson (2006) conducted a similar pilot study in which the ACT model was applied to adolescents suffering with chronic pain. The ACT treatment, which emphasized values, defusion, acceptance and exposure (and is described in detail in the article), was administered weekly for an average of 15 sessions. Results indicated that across the 14 participants, at post-treatment, three-month follow-up and six-month follow-up, significant improvements were made in functioning, school attendance and levels of pain intensity.

The results of these studies were encouraging enough to prompt a huge series of research efforts that involved further tests of ACT in this domain. McCracken, MacKichan and Eccleston (2007) found that highly disabled patients with chronic pain, exposed to a three-week ACT treatment, improved significantly in pain-related distress, psychosocial and physical disability, depression, pain-related anxiety, sit-to-stand performance, daily rest due to pain and increased acceptance of pain. These clinically meaningful results were maintained at three-month follow-up.

Vowles and McCracken (2008) later published another treatment-effectiveness study and found similar results across many of the outcome measures previously mentioned. Additionally, the ACT processes of pain acceptance and valued-based action improved, and these improvements were associated with the progression seen in the primary outcome measures. Not only were these gains maintained at three-month follow-up, but a separate publication (Vowles, McCracken, & O'Brien, 2011) indicated, three-years post-treatment, that the functioning of these patients was still significantly improved compared to pre-treatment and that there was good maintenance of gains when compared to three-month follow-up, where participants recorded medium effect sizes on the majority of outcome measures. This is a quite incredible piece of research, as the effects of a three- or four-week ACT protocol were still evident three years after treatment.

In 2008 and 2009, the effectiveness studies published by McCracken et al. (2007) and Vowles and McCracken (2008) were complemented by two RCTs. Wicksell, Ahlqvist, Bring, Melin and Olsson (2008) found that 11 patients suffering from whiplash-associated chronic pain, who were given a ten-session group treatment in which values and acceptance were targeted, recorded significant improvements in pain disability, life satisfaction, fear of movements, depression and psychological inflexibility, when compared to those in the waitlist control group. These improvements were maintained at seven-month follow-up, despite the fact that the patients recorded no improvement in levels of pain intensity. Wicksell, Melin, Lekander and Olsson (2008) later aimed to determine if the same ten-week ACT package could be comparable to the standard pain treatment (a multidisciplinary treatment [MDT] approach including amitriptyline) in helping young people between the ages of 10 and 18 to manage chronic pain. Results indicated that the ACT group

($n = 16$) showed significant improvements across all measures including functioning and quality of life. Significant improvements in the MDT group suggested that MDT is also a useful approach, but between-group comparisons showed ACT's superiority in pain intensity, pain interference and quality of life.

In addition to comparing ACT with TAU, it is also important to compare it to other successful psychological treatments used for managing pain. Vowles, Wetherell and Sorrell (2009) began the initial steps of comparing ACT with the gold-standard treatment of chronic pain: CBT. Their pilot study showed that ACT was comparable and even outperformed CBT on some measures. However, later work by Wetherell et al. (2011) showed, in RCT format, that while ACT ($n = 49$) and CBT ($n = 50$) both improved the lives of their patients, no difference between the groups emerged on any outcome measure. However, the authors point out that participants assigned to the ACT group rated ACT as more satisfactory than those in the CBT group rated CBT.

Following these studies, there has been much variability in the type of ACT research conducted with chronic pain in terms of the targeted population. For example, one pilot study showed ACT to be useful to elderly people suffering with chronic pain of a musculoskeletal nature (Alonso, Lopez, Losada, & Gonzales, 2013). Another showed that ACT could be used to improve functioning in children (Ghomian & Shairi, 2014). A small RCT showed ACT to be effective in reducing disability and affective distress in a sample of participants with chronic headaches (Mo'tamedi, Rezaiemaram, & Tavallaie, 2012). Two further RCTs showed that ACT outperformed an education intervention (Steiner, Bogusch, & Bigatti, 2013) and waitlist control group (Wicksell et al., 2012) on a number of outcome measures in the treatment of fibromyalgia, a condition characterized by widespread pain and co-morbid conditions such as fatigue and depression.

With the increasing interest in improving access to psychotherapeutic interventions, ACT has also been tested in a number of delivery formats. Although most of the ACT chronic-pain studies described in this book have delivered ACT in group format, McCracken, Sato and Taylor (2013) found that a brief group intervention (four sessions of four hours) reduced depression and increased overall improvement at post-treatment in comparison to TAU, and improved disability, depression and pain acceptance at three-month follow-up. Two further RCTs found that self-help interventions with minimal therapist contact can also benefit chronic-pain patients. Johnston, Foster, Shennan, Starkey and Johnson (2010) found that a self-help ACT book significantly improved quality of life compared to a waitlist control group, while Thorsell et al. (2011) found that compared to applied relaxation, an ACT manual improved acceptance, satisfaction with life, functioning and pain intensity. Finally, one pilot study (Ljótsson et al., 2014) and two RCTs (Buhrman et al., 2013; Trompetter, Bohlmeijer, Veehof, & Schreurs, 2014) detail how a web-delivered ACT protocol improved a number of outcomes at post-treatment and follow-up.

ACT has been tested with people of different ages presenting with different types of chronic pain. It has been tested in pilot studies, effectiveness studies and RCTs, and it has been delivered in brief format, via self-help intervention and web-based intervention. Most of the research leads to the same significant conclusion: ACT is powerful in this domain. For information about one of the leading researchers in the area of chronic pain, please see the researcher profile and future directions of Dr Kevin Vowles below.

Researcher profile: Dr Kevin Vowles

Kevin Vowles completed his PhD in Clinical Psychology at West Virginia University in 2004 and Post-doctoral Fellowship within the Department of Anesthesiology at the University of Virginia the following year. From 2005 to 2009, he worked as a senior research fellow and clinical psychologist within the Centres for Pain Research and Services, which are based within the School for Health, University of Bath and Royal National Hospital for Rheumatic Diseases NHS (National Health Service) Foundation Trust.

In 2009, he accepted a position as Consultant Clinical Psychologist with the Haywood Hospital and Arthritis Research UK Primary Care Centre at Keele University and successfully helped to develop a novel interdisciplinary pain-rehabilitation program to be delivered at the interface of primary and secondary care. After three years of trial funding, this program was deemed by the UK's NHS to be highly effective in both clinical and financial terms, and permanent funding was secured. The service was also the winner of the UK Health Integration Award in the autumn of 2013. In 2012, Kevin moved back to the USA to take up a position within the Department of Psychology at the University of New Mexico (UNM). He was promoted to the rank of associate professor with tenure the following year. He has continued his work in pain rehabilitation since moving to UNM, particularly as it relates to the facilitation of effective, meaningful functioning in those with chronic pain. In addition, recent work has expanded his focus to issues surrounding appropriate and inappropriate opioid use in this area. Current projects are funded by the USA NIH and Robert Wood Johnson Foundation. Since beginning his doctoral training in 2002, Kevin has published over 60 scientific articles.

My doctoral training was steeped in learning the experimental analysis of behaviour and the clinical applications that can be derived from it. Further, as an undergraduate, I was fortunate to work with a clinical psychologist working in chronic pain. Behaviour analysis provides an adequate and coherent account of what the "problem" is in chronic pain. This account was eloquently captured in Fordyce's 1976 book titled, *Behavioural Methods for Chronic Pain and Illness*. In essence, the problem is not the pain itself, but the ways that persistent pain can lead to a narrowed behavioural repertoire focused upon pain avoidance at the cost of engaging in activities that matter. Behaviour analysis, therefore, seeks to expand the narrowed and avoidant repertoire. From these foundational assumptions, the model of ACT provides some clear expansions. For example, increasing the amount of, and enhancing the quality of engagement in, valued activities can provide clear directions for behaviour in response to pain. Furthermore, altering the ways in which pain interferes with functioning, for example by responding to it with a willingness to experience it in the service of something that matters, is a message inherently filled with promise. These are the aspects of behaviour analysis and ACT that attracted me as they pertain to pain.

I think the literature on ACT and chronic pain is fairly strong. We have reasonably good measures, which in turn have reasonably good psychometric properties. We have a fairly established base of data with regard to treatment effectiveness and also evidence of sustained gains up through follow-ups of as long as three years. We have evidence from studies using sophisticated statistical analyses that suggest increases in willingness to have pain, awareness of the present, self-compassion and engagement in valued activities are related to important treatment gains, such as reduced disability and healthcare utilization. These data include a diversity of samples, including pain locations and diagnoses, age and ethnicity (e.g. adolescents, adults) and treatment formats (e.g. groups, individuals, interdisciplinary, psychology only). That is the good news – we have made great gains over a rather short period of time. Such successes should be recognized and celebrated. For example, ACT for chronic pain is listed by the American Psychological Association's Division of

Clinical Psychology (Div 12) as an empirically supported treatment with "strong" support, the highest grading possible.

There are, of course, areas where concerted work is needed. Just like the areas of success, deficits should be recognized, and also addressed in an honest, forthright fashion, as well as approached from the scientific epistemology that is at the heart of the empirical enterprise.

The treatment-effectiveness data are not always coherent across studies, particularly in relation to treatment format and study design. The ACT model, at its heart, implicitly argues that it should allow us better, more efficient and more durable effects than treatment models that assign unique causal status to private events such as thoughts and feelings with regard to the determination of behaviour. Such a mechanism and reductionism is rejected inherently by behaviour analysis because it constrains the utility of the analysis – ACT for chronic pain, theoretically at least, ought to work better. But the data at this point indicate equivocal effects. I do not think we can afford to rest on the "ACT is young, give us time to do better/more adequately powered/more methodologically sound" reason-giving for the same old effectiveness for much longer.

In addition to that, we could do a better job at determining adequate treatment content and requisite training experiences to adequately provide treatment. At this point, we simply do not know how to differentiate the quality of ACT for chronic pain across studies, nor discern necessary parts of intervention from those that are unnecessary – in short, quality control is uncertain. Rather than rely on authority figures to determine what "is" and "is not" ACT (surely a different kind of epistemology from the scientific one), these issues of accuracy and fidelity can be addressed though data.

Finally, treatment success in chronic pain likely involves adding persistently adaptive responses to a persistently aversive stimulus, that of pain, which naturally occasions escape and avoidance. This is a practical matter – chronic pain is lifelong and therefore adaptive response to it must be lifelong as well. As a field, it seems to me we must figure out the methods to increase the probability of sustained adaptive responding. We are not there yet within the field of ACT, or in chronic-pain treatment more broadly.

We could, for example, conceptualize needed adaptive responses through the ACT model – a lack of needless struggles for pain control, an awareness of present experiences that include pain and are also wider than that, a patience and acceptance of oneself as an imperfect human being, a flexible tenacity in one's engagement in the activities that personally matter – and these responses, if sustained over time, would likely be a reasonable definition of treatment success. These data deserve to be collected and their adequacy as a definition of "success" empirically evaluated.

It is entirely feasible for us as a field to address these shortcomings of the literature on ACT for chronic pain, which are perhaps also applicable to the broader field of ACT. I do not see identifying them as a task that needs to elicit concern necessarily, or feelings of despair for those of us in the field. That being said, if we want the field to move forward, I would contend we must be serious about addressing them through our adopted methods, which are reliant on collecting the data first, with every other outcome as a distant second.

Process and component research in chronic pain

In addition to the aforementioned outcome studies, much effort has also been made to investigate the role of ACT processes in the management of chronic pain. One area that has been thoroughly explored is how higher levels of acceptance may be valuable in helping the patient manage their condition. Studies of this kind tend to involve participants completing a battery of questionnaires in which levels of acceptance are measured against adjustment to pain. These investigations were hugely important in the beginning of this research stream, as finding that those with higher levels of acceptance experience better outcomes suggested that training acceptance might be a useful way of improving the lives of people suffering with chronic pain. The following paragraphs will detail some of these investigations.

McCracken (1998) found that greater acceptance of pain was correlated with lower pain intensity, less pain-related anxiety and avoidance, less depression, better physical and psychosocial ability, more daily time of being up and about and better work status. Importantly, regression analyses showed that acceptance predicted better adjustment on all measures of patient functioning independent of perceived pain intensity; that is, pain did not have to decrease in order for patient functioning to increase. Since this study, a plethora of further efforts have been published lending support to the importance of acceptance in managing chronic pain.

McCracken, Spertus, Janeck, Sinclair and Wetzel (1999) found that patients characterized as dysfunctional chronic-pain sufferers (chronic pain affects their levels of everyday functioning) reported greater pain-related anxiety and less pain acceptance than other types of chronic-pain sufferers. McCracken and Eccleston (2003) found that acceptance of pain was more strongly associated with improvement on a number of outcomes in comparison to "coping" with, or tolerating pain. Although it is important to note that later research by Esteve, Ramirez-Maestre and Lopez-Martinez (2007) suggested that acceptance and coping may be complementary approaches. Finally, McCracken (2005) displayed how the influence of social context can affect acceptance of pain, where those who receive solicitous, punishing and distracting responses from people around them tend to record lower levels of acceptance and thus lower engagement in activity.

In the past two years, a number of further investigations from various research groups have continued to link acceptance with better adjustment to pain. Pinto-Gouveia, Costa and Maroco (2013) found that those with greater acceptance of pain reported experiencing less pain, physical limitation and depression. Baranoff, Hanrahan and Connor (2014) found that lower acceptance of pain was associated with greater pain intensity and depressive symptoms in athletes who had received anterior cruciate ligament reconstruction. Dindo, Recober, Marchman, Turvey and O'Hara (2012) found that low acceptance was related to higher rates of depression and disability in migraine sufferers. And a couple of interesting studies found that a CBT chronic-pain protocol increased acceptance in its patients, that those increases in acceptance contributed to treatment outcome and that at six-months post-treatment, participants who reported decreases in acceptance also reported higher levels of deterioration and depression (Baranoff, Hanrahan, Kapur, & Connor, 2013; Baranoff, Hanrahan, Kapur, & Connor, 2014).

Thus far this section has described research in which participants complete a number of questionnaires that assess the relationship between acceptance and pain adjustment at specific time points, but there are other ways to link the concepts. McCracken and Eccleston (2005) measured acceptance of pain on two occasions, roughly 3.9 months apart. Results indicated that acceptance of pain at the beginning of the 3.9 months was significantly related to patient functioning at the end. This implies that willingness to have pain and engage in valued activities can lead to healthy functioning. McCracken, Vowles and Gauntlett-Gilbert (2007) conducted a similar study and found that those who indicated a propensity for trying to control their pain had significantly worse functioning than those willing to persist in activities while acknowledging that pain is present. Kratz, Davis and Zautra (2007) found that acceptance moderated the relation between pain and negative affect in women with osteoarthritis and fibromyalgia over a 12-week period. In other words, participants with higher levels of acceptance were better able to manage their condition, such that when they experienced sharp increases in pain, the expected increases in negative affect did not occur.

Other research studies have been conducted in which other ACT processes have been linked to chronic pain. McCracken and Yang (2006) and McCracken and Vowles (2008) found values-based action to be significantly related to patient functioning, and McCracken and Zhao-O'Brien (2010) and McCracken and Velleman (2010) found that being high in PF may reduce the impact of chronic pain. However, Vowles, Sowden and Ashworth (2014) conducted arguably the most thorough investigation of the relationship between ACT processes and patient functioning. Through a complex analysis, they found that each of the ACT processes was related to pain intensity, emotional distress and disability, suggesting that the ACT model is a good fit in the treatment of those with chronic pain.

In addition to determining if higher baseline levels of ACT processes improve the likelihood of therapeutic success, much work has also been conducted to determine if changes in ACT processes throughout treatment mediate the improvements seen in primary outcome measures. Vowles, McCracken and Eccleston (2007) were among the first to do this when they asked participants to complete a number of measures prior to treatment, immediately following treatment and at three-month follow-up. Although the authors point out that the aim of the investigation was not to study the outcome of treatment, participants recorded significant gains across all outcome measures. The article's primary purpose was to investigate the mediating role of acceptance. Results indicated that changes in acceptance of pain accounted for a significant unique variance of the improvements seen in depression, pain-related anxiety, physical disability, daily rest and physical performance. In a later study, the same authors found that acceptance mediated the effects of catastrophic thinking (a process that often accompanies chronic pain) on depression, anxiety and physical and psychosocial functioning (Vowles, McCracken, & Eccleston, 2008).

Following these studies, in which acceptance seemed to be an active process contributing to clinical improvement, researchers began to re-analyse past data to determine the role of ACT processes in therapeutic outcome. For example, Vowles and McCracken (2010) conducted a secondary analysis of their previous outcome study (Vowles & McCracken, 2008). In this process analysis, they aimed to examine how changes in traditional methods of "coping" with chronic pain compare to PF in relation to improvements in functioning. Results indicated that while changes in PF were persistently related to improvements in functioning, coping was unrelated to improvements. This study is a great example of why a process analysis is important – because it is not enough to know *that* a treatment package works, it is crucial to know *how* it works. According to these authors, coping methods thought to be useful with this population may not be related to treatment improvement, but changes in PF seem to make an important contribution. In the following couple of years, two further mediational analyses of earlier outcome studies were published. Wicksell, Olsson and Hayes (2010) took the data from the Wicksell et al. (2008) whiplash study. Results indicated that PF mediated improvements seen in pain disability and life satisfaction. Interestingly, a number of process variables important in CBT did not mediate improvements seen in many of the outcome measures. Wicksell, Olsson and Hayes (2011) then took the data from the Wicksell et al. (2008) paediatric study and found similar results. Namely, that variables consistent with PF mediated outcome.

Recently, two further studies have been published investigating mediation and process. Vowles, Witkiewitz, Sowden and Ashworth (2014) published an open trial in which 117 patients were given a brief ACT-based intervention. Results indicated that 46.2% of patients had achieved clinically significant change by three-month follow-up. Importantly, changes in PF were found to mediate the improvements found in disability, depression, pain-related anxiety, number of medical visits and the number of prescribed analgesics (pain killers). Finally, Vowles, Fink and Cohen (2014) asked participants to complete a weekly diary that assessed pain control and engagement in valued activities over the course of a four-week ACT intervention for chronic pain. In terms of outcome, 47.6% of the patients evidenced reliable disability reduction. In terms of process, the expected pattern of change occurred for 81% of participants, where decreases in pain control and increases in engagement with valued activities reliably reduced disability, and the absence of the pattern was associated with a lack of reliable change.

This area of ACT research has accumulated much empirical evidence. Consequently, it has been difficult to describe every study in detail. For that reason, we would point you towards a systematic review (Hann &

McCracken, 2014) and three conceptual articles that summarize the area exquisitely (Thompson & McCracken, 2011; McCracken & Montesinos-Marin, 2014; McCracken & Vowles, 2014). We would also encourage you to find some of the articles mentioned in this chapter and notice for yourself the huge participant numbers, the strong designs, the complex analyses and the convincing argument that acceptance is a useful strategy for sufferers of chronic pain. For information about a hugely respected academic and his thoughts on the future directions of this research area, please see Dr Lance McCracken's researcher profile below.

Researcher profile: Dr Lance McCracken

Lance M. McCracken is Professor of Behavioural Medicine at King's College London in the Health Psychology Section of the Psychology Department. He is also Consultant Clinical Psychologist and the Psychology Lead at the INPUT Pain Management Centre at St Thomas' Hospital in London. He has published more than 150 scientific papers and chapters, and two books. He is on the editorial boards for *Health Psychology*, the *Journal of Behavioural Medicine, Journal of Pain*, and the *European Journal of Pain*, among others. He has also been named a Fellow of the Association for Contextual Behavioural Science. His primary research interests are in chronic-pain treatment development, behavioural theory, contextual approaches within the cognitive behavioural therapies and PF.

Some people may not know that ACT for chronic pain probably started some time before 1992, the year a doctoral dissertation on "Acceptance-Focused Treatment...in Chronic Pain" was completed by David S. Geiser at the University of Nevada in Reno. According to that starting point, ACT now has a 23-year history in addressing chronic pain. In 23 years it has amassed 100s of related studies, about 20 treatment-outcome studies and at least 11 RCTs. One therapeutic facet underlying ACT, acceptance, is widely regarded as an important process in chronic pain. The paper presenting the instrument to assess acceptance has been cited more than 485 times since it first appeared in 1998. Based on current published evidence, it appears that ACT is as efficacious as traditional cognitive behavioural therapy (tCBT) for chronic pain. It appears to have better evidence for processes of change, if reflected as a ratio of evidence per RCT. There are also suggestive findings that ACT may be preferred by people seeking treatment and by clinicians who deliver the treatment. So, where ought we to go in the next ten years?

If ACT is to succeed, there are several challenges it will need to meet soon. One of these is to avoid being swept up in trends that have engulfed tCBT. tCBT for chronic pain achieved early success more than 30 years ago. It gained this success within a domain dominated by a medical model. The tCBT model, including packages of treatment methods focused on changing coping and beliefs as a means for reducing distress and disability, gained wide popularity. In part, it achieved this success by selling itself as an expansion of the medical model and not a way to replace it. Within this early success, however, lay the seeds of difficulty. This included the way that tCBT became very good at (1) showing more and more ways that psychological variables relate to, and seem to hold the potential to create change in, pain-related outcomes; and (2) building a larger and larger base of evidence showing that tCBT is effective. tCBT played very well to an interdisciplinary audience. What it did less well was to work within itself to organize a focus of continued research and treatment development, on more and more precisely defined, highly impacting and generally applicable treatment processes, and on designing future treatments that are better than the treatments of today. We often say that it was very good at inventing new variables but not very good at integrating and clarifying important psychological dimensions underlying these.

Selling tCBT may have become slightly too important, and producing the next, possibly radically new treatment, was not important enough. In many ways this is entirely natural, as this is what the times required, and yet it could be good to move on. Some of the collateral effects of the success of tCBT, however, include "over dissemination" and a loss of focus on such factors as competency and fidelity. The message of tCBT was crafted in such an easy-to-understand fashion, and its key terms appeared immediately understandable to anyone, that it looked easy to do. Soon professionals from most disciplines were doing a little CBT, and doing CBT was beginning to look like talking, teaching, lecturing and persuading and not like behavioural experiments, exposure therapy, Behavioural Activation, skills training and such. At some point, effect sizes for tCBT were not getting bigger anymore and certainly the methods were not being significantly refined. In essence, a highly technical activity requiring great skill had become DIY CBT.

One of the lessons from chronic-pain treatment development is in seeing the difference between promoting a treatment versus promoting a treatment-development strategy. Ironically, if ACT wants to grow and prosper, it has to do the latter and not the former. This is not an original idea. All or most of the key opinion leaders in the CBS community appear to be highlighting the same issue. ACT cannot stay the ACT of today if it wants to succeed according to its own goals.

What does this mean more particularly in chronic-pain research and treatment development? I feel we have followed a good road of digging into the current concepts and processes we have at hand, at getting data on these and seeing where they lead us. "Acceptance" as a process has been well researched and so far has been very fruitful – although even here I think we are far from done. "Values" was another natural variable to pick up and so far this has been productive too. "Present-focused attention", "cognitive defusion" and "committed action", although each far behind the work on acceptance, have all provided guides, given us questions to ask and are yielding data that feed back into our treatment-development work. "Self" and therapeutic stance are the newest frontiers for us and we have begun empirical work here too. All the while in the back of our mind sits the notion that each of these seems like a basis for a next step into the unknown, and any one of these terms may one day need a radical overhaul, or may be dropped in favour of a term that organizes our work even better.

The other more particular message from our past that registers here is the goodness and necessity of model, fidelity and competency. Twenty years ago when I first began collecting data on a facet of what later has become psychological flexibility, I could not have imagined that the wide popularity of ACT could be frightening. Yet, it certainly can be. I don't know how to address this, yet I feel it is important to do so. In day-to-day life, we tend to treat things as if they are what they are called. I think succeeding with ACT will probably require that somehow we assert consistently, and with effect, the notion that ACT is not ACT when it does not enhance psychological flexibility and otherwise follow principles of what is ACT. Just because it is called ACT, doesn't mean it is ACT.

There is a point to make about one of the issues already raised. In the multidisciplinary audiences that psychologists encounter in physical health, there is often a tendency to keep our language and concepts simple so that we do not use words that confuse others. It seems to me an effect of this is that we cannot use our own technical language or say some things with precision. This is a curiously non-mutual arrangement. When I read studies in neurophysiology, genetics, or pharmacology, I see immediately that my colleagues in these fields do not aim to protect me from terms I do not understand. Psychological flexibility and its facets are considerably more difficult to understand than the term "coping", yet, if we cannot use our words, our work becomes extremely difficult to develop, do and report. We need to find ways to improve ourselves in our ability to keep speaking with different audiences and not let the need to please one of these audiences restrict our ability to use our own tools. Somehow we need to act more sensitively and more boldly.

In summary, future success of ACT for chronic pain may include the following: (1) building on existing evidence in a progressive fashion; (2) investigating interesting findings on therapist and treatment participant preferences (or positive side effects) of ACT; (3) presenting ACT as an expansion and not a replacement of what is currently done; (4) keeping our eye on a strategy of development rather than a type of therapy; (5) following a process-focused model; (6) assuring that fidelity and competency are included, particularly in research trials; and (7) finding ways to use our own assumptions, principles and terms to guide our work, even if they risk confusion from others, and bridge the gap of translation to others when possible too.

13
Other Health Conditions

Thus far, the application of ACT to eating behaviour, smoking behaviour, substance abuse and chronic pain have displayed that the model is useful across a number of health behaviours. However, there are a variety of other health conditions in which significant research has been conducted. The aim of this chapter is to provide an overview of these investigations.

Tinnitus

Tinnitus can be defined as the conscious perception of internal noises without any appropriate external sound source (Andersson, Baguley, McKenna, & McFerran, 2005). For many, tinnitus is not a source of great distress, however for 10%–20% of sufferers, it disrupts everyday activities and is linked with sleep disturbances and mood disorders (Davis & El Rafie, 2000). Following a questionnaire study in which acceptance played a mediating role in a number of tinnitus-related outcomes (Westin, Hayes, & Andersson, 2008) and an experimental study where participants that tried to control (avoid) their tinnitus reported greater interference and worse cognitive functioning (Hesser, Pereswetoff-Morath, & Andersson, 2009), researchers felt that an acceptance-based treatment might be useful with the disorder.

Hesser, Westin, Hayes and Andersson (2009) conducted the earliest intervention study and found that levels of defusion and acceptance predicted symptom reduction at six-month follow-up in a sample of 24 tinnitus sufferers, however, the two major investigations were conducted in RCT format in the following two years. Westin et al. (2011) compared ten weekly one-hour sessions of ACT with tinnitus retraining therapy (TRT). TRT is an intervention that involves directive counselling based on a neurophysiological account of tinnitus in combination with sound therapy; that is, the use of devices that generate noise. Both parts are used to recondition the mechanisms of the nervous system to habituate the brain to the tinnitus signal. In the current study, TRT was chosen as an active treatment comparison given its popularity and success in treating the disorder (Henry, Zaugg, Myers, & Schechter, 2008). Results showed that those in the ACT group ($n = 21$) experienced significant improvements in tinnitus impact, sleep quality and anxiety compared to the waitlist control group ($n = 22$). Most importantly, at post-treatment, six-month follow-up and 18-month follow-up, those in the ACT group reported significantly greater improvements in tinnitus impact and sleep quality when compared to TRT. In fact, at six-month follow-up, 54.5% of the participants showed clinically significant and reliable change in the ACT group compared to 20% in the TRT group. Finally, process analyses found that increases in acceptance mediated the primary outcomes in the ACT group.

A year after this study, Hesser et al. (2012) compared an internet-delivered ACT protocol ($n = 33$) with an established CBT protocol ($n = 27$) for the treatment of tinnitus. Results indicated that both conditions caused a high percentage of clinically significant change in tinnitus distress at post-treatment, eight-week follow-up and one-year follow-up when compared to control ($n = 32$). However, no difference was observed between ACT and CBT on any of the outcome measures, prompting the authors to conclude that ACT is a viable alternative to CBT.

Epilepsy

Given that tinnitus has already accumulated two RCTs, one could consider the area to be quite well developed. Another domain that has received attention, despite being a relatively uncommon issue, is that of epilepsy. Following a conceptual article published in *The Behaviour Analyst Today*, which discussed the potential utility of the ACT model in treating epilepsy (Dahl & Lundgren, 2005), a pilot RCT was conducted on a sample of individuals from South Africa suffering with drug refractory epilepsy (those for whom drug treatment does not work). Lundgren, Dahl, Melin and Kies (2006) found that those assigned to receive a four-session ACT protocol ($n = 14$) showed significant improvements in quality of life and seizure index (frequency × duration of epileptic fits) in comparison to those assigned to receive supportive therapy (ST), a protocol in which the therapist is employed to listen and support, but not to give advice. These gains were recorded at post-treatment and maintained at six-month and 12-month follow-up. Although no process analysis occurred at the time, a later publication (Lundgren, Dahl, & Hayes, 2008) found that acceptance, defusion, values attainment and persistence in the face of barriers mediated the seizure-index and quality of life outcomes.

Lundgren, Dahl, Yardi and Melin (2008) later conducted another RCT to investigate how useful ACT could be in comparison to a yoga-based treatment, following evidence suggesting that yoga may provide a novel and useful approach for managing epilepsy. Results indicated that although both ACT ($n = 10$) and yoga ($n = 8$) improved seizure index and quality of life from post-treatment to six-month and 12-month follow-up, the ACT group fared better on the seizure-index measure. Given the potential similarities between ACT and yoga-based treatments, the authors recommend that future research include an analysis to discover the active processes contributing towards successful outcome. They also discuss the interesting finding that ACT outperformed yoga on one quality of life measure, while the reverse was found for a second quality of life measure, which is another example of measurement issues in clinical research. Finally, the authors suggest that a large-scale RCT is now needed to determine the effectiveness that ACT might have in treating epilepsy. For information about the leading researcher on these studies, please see the researcher profile of Dr Tobias Lundgren below.

Researcher profile: Dr Tobias Lundgren

Tobias Lundgren, PhD, is a clinical psychologist and licensed psychotherapist. He finished his PhD and clinical psychology program at the Psychology Department at Uppsala University. Tobias' doctoral thesis was mainly conducted in India and South Africa, where he developed, implemented and investigated an ACT approach to reduce seizures and increase quality of life for persons suffering from epilepsy. Tobias has mainly published in the clinical psychology area related to development and evaluation of ACT-based psychological treatments, for problem areas such as epilepsy, pain, Asperger's syndrome, self-harm, and, more recently, psychosis and the enhancement of elite athlete performance. In 2006, he was awarded the Swedish epilepsy organization's award for his work with the development of treatments for those who suffer from epilepsy. Furthermore, he has co-authored two books: *The Art and Science of Valuing in Psychotherapy* and *Living beyond Your Pain*. He is currently on the editorial board for the *Journal of Sport Psychology* and a reviewer for numerous scientific journals. After working as a faculty member at the Department of Psychology, Stockholm University, he now serves as Head of the Center for Psychotherapeutic Excellence at Karolinska Institute, Stockholm City Council, Sweden.

Epilepsy has traditionally been seen as a medical problem that needs to be "fixed" through treatments based in the medical paradigm. To simplify the traditional view, it is assumed that a dysfunction in the brain causes epileptic seizures in a direct causal manner (Zaccara, Gangemi, & Cincotta, 2008). A contextual behaviour approach to epilepsy and related problems assumes that there are no simple one-way causal relations between damaged brain cells and seizures. Instead epileptic seizures are seen as complex, triggered and maintained through specific individual contexts. From a CBS perspective those contexts need to be analysed and influenced through various therapeutic perspectives. Our research has shown that the combination of medical treatment and contextual behavioural psychological treatments show better results than medical treatment alone (Lundgren, Dahl, Melin, & Kies, 2006; Lundgren, Dahl, Yardi, & Melin, 2008). Epileptic seizures can be influenced with psychological interventions and quality of life can be enhanced for those who suffer from recurrent seizures. One major future direction for the treatment of epilepsy and related problems is to work for integration of knowledge from different paradigms such as the medical, psychological, technical, neurological, social and evolutionary in order to serve those who suffer as effectively as possible.

To stimulate this integration from different disciplines, there is a need for development in a range of areas. Two of them are education and research.

Starting with education, there is a need to protect the philosophical part of our medical and health education programs in order to help our students to be able to challenge already established "truths". For example, the one-way medical assumption between damaged brain cells and seizures doesn't necessarily serve the development of effective treatment methods for epilepsy best. Although one context might develop effective treatments, it doesn't necessarily serve the development of further development of treatment methods for those who suffer from recurrent seizures best. Something else might, thus, no "truths" per se are of interest, but instead effectiveness towards certain chosen goals are. Education in philosophy helps us challenge our truths and that is important in order to stimulate development.

Education regarding the effectiveness of psychological interventions for epilepsy needs to be included in both medical education programs and psychological training programs. A range of researchers in the field suggest that there is a need for collaborating efforts to best be of service to those who suffer (Beyenburg, Mitchell, Schmidt, Elger, & Reuber, 2005; Elger & Schmidt, 2008; Mittan, 2009) and therefore knowledge of different methods for treatment from different fields need to be included in education programs from different fields. As a starter, psychologists need the knowledge that they have something to offer not only in testing procedures but also treatment wise in relation to epilepsy. Furthermore, Medical doctors need to know that there are available complimentary treatment procedures that can be of use for those who suffer. There is much to be done in the field of education in order to help treatment personnel to better serve those who suffer from epilepsy.

Research wise there is much to do both inside the field of psychology and through collaborating approaches. Starting inside the field there is a need to do randomized group studies with an increased number of participants and more stringent methodology. However, group studies are not the best methodology per se for our purposes. We need diversity in research and therefore I would also suggest more single subject designed studies, mediational designs, dissemination studies that help us understand more regarding effective treatment components, the process of seizure development and what maintains seizures.

Psychology has a lot to offer in collaborating approaches. For example, patients use vagus nerve stimulators in order to influence the seizure process. But these are often used ad hoc. Operant psychology and a contextual approach may help clients to better understand how to use the stimulator in order to influence the seizure process most effectively. An analysis regarding seizure triggers and maintenance factors may help create hypotheses about when to best use the stimulator. Also, knowledge in $n = 1$ research methods could help test the hypotheses in a more scientific manner. This is only one of many examples of when a collaborating approach could be beneficial.

Neurologists and staff at neurological centres often have a heavy workload. Implementation of new methods and collaborating approaches take time and effort. A future line of research would therefore be development and evaluation of implementation approaches.

Measurement of cost effectiveness research, clinical effectiveness and a sense of work satisfaction may be important ways to move in order to evaluate if the effort of collaboration and implementation of new ways of working is worthwhile.

Serious health conditions

Although tinnitus and epilepsy are serious health issues, ACT research has also been conducted with what might be considered the most serious health conditions. For example, Sheppard, Forsyth, Hickling and Bianchi (2010) found that a half-day ACT workshop, conducted on 15 participants presenting with multiple sclerosis (MS), improved depression, impact of pain on behaviour and quality of life at three-month follow-up. Pakenham and Fleming (2011) complemented this study a year later when asking 128 people with MS to complete a batch of questionnaires, including a newly developed Multiple Sclerosis Acceptance Questionnaire (MSAQ). Results indicated that greater acceptance was related to better adjustment, as calculated by measuring positive affect, subjective health status and life satisfaction. In addition to MS, ACT has also been used to treat sickle cell disease in case-study format (Masuda, Cohen, Wicksell, Kemani, & Johnson, 2011), and may be useful in medical rehabilitation (Kortte, Veiel, Batten, & Wegener, 2009) and post-surgical recovery (Fernandez, Luciano, & Valdivia-Salas, 2012).

ACT has even been used to treat diabetes. In a classic study, Gregg, Callaghan, Hayes and Glenn-Lawson (2007) conducted an RCT to compare education alone ($n = 38$) with a combination of education and ACT ($n = 43$). Following only a one-day workshop, results indicated that those in the ACT group were more likely to be using ACT strategies, reported better diabetes self-care and had glycated-haemoglobin values in the target range (higher levels of glycated haemoglobin increase the likelihood of developing diabetes-related complications). This is quite a remarkable result as it provides evidence that the ACT protocol directly impacted behaviour. Further analysis revealed that self-management and acceptance mediated outcome.

Traumatic brain injury (TBI) is another serious condition to which ACT has been linked in the past few years. For example, two conceptual articles (Soo, Tate, & Lane-Brown, 2011; Kangas & McDonald, 2011) detail how ACT may be useful in helping those who have suffered a TBI to manage their mental health. However, although Whiting, Simpson, McLeod, Deane and Ciarrochi (2012) published an ACT protocol to be used with an RCT, Whiting, Deane, Ciarrochi, McLeod and Simpson (2014) developed a psychological flexibility measure for people with acquired brain injury and Williams, Vaughan, Huws and Hastings (2014) published a qualitative analysis detailing the utility of ACT in helping spousal caregivers manage the stresses of caring for someone with a TBI; as of yet, no intervention research has been conducted with this population.

Arguably, the most feared medical illness is cancer. Researchers have attempted to use the ACT model to help cancer sufferers manage their condition and their mental health with a variety of experimental designs. For example, two case studies (Montesinos, Hernandez, & Luciano, 2001; Karekla & Constantinou, 2010) and two small-scale investigations (Montesinos & Luciano, 2005; Paez, Luciano, & Gutierrez, 2007) showed promise in the treatment of distress associated with breast cancer, and a questionnaire study indicated that living one's values was significantly related to improved well-being and decreased distress in a sample of 107 patients suffering from a variety of cancers (Ciarrochi, Fisher, & Lane, 2011). However, it was not until 2011 that a larger investigation was published with this population. Feros, Lane, Ciarrochi and Blackledge (2011) conducted a preliminary study in which 45 cancer patients received nine therapy sessions that aimed to cover defusion, mindfulness, SAC and values clarification. From pre- to post-intervention, the patients showed significant improvements in distress, mood disturbance and quality of life, and these gains were maintained at three-month follow-up. The effect sizes for improvement were comparable to other interventions with this population and a process analysis revealed that changes in PF predicted the changes seen in the three outcome measures.

The seminal investigation in this area was conducted by Rost, Wilson, Buchanan, Hildebrandt and Mutch (2012). In RCT format, these researchers compared 12 sessions of ACT ($n = 25$) with TAU ($n = 22$) in the treatment of emotional distress among women with late-stage ovarian cancer. Results showed that although both groups displayed improvements in mood and quality of life following the intervention, the ACT group showed greater improvements. The authors discuss that whilst one would expect improvements in quality of life in the ACT condition given the emphasis that ACT places on behaviour, they expected no difference between ACT and TAU in levels of improvement in depression and anxiety. Nevertheless, those in the ACT group showed greater improvements on those measures as well. Given the fact that the TAU group showed improvements that were comparable to other TAUs with this population, and given that reductions in avoidance mediated successful outcome, the study provides justification for further research investigating ACT's usefulness in treating cancer-related distress.

Following this seminal study, a group of researchers from Australia have been making huge strides applying ACT to the area of colorectal cancer. Firstly, Hawkes, Patrao, Green and Aitken (2012) conducted a pilot study in which people at risk of developing colorectal cancer were given six ACT-based telephone-coaching sessions. Results indicated that participants ($n = 22$) positively changed their behaviour from post-intervention to six-week follow-up across a number of behaviours: physical activity, processed meat intake, vegetable intake, alcohol intake, waist circumference and BMI. Improvements were also recorded for physical and mental health, and quality of life. Following this pilot study, the same research group conducted a large-scale RCT to determine if a similar protocol could positively impact the behaviours of colorectal cancer survivors (Hawkes et al., 2013). Results once again indicated that, compared to TAU ($n = 205$), the ACT intervention ($n = 189$) positively changed behaviour by 12-month follow-up. A later publication, in which the authors returned to the data from their RCT, found that participants who received the intervention also reported improved psychosocial outcomes and quality of life (Hawkes, Pakenham, Chambers, Patrao, & Courneya, 2014). What is interesting about these publications is that they do not explicitly name ACT in the title of the article. This means that many may not have come across these important investigations in which ACT has been used, in a multidisciplinary context, as a vehicle for behaviour change. For interested readers, a separate publication details exactly how ACT is used within their protocol (Hawkes et al., 2009).

In the last year or so, two further articles have been published that link ACT to cancer. Gholamhosseini and Mojtabaie (2015) provided more evidence that ACT has cross cultural appeal by reducing anxiety in Iranian women diagnosed with breast cancer and Hulbert-Williams, Storey and Wilson (2014) published a conceptual article detailing how the ACT model may be useful in this domain. Indeed, the first author of that conceptual article, Dr Nick Hulbert-Williams, who is heavily involved in researching ACT's utility in treating cancer in the UK, is the profile researcher in this section.

Researcher profile: Dr Nick Hulbert-Williams

Nick Hulbert-Williams is Coaching Psychologist and Reader in Psychology at the University of Chester (UK), where he directs the Chester Research Unit for the Psychology of Health (CRUPH). Nick has been researching the psychological impact of cancer diagnosis and treatment, and the consequences for both patients and their family members, for the past ten years. He is currently leading a programme of work dedicated to developing clinically and cost-effective interventions for cancer patients, within which ACT features heavily. Nick is Past Chair of the British Psychosocial Oncology Society (BPOS) and is a member of the UK National Cancer Research Institute Psychosocial Oncology and Survivorship Clinical Studies Group. He sits on the editorial board of the *European Journal of Cancer Care* and is a member of the International Psycho-Oncology Society Research Committee. He is a member of the Professional Advisory Board for Maggie's Centres, a UK charitable trust dedicated to providing holistic psychosocial care to those affected by cancer.

The need for psychosocial and supportive care for people with cancer is well established: a survey carried out by Macmillan Cancer Support in the UK, found that 75% of all patients experience anxiety, and 49% experience depression, as a result of their diagnosis (Macmillan, 2006), and we know that this often continues into survivorship (Watson et al., 2012) with fear of cancer recurrence being a prevalent and on-going concern (Hodges & Humphris, 2009). There is a fairly substantial literature on the effectiveness of various psychological interventions (particularly CBT) in cancer, but across the board, these have demonstrated rather modest salutary outcomes. It's no surprise then that the integration of psychological support is still often not prioritized by medical services. Very brief screening measures (often not psychometrically robust) are used to limit the affordance of psychological support to those with only the highest levels of clinical need, with the majority of patients (and, indeed, carers and family members) being relegated to a postcode lottery of supportive care programmes, not all of which adhere to the highest standards of evidence-based care.

Psychosocial oncology has been making a strong case to normalize cancer-related distress for decades, but this is somewhat at odds with the continued strong emphasis towards the use of CBT. More so, outside of this small corner of the oncology community, the military metaphor often prevails, and we continue to hear of patients being encouraged to adopt a "fighting-spirit" approach and to think more "positively". In our recent review paper (Hulbert-Williams, Storey, & Wilson, 2014), we argued that this kind of pressure and expectation is neither appropriate nor helpful for patients, and that the ACT model provides a very real alternative. This is our first challenge: to disseminate the idea that suffering and distress are perfectly reasonable responses to cancer. The aim in CBT to challenge irrational thinking might apply adequately to extremely hopeless thinking in those with a good prognosis, but otherwise, we must surely recognize that virtually anyone would find a diagnosis of a life-threatening illness distressing. In ACT, we can help clients accept difficult private experiences – difficult thoughts and unpleasant emotions – and still live a personally meaningful life, no matter how short it might be.

There are only a handful of papers to be found reporting ACT interventions for this patient group; what we really need are more robustly designed studies to generate a strong evidence base. These need to be comparative trials so that we can, once and for all, determine which interventions are worth providing and which should be sidelined. Psychological interventions, whether that be ACT or any other intervention, are only ever going to be part of standard cancer care when they are demonstrated to be cost effective; we have to move away from trials assessing only acceptability and patient-reported outcomes, and I strongly believe that integrated health economic evaluation could be a game changer for ACT.

Here in the UK, one of our biggest successes in psychosocial oncology may be one of our biggest threats: supportive care is now very much seen as the domain of the charitable sector and they do fantastic work. But they aren't research institutions; they develop interventions and audit and evaluate them. Rarely do cancer charities have the funding to prioritize basic or applied research in psychological interventions. What I would really like to see is a return to science and theory in psychosocial oncology. Stanton, Luecken, MacKinnon and Thompson (2013) wrote a fantastic paper advocating the importance of component analysis in intervention research and I couldn't agree more; let's not just work out whether ACT works, but how we can make it better by identifying the effective and active components and concentrating on making these even better. The reticulated model of ACT and RFT provides us with a framework to do this, and yet to date we have primarily studies testing out whole ACT protocols. That way stagnation lies.

My final point: let's broaden our scope beyond the word "therapy". In many contexts and client groups, it's entirely appropriate, but

I'm just not convinced that it is helpful within the cancer context. It implies an underlying disorder at play. In some cultures it carries profound stigma. And it tends to put healthcare commissioners in mind of the medical model, with the result that psychological services are restricted for the privileged few who score highly enough on clinical screening tools. ACT doesn't have to, and shouldn't, be restricted to this way of thinking.

Everyday health

In addition to these serious health issues, ACT research has also been used to improve everyday health issues. Heffner, Eifert, Parker, Hernandez and Sperry (2003) found ACT to be useful in treating alcohol dependence in case-study format and Metzler, Biglan, Noell, Ary and Ochs (2001) published a large study, in RCT format, in which ACT was compared to usual care in attempting to reduce high-risk sexual behaviour among 339 adolescents. Results indicated that at six-month follow-up, those who received five weekly sessions of ACT reported fewer sexual partners, fewer non-monogamous partners, less sexual contact with strangers within the past three months and less marijuana use before or during sex. Those in the ACT group even performed better on an experimental measure that required them to manage a difficult sex situation. It is important to note that the protocol seemed ineffective with participants from a minority background, suggesting that in this context, more effort would need to be made to create interventions that would work cross-culturally.

Overall, the variety of areas in which the ACT model has shown promise in improving health issues is encouraging. The research in these areas could be enhanced by both larger investigations and single-case studies with high experimental control, in line with the suggestions from Drs Lundgren and Hulbert-Williams. What is interesting is that the disorders presented in this chapter are often well researched as biological or medical problems, and sometimes the psychological aspects of the issues have been underemphasized. Some might argue that ACT might struggle to sit within contexts in which symptom reduction is seen to be so important; however, although the target of ACT protocols is not to reduce symptoms, we often see that letting go of trying to control symptoms actually may reduce their frequency. We have seen that ACT shows promising results not only for coping with the psychological impacts of, for example, cancer, tinnitus or epilepsy, but that it might also help people to thrive. The importance of enabling people to live with health issues is really emphasized in Dr Hulbert-Williams' researcher profile above; how we can help clients to "live a personally meaningful life, no matter how short it might be". Being able to give someone who has been told that they do not have that long to live the chance to live whatever time they have left in a way that they would choose is a worthy cause to pursue in the journey ahead. It will be very interesting to see the development of research in these areas in the next decade.

14
Work

Over the past 14 years, much empirical work has been done to determine whether ACT could be useful in the workplace. The research in this area tends to fall into two categories: questionnaire studies and intervention studies. Although some important questionnaire-based research has been conducted with a variety of workforces displaying the often-predictive relationship between acceptance/PF and better mental health, job performance, learning and job satisfaction (Bond & Bunce, 2003; Donaldson-Feilder & Bond, 2004; Bond & Flaxman, 2006; Bond, Flaxman, & Bunce, 2008; McCracken & Yang, 2008; Onwezen, van Veldhoven, & Biron, 2014), it is the research in which workers have received an ACT intervention that will be the focus of this chapter.

Bond and Bunce (2000) conducted the first of these studies, and indeed one of the earliest ACT RCTs in general, when they investigated how useful the ACT model could be at helping people manage work-related strain. In their study, they compared an ACT-based emotion-focused stress-management intervention (SMI) versus a problem-focused SMI named an innovation-promotion program (IPP). This comparison was an important one because ACT had previously not been used as an intervention in the workplace and IPP had been used to decrease job-related strain (Bunce & West, 1996). Participants, recruited from a large media organization, were randomly allocated to receive nine hours of ACT ($n = 30$) or IPP ($n = 30$). A waitlist control group condition ($n = 30$) was also included. Whereas the ACT intervention aimed to help participants be willing to experience stressors, the IPP approach trained participants to identify and modify workplace stressors. Results indicated that both approaches improved mental health outcomes in its participants and increased their propensity for innovation in the workplace. However, neither intervention increased job satisfaction or motivation. Importantly, the ACT condition outperformed both the IPP and waitlist control group condition in terms of mental health at post-treatment and at three-month follow-up. One of the major aims of the paper was to determine the mechanisms by which successful outcome occurred. The results indicated that acceptance of undesirable thoughts and feelings mediated outcome in the ACT group, whereas the improvements shown in the IPP condition came about via the modifications made to stressors (called "work change" in the article). Like research in other parts of this book, the two approaches achieved success via different pathways. The authors finish the article by suggesting that future research was needed to further contrast SMIs, while taking account of mechanisms of change. They also suggested that in a fast-paced working environment, the brief and flexible nature of the intervention (three sessions of three hours) was a major advantage.

Following this seminal study, the aforementioned questionnaire-based research dominated the area for a decade. However, since 2010, a number of controlled trials have been published in which the ACT model has been used to treat those in the workplace, beginning with Flaxman and Bond (2010a). These researchers conducted an RCT comparing ACT and stress-inoculation training (SIT) in government workers presenting with above average distress. Delivered in two half-day workshops, 37 participants received an ACT protocol that included exposure to each of the six components, 37 participants received a CBT-based SIT that included relaxation training and cognitive restructuring, and 33 participants were allocated to a waitlist control group. Results indicated that the two active approaches were equally effective in reducing psychological distress across the three-month assessment period. Further analysis revealed that outcome in the ACT group was mediated by increases in PF and not cognitive change, while the beneficial impact of SIT was not mediated by a reduction in dysfunctional cognition. Interestingly, outcome in the SIT group was partially mediated by increases in PF, suggesting that there may have been some overlap in the topography of the two treatments. This finding once again highlights the importance of process. In some studies, the comparison treatments achieve success via very different mechanisms, yet in others it seems as though the comparison treatment works, in fact, by moving mechanisms that are important in ACT.

In the same year, the same authors published a hugely interesting study by examining under what circumstances an ACT-based SMI would work best (Flaxman & Bond, 2010b). Specifically, the authors contended that psychologically healthy individuals might dilute the effectiveness of good interventions. Therefore, in RCT format, they compared ACT ($n = 177$) to a waitlist control group ($n = 134$) in an effort to reduce employee distress. Following three half-day training sessions, those in the ACT group recorded a significant reduction in distress. Most importantly, the impact of the intervention was moderated by distress, where the largest effects were found for a sub-group of participants who recorded higher levels of baseline distress. Of these workers, 69% improved to a clinically significant degree. The authors rightly point out that future interventions of this kind would need to take into account moderating factors before rollout.

Brinkborg, Michanek, Hesser and Berglund (2011) later conducted an RCT to assess the utility of ACT in treating stress amongst social workers. In group format, 63 participants received four three-hour sessions of ACT, while 36 participants were allocated to the waitlist control group. The participants were also divided depending on whether they recorded low or high levels of baseline distress. Results indicated that the entire sample benefited from the treatment in terms of reductions in stress and burnout, and better general mental health. Indeed, whereas only one person deteriorated across treatment, 22 reached the criteria for clinically significant change. Similar to Flaxman and Bond (2010b), the authors found that the treatment was especially effective for those who present with higher levels of baseline distress. Interestingly, the investigation used both experienced and inexperienced therapists, but this had no impact on the effect of the intervention. Finally, changes in PF correlated with greater improvements. The take-home message presented in the discussion was that such a brief and low-cost intervention could be administered to social workers in the public sector with great ease, but future research should include a comparison to another treatment approach and long-term follow-up.

Two further RCTs of note have been published in the last couple of years. Firstly, Lloyd, Bond and Flaxman (2013) gave 43 participants three half-day ACT workshops, while 57 participants were assigned to a waitlist control group. Results indicated that significant reductions in emotional burnout and strain were recorded in the ACT group during treatment and at six-month follow-up. Additionally, a process analysis found that increases in PF mediated the decreases seen in emotional exhaustion at follow-up. Secondly, Ly, Asplund and Andersson (2014) gave 36 middle managers an ACT-based smartphone App to aid with stress management. The six-week intervention, which focused on mindfulness, acceptance and values, caused improvements in stress and general health in the ACT group alone. However, no improvement was recorded in transformative leadership. According to the authors, future research should include appropriate process and follow-up measures.

In addition to the research conducted in office settings, a few investigations have been published in which ACT interventions have been administered to teaching staff in a school setting and carers for those with intellectual disabilities. In a small-scale study, Biglan, Layton, Jones, Hankins and Rusby (2011) found that two 3.5-hour workshops improved acceptance, reduced stress and increased levels of efficacy in a sample of early childhood special-education staff, when compared to those allocated to the waitlist control group. Furthermore, pre-intervention levels of experiential avoidance and mindfulness in the sample were related to depression, stress and burnout, but at post-intervention, those in the ACT condition reported reduced experiential avoidance, greater mindfulness and greater valued living.

Jeffcoat and Hayes (2012) later conducted a larger scale study comprised of 236 participants involved in the education system. Of these, 121 participants received an ACT workbook (*Get out of Your Mind and into Your Life*; Hayes & Smith, 2005) designed to increase psychological well-being, while 115 participants were allocated to a waitlist control group. Results indicated that reading the workbook over an eight-week period positively impacted general psychological health, depression, anxiety and stress for people suffering in those areas. Clinically significant change was recorded in 38% of the ACT group, in comparison to 16% in the waitlist control group, while the number of those who deteriorated was also far less in the ACT group. Many of the effects were maintained at ten-week follow-up, especially in those who showed greater interaction with the material, as indicated by self-report and scores on weekly quizzes. A process analysis revealed that increases in PF were related to improvements at follow-up. Finally, three small pilot studies (Noone & Hastings, 2009, 2010; Bethay, Wilson, Schnetzer, Nassar, & Bordieri, 2013) and a large scale RCT pilot (McConachie, McKenzie, Morris, & Walley, 2014) have recently been conducted in which ACT has been used successfully to aid support staff managing the distress that arises from caring for someone with intellectual disabilities. A subsequent process analysis suggested that PF might be the mediator by which reductions in stress are seen in this population (Kurz, Bethay, & Ladner-Graham, 2014).

The large number of controlled trials conducted in the workplace suggests that ACT is a useful treatment in this context. Indeed, this research has had a ripple effect, whereby it has inspired laboratory-based empirical work investigating the utility of acceptance in increasing task performance and lowering stress (Kishita & Shimada, 2011), the development of work-based measures of PF (Bond, Lloyd, & Guenole, 2013) and a number of conceptual contributions linking ACT principles to organizational psychology (VanStelle, Koerber, & Fox, 2010; Atkins & Parker, 2011; Moran, 2011). Although ACT has not blown its competitors out of the water, in the majority of the controlled trials it has been equally effective as standardized treatments, as tested on a huge number of participants. Having said that, there is always room for improvement, as detailed by a prolific researcher in this area, Dr Frank Bond.

Researcher profile: Dr Frank Bond

Frank W. Bond, PhD, is Professor of Psychology and Management at Goldsmiths' College, University of London, where he is also Director of the Institute of Management Studies. He trained as both a clinical and as an occupational (or industrial/organizational) psychologist, and most of his research focuses on integrating theories and practices from both fields. More specifically, Bond's research often examines ACT's core concept of PF, and how it is an important determinant of mental health and productivity in the workplace. He does this by conducting RCTs of ACT and ACT-enhanced transformational-leadership training, work-redesign experiments, as well as longitudinal studies investigating how PF can enhance the effectiveness of core job-design principles, such as job control and supervisor support. Bond has also taken the lead in creating measures of PF, such as the AAQ-II and the Work-Related Acceptance and Action Questionnaire.

Bond has published this research in approximately 50 peer-reviewed journal articles, and he also describes his work in seven books, two UK government reports and over 20 book chapters, all of which have, together, been cited over 6000 times. Funding for his research comes from the UK Economic and Social Research Council (ESRC), charities, the UK government and a wide range of commercial organizations. Bond is Fellow and Past President of the Association of Contextual Behavioural Science, which is the international society for ACT and other fields of CBS.

> Over the past 15 years, there have been many RCTs that have examined the effectiveness of ACT in performance-related settings (mostly work organizations), and they have, on average, demonstrated ACT's success in enhancing mental health, productivity and beneficial attitudes (e.g. job satisfaction). While more questions need to be asked,

I think that the evidence of ACT's benefits in
ficient to "free up" some researchers to explore
and CBS can be useful in the world of work and
ple, theory development is just getting started c
principles of PF and "translate" them, or scale the
and organizational levels. These efforts lead us to
flexible organization look like? Or, how can we u   ౼ఌmote
organizational-change initiatives and group cohesion? In order to
begin to address these questions, I have started a project to try to
identify aspects of organizational structures, processes and strategies
that functionally map onto the six processes that produce PF. In addition, a group within ACBS has just begun work on a project called
PROSOCIAL. This is an attempt to help groups, of all kinds and sizes,
enhance group characteristics that Nobel Prize-winning research has
shown to be necessary for ensuring group cohesion and effectiveness.
Over the next ten years, a great deal of work will be done on these
two projects, and, no doubt, many more with similar aims.

One finding that is very consistent across most RCTs is that ACT
produces its benefits because it increases PF; in other words, ACT is
working for the theoretical reason for which it should. This is important for academic reasons, but it is also important for applied ones,
as it helps us to design interventions that specifically target PF. If we
are serious about scaling up PF to the group and organizational levels,
we need to develop measures that can assess that scaled-up construct
(e.g. organizational flexibility). We can then use those measures to
ensure that our group and organizational interventions work for reasons that are as theoretically consistent as the ones for which we
know ACT works.

Regarding measuring PF, we need to develop ways to measure it
quickly, in situ. ACT maintains that PF is contextually controlled
and, thus, it can fluctuate depending on the situation. Our current,
primary measures of PF tend to assess this construct as if it were a
trait that does not fluctuate across time, places, moods, relationships
and other contextual variables. While these measures have proved
valuable in terms of research and practice, we can do better by developing Apps, for example, that can let people use their smartphones
quickly to test their PF in relation to the context in which they find
themselves. This would allow clinicians to help their clients more
effectively, and it would help researchers wanting better to learn how
PF relates to different constructs across different contexts.

ally, we need better to promote ACT to organizations and those who consult with them. We have been good at scientifically examining ACT and PF in organizations, but we have been less good at proselytizing their evidence-based benefits. This is beginning to change, but not very quickly. As a community, we need to work more assiduously at talking about ACT at meetings, conferences and in media that attract organizationally focused individuals. I think that we now have a large enough community to do this successfully.

15
The ACT Variety

Thus far, we have considered how ACT has been applied to the best-known psychological issues. Now that we have reached the final empirical chapter of the current volume, we are left to describe ACT research that does not fit into any of the aforementioned topics. While the variety that we are about to describe is one of the most remarkable aspects of the ACT model, from our perspective, there is no tidy and orderly way to describe it. Therefore, instead of trying to create order, we decided to present all of this research in the same chapter via the use of an outrageous pneumonic: ACCEPTS (Academia, Clinical, Component research, Exercise and sport, Parenting, Training and Stigma). Consequently, when reading this chapter, do not expect any coherent story between the sections, instead feel free to appreciate the broad application of the ACT model.

Academia

Students tend to present with low levels of psychological well-being (Blanco et al., 2008). For that reason, researchers have attempted to determine the utility of ACT in improving general mental health with this population. Muto, Hayes and Jeffcoat (2011) published the earliest study of this kind. In RCT format, 35 international students were given an ACT self-help book (*Get Out of Your Mind and into Your Life*; Hayes & Smith, 2005) to complete at their own pace over an eight-week period. The waitlist condition consisted of 35 participants who were given the intervention at a later point. Results revealed that those in the ACT group recorded significant improvements in general mental health at post-treatment and two-month follow-up, especially in distressed individuals. These improvements were mirrored in the waitlist control group when they received the intervention. Finally, increases in PF mediated follow-up outcome and most improvement was seen in participants who were less psychologically flexible at baseline.

Given that college populations tend to have problems accessing psychological support, Levin, Pistorello, Seeley and Hayes (2014) followed the lead of Muto, Hayes and Jeffcoat (2011) by investigating the use of a web-based ACT intervention. Of 76 students, 37 were required to complete a two-lesson ACT protocol, within a three-week period, which focused on values and willingness, while those in the waitlist control group ($n = 39$) were simply instructed to wait until the next assessment. Given the preliminary nature of the study, the major aim was to determine if such a web-based package was feasible with college students. Results indicated that acceptability was high. Additionally, those in the ACT condition recorded significant improvements in ACT knowledge, education values and depression; these improvements were maintained at three-week follow-up. As with previous research, further analysis found that the intervention was most effective with students presenting with baseline distress. However, contrary to expectation, PF did not improve over the course of the study. The authors account for this by suggesting that participants were only exposed to two of the six components and that trends in the data suggest that longer follow-up assessments might better highlight the importance of PF as a contributing process. In the discussion, the authors are very tentative in their claims and suggest that this is the start of a research stream, rather than the end product.

Although Cook and Hayes (2010) conducted a cross-cultural questionnaire study which found that Asian Americans were more likely to use control-based strategies to manage stress and that control-based strategies were associated with poorer mental health, the final two studies of note in this area involve academic performance and academic procrastination. Chase et al. (2013) found that values training in addition to goal setting improved grade point average (GPA) in a sample of psychology undergraduates, when compared to goal-setting alone and the waitlist control group. Glick, Millstein and Orsillo (2014) found that high levels of procrastination were associated with high levels of anxiety and low levels of PF.

As with most of the sections in this chapter, ACT research with college populations is in its infancy. However, with the development of accessible interventions, this will change in the coming years.

Clinical

It may seem odd to have a section in this chapter about ACT research with clinical issues, given that much of the book involves the description of ACT research with such populations. However, there are a number of further investigations that belong in a chapter dedicated to variety. These studies fall into two areas: case studies and larger intervention studies.

Case studies have displayed the utility of ACT in treating exhibitionism (Paul, Marx, & Orsillo, 2000), distressed couples (Peterson, Eifert, Feingold, & Davidson, 2009), insomnia (Dalrymple, Fiorentino, Politi, & Posner, 2010), self-harm and violence in severe mental illness (Razzaque, 2013), agoraphobia in a pregnant woman (Cullinan & Gaynor, 2014) and conduct disorder with at-risk adolescents (Gomez et al., 2014). Additionally, in a multiple baseline across participants design, Twohig and Crosby (2010) reduced pornography viewing in six adult males at post-treatment and three-month follow-up after exposure to an eight-session ACT protocol. Process analyses suggested that increases in PF were associated with reductions in viewing.

In terms of intervention studies, two pilot studies and three RCTs of note have been recently published. Beilby, Byrnes and Yaruss (2012) found that eight two-hour sessions of group ACT improved psychosocial adjustment and speech fluency in people who stutter ($n = 20$). Subsequently, Hertenstein et al. (2014) gave six weekly two-hour group sessions of ACT to insomniacs ($n = 10$) that had not responded to CBT. Results indicated that subjective sleep quality and sleep-related quality of life improved at post-treatment and three-month follow-up.

In RCT format, Clarke, Kingston, James, Bolderston and Remington (2014) randomized treatment-resistant participants, who had received at least one other psychosocial intervention, to receive ACT with TAU ($n = 26$), or CBT with TAU ($n = 19$). Results indicated that although no differences emerged between the two groups at post-treatment, reduction of symptoms were evidenced better in the ACT group at six-month follow-up. In the same year, Zarling, Lawrence and Marchman (2014) published an influential study that aimed to determine if ACT could be used to reduce aggression among people who had recently engaged in at least two aggressive acts towards their partner. Participants were randomly assigned to receive 12 weekly two-hour sessions of group ACT, or were required to attend a support and discussion control group. Results indicated that those in the ACT group recorded greater declines in psychological and physical aggression from pre- to post-treatment, and from pre-treatment to six-month follow-up, with experiential avoidance functioning as a mediator. Finally, Yadavaia, Hayes and Vilardaga (2014) found that ACT could be used to increase self-compassion in undergraduate students, when compared to the waitlist control group. This is a timely development given the conversations currently taking place between advocates of ACT and compassion-focused therapy (CFT; Gilbert, 2010).

Component research

ACT is comprised of six core components: acceptance, defusion, contact with the present moment, self-as-context, values and committed action. In their classic article, Hayes et al. (2006) suggest that component-based studies, which involve breaking down a therapy to ensure that each process is psychologically active, are crucial for the overall model. Consequently, much research has been conducted in this area, which tends to involve administering a brief single-component intervention and then measuring how that intervention changes the way that participants relate to thoughts and behaviour. Throughout this book, component-based research has been integrated with research into the full ACT model within each diagnosis, implying that a full chapter describing component research is unwarranted. However, there are component investigations conducted on student populations that deserve mentioning, given their role in catalysing this type of research.

Due to the incredible popularity of mindfulness, it is unsurprising that research has displayed the usefulness of brief mindfulness interventions across a whole variety of areas, ranging from spider fear (Hooper, Davies, Davies, & McHugh, 2011) to aggression (Heppner et al., 2008), emotion regulation (Arch & Craske, 2006) and even stereotype threat (Weger, Hooper, Meier, & Hopthrow, 2012). Research has also showed the utility of acceptance (Marcks & Woods, 2005, 2007; Low, Stanton, & Bower, 2008; Luciano et al., 2010), values (Crocker, Niiya, & Mischkowski, 2008) and committed action (Kashdan & McKnight, 2013).

However, although investigations of mindfulness, acceptance, values and committed action are of huge worth, when asked to describe the classic and most-cited component-based ACT research, it is often the early defusion studies that spring to mind. In the first of these studies, Masuda, Hayes, Sackett and Twohig (2004) aimed to determine the impact of a defusion technique (word-repetition exercise; Titchener, 1916) on a self-relevant negative thought. In a series of eight single-case alternating-treatments designs, results indicated that the defusion intervention reduced the discomfort and believability of an unwanted thought, when compared to a distraction task and a thought-control task. A number of similar defusion studies have since emerged with promising results (Healy et al., 2008; Masuda et al., 2009; De Young, Lavender, Washington, Looby, & Anderson, 2010; Hinton & Gaynor, 2010; Masuda, Feinstein, Wendell, & Sheehan, 2010; Masuda et al., 2010; Deacon, Fawzy, Lickel, & Wolitzky-Taylor, 2011; Yovel, Mor, & Shakarov, 2014). Lately, defusion research has moved away from an excessive reliance on self-reported ratings of believability and discomfort via the use of behavioural measures (Hooper, Sandoz, Ashton, Clarke, & McHugh, 2012; Hooper & McHugh, 2013; Kishita, Muto, Ohtsuki, & Barnes-Holmes, 2014).

A recent component meta-analysis published by Levin, Hildebrandt, Lillis and Hayes (2012) identified 75 studies investigating ACT components and combinations of these components in helping people manage unwanted thoughts and behaviour, although only 66 were included in the final analysis. The results indicated positive effect sizes for defusion, acceptance, present moment and values. Thus far, it is evident that very little research has been conducted on the SAC component, with a notable exception in a study comparing two different ways of instructing SAC (Foody, Barnes-Holmes, Barnes-Holmes, & Luciano, 2013). Future investigations also need to include more behavioural measures in order to fully assess the impact of ACT components. For more information about a key researcher in the area, and a person whose name you will find dotted across this volume, please see the researcher profile below of Dr Akihiko Masuda.

Researcher profile: Dr Akihiko Masuda

Akihiko (Aki) Masuda is Associate Professor of Psychology at Georgia State University in the United States. He received his PhD in Clinical Psychology from the University of Nevada, Reno in 2006, under the supervision of Steven Hayes. An author of over 60 peer-reviewed papers and over 15 book chapters, his research encompasses a range of topics, including processes of change in ACT, cultural humility, adult psychopathology, Zen Buddhism, eating disorders, stigma/prejudice and many others. He recently edited the book titled, *Mindfulness and Acceptance in Multicultural Competency: A Contextual Approach to Socio-cultural Diversity in Theory and Practice*, which is published by New Harbinger.

Currently there is much evidence of ACT in theory and practice, and ACT is relatively diversified. More specifically, ACT has been applied to a broad array of individuals, as well as groups/societies. Given the diversification of ACT, many people want to know what ACT is and how it is different from some of the other major paradigms. For example, it is likely that there are even significant disagreements among ACT practitioners/researchers. Ideally, ten years from now, I would like ACT to be construed as a basic and pragmatic framework of change, more so than as a particular set of techniques or a particular mode of treatment delivery. I also would like research to investigate the legitimacy of this perspective. I am hopeful that the increasing interest in ACT will go beyond the arena of psychopathology and behavioural adaptation. More specifically, I would like ACT to promote our commitment to perhaps more fundamental issues, such as searching for meaning in living, at multiple levels of analysis.

Exercise and sport

In the coming decades, in addition to managing obesity by helping people commit to healthy eating, it will be important for researchers to use ACT to increase exercising behaviour. Although an early study by Burton, Pakenham and Brown (2010) found that an ACT intervention increased resilience, physical activity and well-being among 16 participants, Butryn, Forman, Hoffman, Shaw and Juarascio (2011) conducted the first major investigation in this area. In RCT format, they compared a four-hour ACT protocol ($n = 35$) with an education-alone protocol ($n = 19$) in trying to increase physical activity in female university students. Results indicated, as measured by a brilliant behavioural dependent variable where participants swiped a card each time they entered the university gym, that those in the ACT group significantly increased their physical activity compared to both baseline and education alone. In the discussion section of the paper, following a process analysis, the authors suggest that defusion may be a particularly important technique in this domain. Although improvements could be made in future research, the take-home statistic is that ACT participants doubled their physical activity from baseline to post-intervention.

In the same year, researchers from the same lab aimed to determine if an acceptance-based intervention could improve diet and physical activity among cardiac patients; that is, patients referred by their doctors due to having a high risk of coronary artery disease. Goodwin, Forman, Herbert, Butryn and Ledley (2011) supplied four 90-minute group sessions to 16 cardiac patients in an effort to determine if the approach was feasible with this population. Firstly, the program was reported to be helpful to participants and feasible to deliver. Consequently, it maintained a moderately high retention rate. Incredibly, given that participants were only supplied with a six-hour intervention, large improvements were seen in weight loss, physical activity, and calorie, saturated fat and sodium intake. These results compare favourably to other programs for this population and the important psychological mechanisms of acceptance, mindfulness and defusion mediated outcome.

Finally, two engaging RCTs have recently been published, both with creative dependent variables. Firstly, Moffitt and Mohr (2014) randomly allocated participants to receive a standard 12-week pedometer walking program, with or without a supplementary ACT DVD. Results indicated that those assigned to the ACT group achieved a significantly greater increase in physical activity at post-intervention and reported a higher step count than those who only completed the standard program. Secondly, Ivanova, Jensen, Cassoff, Gu and Knauper (2014) found that a 40-minute ACT intervention increased exercise tolerance in sedentary women by 15%, from a pre-intervention cycle test to a post-intervention cycle test 48 hours later. Those assigned to the no-intervention control group recorded an 8% reduction in tolerance across the two tests. Given the research presented thus far in this book, it is possible that ACT could be used to target both weight loss by healthy eating and weight loss by increases in physical activity, which may be a potentially potent mix.

In addition to increasing exercise behaviour, ACT has also been used to improve performance in sports. Perhaps the best-explored sport in which ACT has been successfully applied is that of chess. Following a case study in which interference and believability of unwanted thoughts was reduced and performance was improved (Ruiz, 2006), Ruiz and Luciano (2009) compared the efficacy of a five-day group ACT intervention to a no-contact control group. The results indicated significant performance improvements in five of the seven participants in the ACT group, while none of the control group reached the established change criterion. The same authors supplemented their previous study with the finding that a four-hour ACT intervention significantly reduced interference and believability of unwanted thoughts when compared to a matched no-contact control group (Ruiz & Luciano, 2012). Additionally, all five of the participants showed improvements in performance in the seven months following treatment, compared to none of the participants in the control group. In both studies, experiential avoidance and believability were found to be important processes.

Unsurprisingly, acceptance and mindfulness approaches are now becoming more prevalent in sporting contexts other than chess. For example, case studies have shown these approaches to improve performance in swimming and weightlifting (Gardner & Moore, 2004), springboard diving (Schwanhausser, 2009), basketball performance (Gardner & Moore, 2007) and lacrosse (Lutkenhouse, 2007). Furthermore, larger trials have found that ACT improved the number of repetitions in an inclined rowing exercise (Fernández, Secades, Terrados, García, & García, 2004) and competition performance in seven young elite golfers (Bernier, Thienot, Cordon, & Fournier, 2009). What is most interesting about these studies is that the mindfulness–acceptance–commitment (MAC) approach of Gardner and Moore (2004) has been employed successfully in most of them. This is important because it suggests that an ACT protocol is useful across a number of different sports and across a number of different types of athletes. For example, it has been used with both the young and the old, and it has been used with both aerobic and anaerobic sports. As psychology in sport grows, it will be important to continue to research MAC in this context.

Parenting

Although a few studies about the use of ACT with adolescents can be found in various places throughout this book, there is lack of empirical research showing that ACT is useful with this population. Recently, Murrell, Steinberg, Connally, Hulsey and Hogan (2014) found that an ACT intervention improved value-consistent behaviour in a group of nine adolescents presenting with ADHD, but over and above this study, you will only find a couple of well-detailed conceptual papers linking ACT principles with adolescents and children (Murrell & Scherbarth, 2006; Coyne, McHugh, & Martinez, 2011).

ACT research for parenting, however, is far more developed. The earliest investigation involved using ACT to help parents of autistic children. These parents tend to experience chronic stress (DeMyer, 1979) and tend to have difficulty managing feelings of guilt, shame and responsibility. Blackledge and Hayes (2006) designed a two-day (14-hour) workshop for 20 parents of children diagnosed with autism in an attempt to improve their psychological well-being. Results indicated that at post-treatment, improvements were recorded on levels of depression and psychological distress. These results were maintained at three-month follow-up. The results also indicated a significant improvement in general health from pre-treatment to follow-up, and mediational analyses further suggested that increases in defusion and decreases in experiential avoidance contributed to the various improvements.

In the past few years, a number of further research studies have emerged. Questionnaire studies have shown that experiential avoidance predicts maternal attachment and psychological symptoms (Evans, Whittingham, & Boyd, 2012), that experiential avoidance predicts burden and chronic sorrow symptoms in parents of children with cerebral palsy (Whittingham, Wee, Sanders, & Boyd, 2013) and that PF is a possible moderator in the relationship between parent and child distress (Moyer & Sandoz, 2014). Additionally, two publications described trial protocols to be used with parents of children with an acquired brain injury (ABI) (Brown, Whittingham, McKinlay, Boyd, & Sofronoff, 2013) and cerebral palsy (Whittingham, Sanders, McKinlay, & Boyd, 2013). Finally, in a preliminary intervention study, Casselman and Pemberton (2015) found that ACT improved parenting behaviour in seven veterans suffering from PTSD.

Despite these efforts, it is two recent RCTs that have invigorated the area. In the first study, Brown, Whittingham, Boyd, McKinlay and Sofronoff (2014) compared a combination of the well-established Stepping Stones Triple P (SSTP) intervention plus ACT ($n = 30$) with a waitlist control group ($n = 29$). SSTP is a behavioural family intervention that seeks to develop parenting skills, knowledge and confidence in the prevention of child emotional and behavioural difficulties. In this particular study, the intervention was used with parents of children with an ABI and mild behavioural problems. Over the course of ten weeks, participants received two ACT sessions and nine sessions of STTP. Results indicated that the intervention significantly reduced behavioural and emotional problems in the child and it also reduced the dysfunctional parenting styles of laxness and over-reactivity. Although the majority of these gains were maintained at six-month follow-up, child emotional problems returned to baseline at that point. The authors correctly indicate that such a program would need development, especially in terms of booster sessions, but the fact that the program worked is encouraging in a practical sense. From a research perspective, however, there is no way to determine the relative contributions of ACT and STTP.

In a later study, Whittingham, Sanders, McKinlay and Boyd (2014) addressed the issue of whether ACT adds anything to STTP by comparing STTP alone ($n = 22$), STTP plus ACT ($n = 23$) and a waitlist control group ($n = 22$) in the treatment of parents with children who have cerebral palsy. Results indicated that although improvements were recorded in behavioural and emotional problems in both active groups, the combined STTP plus ACT intervention was associated with reductions in child hyperactivity, parental over-reactivity, parental verbosity and child behavioural problems when compared to STTP alone. Furthermore, at six-month follow-up, the STTP plus ACT condition showed reductions in child hyperactivity, parental laxness and parental verbosity in comparison to STTP alone. Although this research suggests that the addition of ACT supplemented STTP, the results are tentative, with one finding suggesting that STTP alone better decreased child emotional symptoms than STTP plus ACT. Future research of this kind is needed, and the inclusion of a process analysis to determine that ACT processes mediate outcome would be crucial. For further information about the utility of ACT for parenting, please see two recent conceptual papers (Whittingham, 2014; Whittingham & Douglas, 2014), and for the future directions that ACT research must take in this area, please see the researcher profile below of Dr Koa Whittingham.

Researcher profile: Dr Koa Whittingham

Dr Koa Whittingham is a psychologist with specialisations in both clinical and developmental psychology, as well as a research fellow at the Queensland Cerebral Palsy and Rehabilitation Research Centre, the University of Queensland. She completed her PhD at the University of Queensland in 2007 and currently holds a National Health and Medical Research Council (NHMRC) postdoctoral fellowship. Koa's research program covers three key interests: parenting and parenting intervention, neurodevelopmental disabilities and ACT. She is particularly passionate about the application of CBS to parenting. Koa was awarded the Early Career Research Award at the international Helping Families Change Conference in 2010 and the Award for Best Paper for Effective Intervention at the Australasian Academy of Cerebral Palsy and Developmental Medicine Conference in 2014. Koa is part of the research team of Possums for Mothers and Babies, a charitable organization committed to promoting evidence-based, interdisciplinary practice in the care of mothers and babies (http://www.possumsonline.com/). In addition, she is the author of *Becoming Mum*, a self-help book for the transition to motherhood grounded in ACT (http://becomingmum.com.au/). Koa regularly blogs about parenting issues on her website blog *Parenting from the Heart*, often from a CBS perspective (http://www.koawhittingham. com/blog/).

We are really only at the beginning of applying contextual behavioural science to parenting and there is much to be done. Established behavioural family intervention approaches are grounded in research identifying the parenting practices and behaviours that predict child behavioural and emotional problems. While this has been incredibly useful, and established behavioural family interventions are some of the most effective psychological interventions in existence, from an ACT perspective, a different question needs to be asked: which parenting practices and behaviours predict the development of child psychological flexibility? If our aim is not to decrease the frequency of childhood behavioural and emotional problems, but to maximize childhood psychological flexibility, then new parenting strategies may emerge and existing strategies may need to be tweaked. In essence, behavioural family intervention needs to be taken apart and rebuilt with contextual behavioural science at its heart. In the future, we may see RCTs comparing contextual ACT-integrated behavioural family intervention to the established behavioural family intervention approaches we are familiar with today.

In addition, it is vital that contextual behavioural scientists reclaim an aspect of family life that is so important to all of us, and yet has been neglected by much behavioural family research: the parent–child relationship. At present, many published trials of behavioural family interventions, including some of my own, fail to even measure the relationship between parent and child. Yet, what could be more important? Psychodynamic understandings of the relationship between parent and child dominate the psychological literature. Yet, it is possible to understand attachment theory and parental responsiveness from a contextual perspective. Building clear contextual understandings of healthy, happy parent–child relationships, of attachment theory and of parental responsiveness is crucial to overcoming the hostile and unworkable divide between the attachment and behavioural literature; a divide that is blocking scientific progress. Further, ACT, with its ability to foster acceptance, psychological presence in the here-and-now, emotional awareness and liberation from rule-governed behaviour, has the potential to be exactly the right therapy to promote healthy parent–child relationships.

Training

Although a hugely interesting study has recently been published in which ACT was used to train children to make novel food choices (Kennedy, Whiting, & Dixon, 2014), the majority of investigations in this section will describe research which has the aim of improving therapist behaviour in some way. In the earliest of these studies, Luoma et al. (2007) conducted an RCT to determine if a supplementary eight-week ACT course could help trainee psychologists overcome barriers that might stop them from implementing group drug-counselling (GDC) methods. Results indicated that those assigned to receive just the one-day GDC training course ($n = 14$) were significantly less likely to implement and make use of GDC at two-month and four-month follow-up than those who received the supplementary ACT course. The authors recommend that future studies use more participants, include a process analysis and rely less on self-report measures.

Varra, Hayes, Roget and Fisher (2008) followed this initial preliminary investigation with a similar RCT that aimed to determine if ACT could increase clinician willingness to use evidence-based pharmacotherapy. Drug and alcohol counsellors were either assigned to receive a one-day ACT workshop ($n = 30$) or a one-day education-alone workshop ($n = 30$). Subsequently, all participants were given a two-day workshop on using evidence-based treatments for substance-abuse disorder. Results indicated that those assigned to the ACT condition showed significantly higher rates of referrals to evidence-based pharmacotherapy at three-month follow-up. Additionally, they rated barriers to learning new treatments as less believable and became more psychologically flexible at post-treatment and follow-up. Finally, process analyses indicated that believability and PF mediated outcome.

These two research studies are important as they illustrate that therapists need PF in their working environment in order to properly support their clients. However, research has also been conducted in which ACT has been used to support the psychological needs of therapists themselves. Firstly, Stafford-Brown and Pakenham (2012) used a ten-week group ACT protocol as a stress-management tool for trainee psychologists. Results indicated that, compared to waitlist control group, those assigned to receive the ACT intervention recorded significant reductions in distress and increases in positive therapist qualities. Subsequently, Pakenham (2014) had 32 clinical-psychology trainees complete 12 two-hour weekly ACT workshops. Results indicated that, at post-intervention, therapists had improved across a number of outcome measures: self-efficacy, self-kindness, client–therapist alliance and the ACT processes of defusion, mindfulness, acceptance and values.

In a related study, Luoma and Vilardaga (2013) aimed to increase PF in therapists. Results indicated that those who completed a two-day ACT workshop in combination with phone consultation reported significantly higher PF at three-month follow-up than those who attended the ACT workshop with no additional contact, suggesting that greater exposure to ACT results in greater PF. Importantly, both groups recorded improvements in burnout, personal accomplishment and ACT knowledge. Recording whether or not participants experience increases in ACT knowledge may seem like an odd outcome measure given that they are explicitly exposed to the ACT model. Nevertheless, evaluation studies that assess the various ways an intervention have impacted the knowledge of its attendees are ever important as demand for ACT training increases. Only one other such study has currently been published with this aim; Richards et al. (2011) found that a one-day ACT workshop given to psychologists increased ACT knowledge, stimulated interest, was received positively and influenced clinical work.

Finally, two further publications have recently become available in this domain. Wardley, Flaxman, Willig and Gillanders (2014) qualitatively described the experiences of eight psychological practitioners following exposure to ACT training and Brock, Robb, Walser and Batten (2015) published a conceptual article in which they describe the common mistakes that ACT therapists make. Overall, ACT views clinicians as people who can suffer in the same way as their clients. It is therefore admirable that this research stream has developed, because the psychological health of clinicians is crucial as the demand for mental health services increases. For future directions in this area, please see the research profile of Dr Kenneth Pakenham below.

Profile researcher: Dr Kenneth Pakenham

Kenneth Pakenham, PhD, is Professor of Clinical and Health Psychology in the School of Psychology at the University of Queensland, Australia. Inspired by the resilience of some people with serious illnesses, he has committed much of his career to investigating the processes that foster personal growth in the context of health adversities and to translating his findings into interventions that help people live fully with illness. This passion has driven his empirical, theoretical and translational research, curriculum development, and clinical training and supervision. Importantly, his work has included not only the person with chronic illness, but also his or her network, particularly the carer. Through his 120 publications, over 60 conference presentations and more than two million dollars of competitive grant funding, he has become a leader in the application of positive health frameworks to several chronic illnesses and to caregiving in these contexts. His research has helped to inform government policies, particularly those related to carers, and establish interventions and assessment protocols within government and community services. The "living fully with illness" theme integrates his early research in stress/coping theory, his mid-career shift to incorporate the rise of positive psychology, and his current and future focus on ACT. Using ACT to extend his research on living fully with illness has also invigorated his teaching. He developed the first ACT university course in Australia. This course integrates training in therapist competencies and self-care skills and shows published empirical evidence of fostering competent and resilient clinicians. Through peer-reviewed publications, conference and keynote presentations, and a university teaching award, he has become a leader in integrating training in therapist and self-care competencies into clinical-psychology curricula using an ACT framework. He has supervised the postgraduate research of 53 students. He has served in many influential professional roles including: Chair of the Registration Committee of the Psychologists Board of Queensland for over ten years, Director of the University of Queensland Psychology Clinic for seven years, Honours Convenor for three years, and he is a member of the editorial boards for six international journals.

The ACT psychological-flexibility framework links the basic contextual behavioural science and theory (RFT) with the applications of ACT to alleviate human suffering. The ACT psychological-flexibility framework consists of mid-level terms and, unapologetically, they therefore lack the precision of constructs used in basic science. However, more work is needed to tighten the ACT framework including clearer and more accurate conceptualization, definition and measurement of each of the six core ACT processes that serve to foster psychological flexibility, and further clarification of the interrelations among the core processes. For example, it is problematic conceptually to have a measure of the umbrella construct, psychological flexibility (Acceptance & Action Questionnaire), which is also a measure of one of the core ACT processes, acceptance, that is subsumed by the overarching construct (psychological flexibility). In addition, few studies have examined the effects on outcomes of all six processes of the model simultaneously; most studies focus on one or two. Hence, there is a need for more sophisticated tests of the ACT framework.

There is a need to develop measures that assess outcomes in clinical trials involving ACT that better reflect the philosophy and theory underlying ACT. For example, many clinical trials have as a primary outcome decreases in distress (e.g. anxiety, depression, stress). However, the focus of ACT is not the removal of symptoms or distress, but "working" with the discomfort to fulfil one's values. Although this is likely to lead to an overall net reduction in distress over time, this is not the explicit goal of ACT. Understandably, research funders and/or consumers focus on the removal or decrease of symptoms, and researchers are, therefore, obliged to assess such outcomes. However, it is also possible to measure outcomes more consistent with ACT including increases in valued living and decreases in the extent to which participants are bothered by their distress etc.

Further work is needed to understand the effects of ACT training on trainees and the most effective ways to deliver training, and whether these vary according to who is being trained (e.g. qualified vs trainee health professionals vs paraprofessionals vs volunteers). Very few studies have examined these issues, despite the widespread uptake of ACT by practitioners. Furthermore, the most frequently measured effects of training are knowledge of ACT and self-reported changes on psychological flexibility and the ACT processes. More work is required to develop measures of behavioural changes in trainees, acquisition of ACT competencies and impacts on clinical practice and clients.

Future research should focus on determining under which conditions traditional CBT techniques are most effective and under which conditions ACT strategies are most effective. Although there are preliminary data on this topic, it needs to be extended. This type of research is important because it is likely to clarify the theoretical distinctiveness of each approach and where there is overlap or common ground. It will also likely diminish the "all or nothing" or "black and white" approach to ACT and CBT. For example, preliminary data on cognitive restructuring vs defusion suggest that the relative effectiveness of these strategies may vary according to client characteristics. In addition, both defusion and cognitive restructuring may achieve psychological distance from cognitions and, therefore, both may increase meta-cognitive awareness. Thinking is a profoundly important and adaptive human function – defusion is one useful strategy for dealing with unhelpful thoughts, but there are other useful non-defusion strategies similar to cognitive restructuring such as reframing, rethinking a situation to get another perspective and employing a cognitive search for meaning in adversity etc.

Interestingly, some of these latter strategies are encouraged through some ACT techniques. There has been commentary on the possibility of developing "hybrid strategies" that incorporate both ACT and traditional CBT techniques, but there is little research on this topic. However, the reality is that in practice many practitioners tend to embrace an eclectic approach and end up developing their own hybrid strategies. It is preferable to have data that can inform such practices.

Research is needed to increase our understanding of the development of psychological flexibility and the core ACT processes in children and adolescents. In general, there is a lack of ACT-related theoretical and intervention research with youth and, therefore, the research agenda is very broad. This became very evident to me when I searched the ACT literature on youth in preparation for developing a study that incorporates psychological flexibility in a proposed model that explains the effects of family illness and youth caregiving on youth and family functioning. There was an absence of data on how ACT processes, especially psychological flexibility, develop and/or fluctuate over developmental phases in young people.

Stigma

People with psychological illness tend to suffer much stigmatization (Crisp, Gelder, Nix, Meltzer, & Rowlands, 2000). And despite being responsible to their clients, many health care providers may hold negative beliefs about recipients of care (Maslach, Jackson, & Leiter, 1986). Researchers have felt that ACT, with its emphasis on reducing the impact of negative thoughts via acceptance, may be helpful in this domain, especially given that avoidance attempts have been shown to exacerbate stigma (Macrae, Bodenhausen, Milne, & Jetten, 1994). Hayes et al. (2004) published a classic study testing whether a one-day ACT workshop could reduce stigma in a group of therapists. They also suggested that reducing stigma might reduce the likelihood of burnout as "difficult" clients may be viewed as less difficult. In RCT format, the researchers compared ACT with two well-known stigma interventions: multicultural training and a biologically-oriented education-alone control group. Results indicated that ACT had a positive impact on stigma at three-month follow-up and reduced burnout at post-treatment and follow-up. Even though multicultural training resulted in decreases in stigma and burnout, the burnout gains in the ACT group at follow-up outperformed those in the multicultural training. Process analyses showed that believability changed throughout therapy and that these changes mediated follow-up stigma and burnout. Masuda et al. (2007) later conducted a similar RCT where they attempted to reduce stigma in college students. Results indicated that those assigned to receive a 2.5-hour ACT workshop ($n = 52$) recorded reduced mental health stigma at post-treatment and one-month follow-up when compared to education alone ($n = 43$). Importantly, the education-alone workshop only reduced stigma in those who scored highly on PF, whereas the ACT workshop reduced stigma regardless of baseline levels of PF.

Four further investigations have been conducted in the area of stigma. Firstly, Luoma, Kohlenberg, Hayes, Bunting and Rye (2008) aimed to determine if ACT could be useful in reducing the self-stigma that results from identification with a stigmatized group. A six-hour ACT workshop that focused on mindfulness, acceptance and values work in relation to stigma was given to 88 participants presenting with substance-abuse disorder. The results, which include a number of outcome and process measures, suggested that the intervention generally reduced self-stigma and levels of experiential avoidance. Secondly, Skinta, Lezama, Wells and Dilley (2014) reported that a combined group-based ACT and compassion focused therapy (CFT) intervention showed promising results in alleviating HIV self-stigma. Although, the author's highlight that future research would need to be conducted on a larger scale, reduce the reliance on self-report measures and include a follow-up measure and a control group.

Thirdly, in questionnaire format, Masuda, Price, Anderson, Schmertz and Calamaras (2009) found that those who hold stigmatizing attitudes tend to suffer from psychological distress themselves. They also found that lower levels of PF were related to higher stigma and distress, and that the relation between stigma and poor psychological outcomes was partially accounted for by PF. Finally, Lillis, Hayes, Bunting and Masuda (2009) found, in a sample of patients completing a weight-loss program, that a one-day ACT workshop ($n = 40$) resulted in improvements in obesity-related stigma, quality of life and psychological distress at three-month follow-up when compared to the waitlist control group ($n = 44$). As predicted, participants also made significant gains in PF and lost more body mass than those who did not take part in the workshop. Most interestingly, the changes recorded in stigma, quality of life and distress were not due to changes in weight. In summary, as well as improving quality of life in obese people regardless of whether they recorded successful weight loss, the ACT workshop also caused explicit weight loss.

In addition to stigma, ACT researchers have investigated the related issues of prejudice and shame. For example, a small-scale RCT found that values clarification buffered against the psychological impact of those who experience racism (West, Graham, & Roemer, 2013). Additionally, Lillis and Hayes (2007) found that a 75-minute ACT intervention reduced racial and ethnic prejudice in a sample of 32 college students, in comparison to education alone. In the discussion, the authors highlight that the participants were able to see that it was possible to both have a prejudicial thought and have positive behavioural intentions. Finally, in RCT format, Luoma, Kohlenberg, Hayes and Fletcher (2012) found that those who were in a residential addiction clinic for substance abuse and received six hours of ACT ($n = 68$) reported small reductions in shame at post-treatment and large reductions in shame at four-month follow-up, when compared to TAU ($n = 66$). Those in the ACT group also showed higher treatment attendance and fewer days of substance use at follow-up.

For further information about the ACT approach towards stigma and prejudice, see the review paper by Masuda, Hill, Morgan and Cohen (2012). And for future directions in this area, see the profile below of a well-known ACT researcher who has substantial interest in stigma and prejudice, Dr Jason Luoma.

Profile researcher: Dr Jason Luoma

Jason Luoma, PhD, is founder of *ACTwithCompassion.com* and a leading researcher in the area of shame, self-stigma and interventions for those difficulties. He is also co-founder of Portland Psychotherapy Clinic, Research, & Training Center, a unique research and training clinic where proceeds from services go to fund scientific research. Jason is an internationally recognized trainer of ACT and author of *Learning Acceptance and Commitment Therapy*, a book popular with professionals for its mixture of sophistication and accessibility. He has over 30 publications on shame, stigma and ACT including publishing the first randomized trial of an ACT approach to shame in the *Journal of Consulting and Clinical Psychology*. He also maintains a clinical practice focused on helping people with chronic shame and self-criticism develop more self-compassion.

> Over the next decade, CBS research needs to move beyond the "name brand" of ACT and focus more on the basic principles that guide effective practices derived from CBS. One way this can happen is

through CBS developing connections with researchers who share a contextual viewpoint, such as most behavioural researchers. In addition, we need to expand beyond the therapy room and into research that helps people in the environments in which they live – home, work, play, school and the community at large. If we want to have a broader scale impact on the world, we need to take greater advantage of technological advances and how they can be used for better experimental designs and new interventions.

Without losing our contextual foundations, CBS needs to increase the depth of our theories, developing stronger links to other levels of analysis, such as the sociological and the biological. To remain relevant and influential, CBS needs to better link to neuroscience, biology and evolution, as these views of behaviour are currently in the ascendance. A unique contribution of CBS could be helping researchers in these areas better understand the role of context, and therefore develop their ability to influence behaviour, in addition to predicting it.

I believe it's essential for CBS to return more to its roots in behaviour analysis through observing actual behaviour in context and reducing the frequency of studies based primarily on self-report questionnaires. Research designs that incorporate other forms of measurement, such as ecological momentary assessment and experimental designs with direct measurement of behaviour, are essential if we want to see the field move forward. Very little remains to be gained from observational studies focusing purely on questionnaire measures.

Part III
The Journey Ahead

16
The Statistics

If you have read this book from beginning to end, it is likely you have been overwhelmed by the sheer amount of ACT research. By now, with a coffee in your hand and a headache, you might feel pretty satisfied with the evidence base. However, although great strides have been made by ACT researchers in the past 30 years, there is still much to do, as we hope to illustrate in this chapter, where we will break down this book into figures. It is important to note that the figures you see presented in this chapter are not "the" figures, as we have likely not found some investigations and as we have been unable to translate research written in languages other than English. Rather these pages will present trends that only take into account the research in this volume.

Over the years, studies in which there are less than ten participants, and in particular, case studies, have been criticized by the research community for lacking generalizability. Of the 265 empirical investigations described in this volume, 54 of them have included less than ten participants. In other words, 20% of ACT research involves small-scale studies. Many may be critical of this, but it is important to remember the context. When a research stream begins, it is vital to test and refine the protocol with a small number of participants and to present detailed findings to academics and clinicians interested in the approach. As ACT is a relatively new therapeutic approach, it is unsurprising that a high percentage of small-scale studies have been published, as researchers are at the beginnings of their research stream and are working their way to full-scale trials.

Of the 265 investigations, 67 of those studies explicitly involve targeting therapeutic processes. Put more simply, just over 25% of ACT research aims to investigate the relationship between ACT processes (PF, mindfulness, acceptance, defusion, values, SAC, committed action) and outcome. We feel, especially as this statistic does not include the scores of outcome studies that also incorporate a process analysis, that ACT researchers have made much effort in this area. And in the coming years, as interest increases in active therapeutic processes, the results of these studies will become ever more important.

The remaining 144 (55%) investigations in this volume are outcome studies in which the number of participants exceeds ten. Of these outcome studies, 108 are RCTs while the remaining 36 are pilot trials, preliminary trials or open trials. Figure 16.1 below illustrates how many of these studies have been conducted across each disorder, while Figure 16.2 illustrates how the 10,080 participants that have taken part in these studies are spread across disorder. It is important to note, at this point, that these studies have been divided in a rather blunt manner. Specifically, the studies have been categorized only according to their primary outcome measure, which may skew the data somewhat. As an example, in Figure 16.1, you will find 17 studies that have explicitly targeted ACT for depression. However, countless other studies throughout this book have measured depression as a secondary outcome.

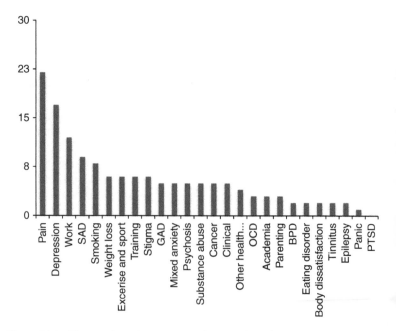

Figure 16.1   The number of outcome studies conducted across each disorder

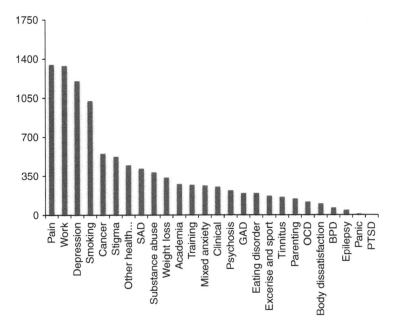

Figure 16.2 The number of participants across each disorder

As you can see, investigations in the areas of pain, work, depression and smoking have been conducted on huge amounts of participants. However, it cannot be denied that many areas need further development. For example, only 221 participants have been involved in ACT research for psychosis, 195 for eating disorders, 117 for OCD and no trial has ever been published with ACT for PTSD that has more than ten participants. Furthermore, these participant totals are not the number of people that have received ACT, but the number of people who have taken part in these experiments, even if randomized to a control condition.

With regards to control conditions, on 47 occasions ACT has been compared to waitlist control group, while on 73 occasions ACT has been compared to an active comparison, whether that is TAU or an alternative therapeutic approach. Of those active comparisons, ACT has been compared to CBT 18 times and compared to CT 6 times. And when you think that on many of those occasions ACT has not outperformed CBT or CT, it is easy to see that many more trials of this nature need to be conducted.

Although quite a few studies involved using a combination of both experienced and novice therapists, it seems that there is quite an equal spread of novice (49 studies) and experienced (57 studies) clinicians in ACT studies (where novice refers to trainee therapists). It is also evident that more research needs to be conducted on elderly people (2 studies), children (1 study) and adolescents (6 studies), as the majority of ACT outcome research has been conducted on adults. Figure 16.3 below illustrates the various formats in which ACT has been delivered. It suggests that many investigations have involved delivering ACT in group and individual format and that the number of studies using technology to deliver ACT is growing (with all of the technology-based studies being published in the last five years). Finally, given the large number of self-help books available to the general public, more research needs to be added to the ACT investigations in this area.

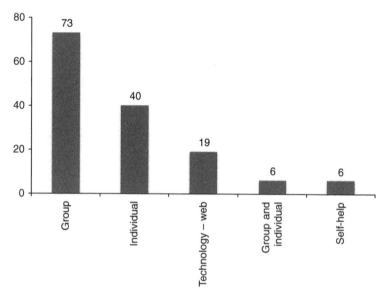

Figure 16.3   The delivery formats of ACT research

Three final statistics are illustrated below. Figure 16.4 shows the average length of treatment across disorder, Figure 16.5 shows the places in the world that have produced the outcome studies and Figure 16.6 details the rate of ACT research since the first study was conducted in 1986.

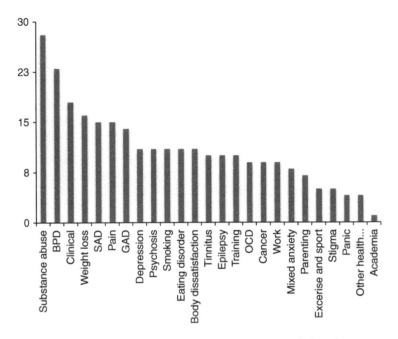

Figure 16.4   The average number of therapy hours across each disorder

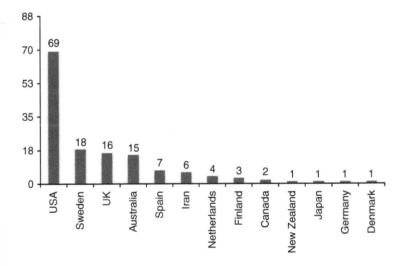

Figure 16.5   The breakdown of outcome studies across countries

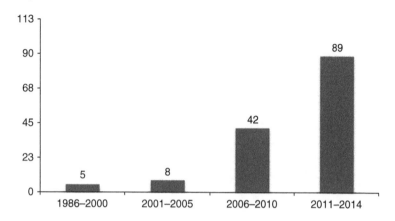

Figure 16.6   The breakdown of outcome studies over the past 30 years

It seems as though the more serious psychological issues require longer interventions, but then again, the average length of treatment for psychosis is only 11 hours, which happens to be the average number of hours given to participants across all of the diagnostic areas. It is no surprise that the USA leads the way with the amount of ACT outcome research, but it is great to see that labs from many different countries are also contributing.

Finally, the numbers from Figure 16.6 are encouraging. In 2014 alone, 30 ACT outcome studies were published. That is one study every 12 days. This level of interest in research activities bodes well for the development of ACT in the coming years. For interested readers, we have a spreadsheet with the breakdown of these statistics that we are more than willing to share. But remember that these statistics are not "the" statistics. They merely illustrate trends about the research presented in this book. Over the coming years, we would like to update the spreadsheet as often as possible. Therefore, if you have published research that we have omitted, or if you publish research from 2015 onwards, please contact us. Then, every so often we will upload the latest version of these statistics to the following blog: http://nichooper.com/blog/.

17
Conclusion

Future directions

So where do we go from here? The ACT journey has so far taken an ever-growing community of scientists, clinicians and practitioners to the empirical point described in this book. The progress, as illustrated in the last chapter, is truly encouraging and pretty remarkable. Some might argue that we can safely say the model works. Others disagree. In this chapter, we will briefly summarize the thoughts of our profile researchers in an attempt to blueprint the ways forward for ACT research.

It cannot be denied that bigger and better controlled RCTs will cement ACT as an evidence-based treatment in the therapeutic world. However, while outcome research on both ACT and its components is crucial, it is important to keep developing the model itself. RCTs are the gold standard for proving that a treatment is effective, and from that we know ACT is effective, but it is far from completely effective. Thus, we need to improve what we put into our RCTs in the service of refining the model. Sample size made from power analyses, longer follow-up periods, stronger moderation and mediational analyses, reduced data attrition and gold-standard comparison groups are certainly very expensive, but ACT is beginning to pull in the kind of funding needed to achieve these things.

In addition to these recommendations, there are a number of measurement-related issues that need to be improved. One of the most shocking aspects of this book is that the majority of ACT studies involve measurements of symptom reduction, and symptom reduction, in turn, is used as a marker for therapeutic success. Yet ACT does not aim to reduce symptoms; it aims to provide people with the PF to experience symptoms and still move in a valued direction. When people look at the comparisons between other treatments and ACT, they often become disheartened if no difference is found between approaches. Indeed, you will see critics of ACT shout these results from the rooftops. But the game, played in this way, is rigged. ACT is not interested in symptom reduction; it is interested in values-based living. Therefore much effort needs to be made to develop sensitive measures of values-based living and to incorporate these measures into our outcome trials. ACT needs to be compared on its own terms, not as a symptom-reducing treatment.

Some have also suggested that better measures of both processes and outcome need to be developed. An example of this is the AAQ-II, which is the standard measure of PF. It holds up to psychometric evaluation and has been shown to mediate outcome in many studies. However, it is still cast mostly as a trait-type measure even though levels of PF will alter moment to moment. In order to address this, a state measure needs to be developed that would be sensitive to real-time increases and decreases in PF. Additionally, it might be interesting to ask, does the AAQ-II measure experiential avoidance as a negative of the PF model or just as a negative of the acceptance process? If it is one, how do we measure the other? With these issues in mind, it has become obvious that more behavioural measures are needed to show that there are effects in people's lives outside circling "7" instead of "2" on a piece of paper. Indeed, behavioural measures are where applications of ACT seem to be doing particularly well. Smoking-cessation and weight-loss research come to mind; that is, research in which the problematic behaviour can be measured objectively.

Being a contextual application, ACT was never constricted to the world of psychotherapy, nevertheless with a name that includes the word "therapy", psychotherapy is where you will find ACT used the most. In the coming years, ACT can, and should, be applied in practical contexts outside of psychotherapy. Some have begun to make these strides. For example, ACT as a workplace intervention can improve productivity, as measured in pounds sterling, and ACT has been used in behaviour-based safety work. We even know of at least four new unpublished studies where ACT has improved training output, passes, interceptions and goal scoring in ice hockey teams. In these settings, the word "therapy" in ACT has sometimes been replaced with the word "training". This not only overcomes issues of mental health stigma, but also is more accurate, since these are not mental health problems that need to be treated with therapy. Instead, these applications of ACT show us how being trained to handle thoughts and feelings differently can positively impact our behaviour in a variety of non-therapeutic contexts.

Getting reliable and predictable results in studies requires reliable and predictable clinical training. How do we know that the people who publish ACT research are actually doing ACT with their participants? How do we supervise clinicians that do ACT? And how do we train them? No doubt these are areas of research that are under-developed in clinical psychology as a whole. Nevertheless, more research is needed so that we can predictably increase ACT knowledge and maintain skilled practitioners and clinical researchers that are able to move PF in clients and participants.

Finally, the ACT model should be able to do more. A person who is able to hold all thoughts lightly, make room for negative emotions, is in contact with their present moment, while also flexibly able to take the perspective of themselves and others over time, seems like a recipe for coping with anything. This means that in the future we need to become better at ensuring that every participant gets psychologically flexible in precisely the context we are researching. This requires progressive model development, enhanced by the other CBS approach of RFT in a reticulated model. It also means holding our terms and models lightly enough that we are able to listen to each other and adapt.

Final thoughts

Arguments about the evidence base for therapeutic approaches should always happen. If we are serious about alleviating human suffering then we have to be critical of our approaches so that we can improve them. Öst (2014) conducted a meta-analysis that did not favour ACT (although a recent meta-analysis found more encouraging results; A-Tjak et al., 2015). Since this publication came to the attention of the ACT community, certain aspects of it have caused controversy, but other aspects of it provide guidance about how to get better. In a similar vein, we hope that this book will also help orient researchers as to how we can move forward in the coming years.

Having said that, the aim of this volume was primarily to inform readers where we are at this moment, rather than where we are going. It aimed to do this by describing the whole ACT research journey and not just the RCTs described in a typical meta-analysis. It is our hope that by being exposed to this research, readers will be able to see the lines of consistency running throughout the book. ACT has been conducted across a number of disorders, it has been delivered by people of varying experience, it has been delivered in treatment lengths that range between one hour and 50 hours, and it has been delivered in various formats and in various languages. The results consistently suggest that ACT is effective and that processes important in ACT mediate outcome. And given the startling rate at which ACT research is increasing, there must be something about the model that resonates with clinicians and their clients at a personal level. But, there is much work to do. Maybe, in ten years' time, we will write a second edition of this book in which the second stage of the ACT research journey is described. Hopefully, however, so much research will have accumulated by then that such a task will be impossible. Only time will tell.

References

Part I

Agras, S., Leitenberg, H., & Barlow, D. H. (1968). Social reinforcement in the modification of agoraphobia. *Archives of General Psychiatry, 19*(4), 423–427.

American Psychiatric Association. (1994). *Diagnostic and Statistical Manual of Mental Disorders* (4th ed.). Washington, DC: Author.

American Psychological Association. (2002). Ethical principles of psychologists and code of conduct. *American Psychologist, 57*(12), 1060–1073. doi: 10.1037//0003-066x.57.12.1060.

Andrew, D., & Dulin, P. (2007). The relationship between self-reported health and mental health problems among older adults in New Zealand: Experiential avoidance as a moderator. *Aging & Mental Health, 11*(5), 596–603.

Baer, R. A. (2005). *Mindfulness-Based Treatment Approaches*. San Diego, CA: Elsevier Academic Press.

Barlow, D. H. (2004). *Anxiety and Its Disorders*. New York: Guilford Press.

Barraca, J. (2004). Spanish adaptation of the Acceptance and Action Questionnaire (AAQ). *International Journal of Psychology and Psychological Therapy, 4*, 505–515.

Barrett, L. (2012). Why behaviorism isn't Satanism. *The Oxford Handbook of Comparative Evolutionary Psychology*, 17–38.

Beck, A. T. (1979). *Cognitive Therapy of Depression*. New York: The Guilford Press.

Beck, A. T., Steer, R. A., & Brown, G. K. (1996). *Manual for the Beck Depression Inventory-II*. San Antonio, TX: Psychological Corporation.

Beck, J. S. (2011). Introduction to cognitive behavior therapy. In J. S. Beck (Ed.) *Cognitive behavior therapy: Basics and beyond* (2nd ed., pp. 1–16). New York: Guilford Publications.

Bloom, D. E., Cafiero, E. T., Jané-Llopis, E., Abrahams-Gessel, S., Bloom, L. R., Fathima, S., Feigl, A. B., & Weinstein, C. (2011). *The Global Economic Burden of Noncommunicable Diseases*. Geneva: World Economic Forum.

Boelen, P. A., & Reijntjes, A. (2008). Measuring experiential avoidance: Reliability and validity of the Dutch 9-item Acceptance and Action Questionnaire (AAQ). *Journal of Psychopathology and Behavioral Assessment, 30*, 241–251.

Bond, F. W., & Bunce, D. (2000). Mediators of change in emotion-focused and problem-focused worksite stress management interventions. *Journal of Occupational Health Psychology, 5*, 156–163.

Bond, F. W., Hayes, S. C., Baer, R. A., Carpenter, K. M., Guenole, N., Orcutt, H. K., & Zettle, R. D. (2011). Preliminary psychometric properties of the Acceptance and Action Questionnaire–II: A revised measure of psychological inflexibility and experiential avoidance. *Behavior Therapy, 42*(4), 676–688.

Borkovec, T. D., Newman, M. G., Pincus, A. L., & Lytle, R. (2002). A component analysis of cognitive-behavioral therapy for generalized anxiety disorder and the role of interpersonal problems. *Journal of Consulting and Clinical Psychology, 70*(2), 288–298. doi: 10.1037//0022-006X.70.2.288.

Butler, A., Chapman, J., Forman, E., & Beck, A. T. (2006). The empirical status of cognitive-behavioral therapy: A review of meta-analyses. *Clinical Psychology Review, 26*(1), 17–31.

Chapman, A. L., & Cellucci, T. (2007). The role of antisocial and borderline personality features in substance dependence among incarcerated females. *Addictive Behaviors, 32*, 1131–1145.

Chiles, J. A., & Strosahl, K. D. (1995). *Clinical Manual for Assessment and Treatment of Suicidal Patients*. Washington DC: American Psychiatric Association.

Chomsky, N. (1956). A review of B. F. Skinner's verbal behavior. *Language, 35*(1), 26–58.

David, D., & Hofmann, S. G. (2013). Another error of Descartes? Implications for the "third wave" cognitive-behavioral therapy. *Journal of Cognitive and Behavioral Psychotherapies, 13*, 111–121.

David, D., & Montgomery, G. H. (2011). The scientific status of psychotherapies: A new evaluative framework for evidence-based psychosocial interventions. *Clinical Psychology: Science and Practice, 18*(2), 89–99. doi: 10.1111/j.1468-2850.2011.01239.x.

Dykstra, T. A., & Follette, W. C. (1998). *An Agoraphobia Scale for Assessing the Clinical Significance of Treatment Outcome*. Unpublished manuscript.

Dymond, S., May, R., Munnelly, A., & Hoon, A. (2010). Evaluating the evidence base for relational frame theory: A citation analysis. *The Behavior Analyst, 33*, 97–117.

Dymond, S., & Roche, B. (Eds.) (2013). *Advances in Relational Frame Theory: Research & Application*. Oakland, CA: New Harbinger Publications.

Ellis, A. (2010). *Albert Ellis*. Fort Lee, NJ: Barricade Books Incorporated.

Ellis, A., & Ellis, D. J. (2011). *Rational Emotive Behavior Therapy*. Washington, DC: American Psychological Association.

Fletcher, L., Hayes, S. C., & Schoendorff, B. (2010). Searching for mindfulness in the brain: A process-oriented approach to examining the neural correlates of mindfulness. *Mindfulness, 1*(1), 41–63.

Forsyth, J. P., Parker, J. D., & Finlay, C. G. (2003). Anxiety sensitivity, controllability, and experiential avoidance and their relation to drug of choice and addiction severity in a residential sample of substance abusing veterans. *Addictive Behaviors, 28*, 851–870.

Gold, S. D., Dickstein, B. D., Marx, B. P., & Lexington, J. M. (2009). Psychological outcomes among lesbian sexual assault survivors: An examination of the roles of internalized homophobia and experiential avoidance. *Psychology of Women Quarterly, 33*, 54–66.

Gold, S. D., Marx, B. P., & Lexington, J. M. (2007). Gay male sexual assault survivors: The relations among internalized homophobia, experiential avoidance, and psychological symptom severity. *Behaviour Research and Therapy, 45*, 549–562.

Greco, L. A., Lambert, W., & Baer, R. A. (2008). Psychological inflexibility in childhood and adolescence: Development and evaluation of the Avoidance and Fusion Questionnaire for youth. *Psychological Assessment, 20*(2), 93–102. doi: 10.1037/1040-3590.20.2.93.

Harris, B. (1979). Whatever happened to little Albert? *The American Psychologist, 34*(2), 151–160. doi: 10.1037/0003-066X.34.2.151.

Hayes, S. C. (1993). Analytic goals and varieties of scientific contextualism. In: S. C. Hayes, L. J. Hayes, H. W. Reese, & T. R. Sarbin (Eds.). *Varieties of scientific contextualism*. Reno, NV: Context Press. pp. 11–27.

Hayes, S. C. (2004). Acceptance and commitment therapy, relational frame theory, and the third wave of behavioral and cognitive therapies. *Behavior Therapy, 35*(4), 639–665.

Hayes, S. C. (2008). Learning from the mistakes of the past? *The Behavior Therapist, 31*(8), 151–153.

Hayes, S. C. (2014). Foreword. In J. M. Stewart, *Mindfulness, Acceptance, and the Psychodynamic Evolution*. Oakland, CA: New Harbinger Publications.

Hayes, S. C., & Brownstein, A. J. (1986). Mentalism, behaviour–behavior relations, and a behavior-analytic view of the purposes of science. *The Behavior Analyst, 9*, 175–190.

Hayes, S. C., Barnes-Holmes, D., & Roche, B. (2001). *Relational Frame Theory*. New York: Springer.

Hayes, S. C., Barnes-Holmes, D., & Wilson, K. G. (2012). Contextual behavioral science: Creating a science more adequate to the challenge of the human condition. *Journal of Contextual Behavioral Science, 1*(1) 1–70. doi: 10.1016/j.jcbs.2012.09.004.

Hayes, S. C., Hayes, L. J., & Reese, H. W. (1988). Finding the philosophical core: A review of Stephen C. Pepper's world hypotheses: A study in evidence. *Journal of the Experimental Analysis of Behavior, 50*(1), 97–111. doi: 10.1901/jeab.1988.50-97.

Hayes, S. C., Luoma, J., Bond, F. W., Masuda, A., & Lillis, J. (2006). Acceptance and commitment therapy: Model, processes and outcomes. *Behaviour Research and Therapy*, doi: 10.1016/j.brat.2005.06.006.

Hayes, S. C., Strosahl, K. D., & Wilson, K. G. (2011). *Acceptance and Commitment Therapy: The Process and Practice of Mindful Change* (2nd ed.). New York: Guilford Press.

Hayes, S. C., Strosahl, K., & Wilson, K. G. (1999). *Acceptance and Commitment Therapy: An Experiential Approach to Behavior Change*. New York, London: The Guilford Press.

Hayes, S. C., Strosahl, K. D., Wilson, K. G., Bissett, R. T., Pistorello, J., Toarmino, D., & McCurry, S. M. (2004). Measuring experiential avoidance: A preliminary test of a working model. *The Psychological Record, 54*, 553–578.

Hofmann, S. G., & Asmundson, G. J. G. (2008). Acceptance and mindfulness-based therapy: New wave or old hat? *Clinical Psychology Review, 28*(1), 1–16.

Hooper, N., Saunders, J., & McHugh, L. (2010). The derived generalization of thought suppression. *Learning & Behavior, 38*(2), 160–168.

Hooper, N., Stewart, I., Duffy, C., Freegard, G., & McHugh, L. A. (2012). Modelling the direct and indirect effects of thought suppression on personal choice. *Journal of Contextual Behavioral Science, 1*, 73–82.

Jacobson, N. S., & Truax, P. A. (1991). Clinical significance: A statistical approach to defining meaningful change in psychotherapy research. *Journal of Consulting and Clinical Psychology, 59*(1), 12–19. Retrieved from http://psycnet.apa.org/journals/ccp/59/1/12/.

Jacobson, N. S., Dobson, K. S., Truax, P. A., Addis, M. E., Koerner, K., Gollan, J. K.,…& Prince, S. E. (1996). A component analysis of cognitive-behavioral treatment for depression. *Journal of Consulting and Clinical Psychology, 64*(2), 295–304.

Jones, M. C. (1960). A laboratory study of fear: The case of Peter. In H. J. Eysenck, *Behavior therapy and neuroses* (pp. 45–51). New York: Pergamon Press.

Kabat-Zinn, J., & Hanh, T. N. (2009). *Full Catastrophe Living.* New York: Random House LLC.

Kanter, J. W., Busch, A. M., & Rusch, L. C. (2009). *Behavioral Activation.* Hove: Routledge.

Karekla, M., Forsyth, J. P., & Kelly, M. M. (2004). Emotional avoidance and panicogenic responding to a biological challenge procedure. *Behavior Therapy, 35,* 725–746.

Kashdan, T. B., & Breen, W. E. (2007). Materialism and diminished well-being: Experiential avoidance as a mediating mechanism. *Journal of Social and Clinical Psychology, 26,* 521–539.

Kashdan, T. B., Barrios, V., Forsyth, J. P., & Steger, M. F. (2006). Experiential avoidance as a generalized psychological vulnerability: Comparisons with coping and emotion regulation strategies. *Behaviour Research and Therapy, 44,* 1301–1320.

Kazdin, A. E. (2007). Mediators and mechanisms of change in psychotherapy research. *Annual Review of Clinical Psychology, 3,* 1–27.

Kessler, R. C., & Üstün, T. B. (2008). *The WHO World Mental Health Survey: Global Perspectives on the Epidemiology of Mental Disorders.* Cambridge: Cambridge University Press.

Khoury, B., Lecomte, T., Fortin, G., Masse, M., Therien, P., Bouchard, V., & Hofmann, S. G. (2013). Mindfulness-based therapy: A comprehensive meta-analysis. *Clinical Psychology Review, 33*(6), 763–771. doi: 10.1016/j.cpr.2013.05.005.

Langer, A. I., Ruiz, F. J., Cangas, A. J., & Luciano, C. (2009). *Spanish Adaptation of Acceptance and Action Questionnaire-II: Factor Structure and Psychometric Properties.* Poster presented at The Third World Conference on ACT, RFT, and Contextual Behavioral Science, Enschede, The Netherlands.

Linehan, M. M., Schmidt, H., Dimeff, L. A., Craft, J. C., Kanter, J. W., & Comtois, K. A. (1999). Dialectical behavior therapy for patients with borderline personality disorder and drug-dependence. *American Journal on Addictions, 8*(4), 279–292.

Longmore, R. J., & Worrell, M. (2007). Do we need to challenge thoughts in cognitive behavior therapy? *Clinical Psychology Review, 27*(2), 173–187.

Masuda, A., Hayes, S. C., Sackett, C., & Twohig, M. P. (2004). Cognitive defusion and self-relevant negative thoughts: Examining the impact of a ninety year old technique. *Behaviour Research and Therapy, 42,* 477–485.

McCracken, L. M., & Zhao-O'Brien, J. (2010). General psychological acceptance and chronic pain: There is more to accept than the pain itself. *European Journal of Pain, 14*(2), 170–175.

Miller, G. A. (2003). The cognitive revolution: A historical perspective. *Trends in Cognitive Sciences, 7*(3), 141–145. doi: 10.1016/S1364-6613(03)00029-9.

Pepper, S. C. (1942). *World Hypotheses.* Berkeley: University of California Press.

Pistorello, J. (1998). *Acceptance, Suppression, and Monitoring of Personally Relevant Unwanted Thoughts in Women Diagnosed with Borderline Personality Disorder.* Unpublished doctoral dissertation, University of Nevada, Reno, NV.

Plumb, J. C., Orsillo, S. M., & Luterek, J. A. (2004). A preliminary test of the role of experiential avoidance in post-event functioning. *Journal of Behavior Therapy and Experimental Psychiatry, 35*, 245–257.

Polk, K., & Schoendorff, B. (2015). *The ACT Matrix*. Oakland, CA: New Harbinger Publications.

Polusny, M. A., Rosenthal, M. Z., Aban, I., & Follette, V. M. (2004). Experiential avoidance as a mediator of the effects of adolescent sexual victimization on negative adult outcomes. *Violence and Victims, 19*, 109–120.

Ramnerö, J. (2012). Exposure therapy for anxiety disorders: Is there room for cognitive interventions? In P. Neudeck & H.-U. Wittchen (Eds.), *Exposure therapy: Rethinking the model refining the method* (pp. 275–297). Springer. doi: 10.1007/978-1-4614-3342-2_16.

Robins, C. J., Schmidt, H., & Linehan, M. M. (2011). Dialectical behavior therapy: Synthesizing radical acceptance with skillful means. In S. C. Hayes, V. M. Follette, & M. M. Linehan (Eds.), *Mindfulness and acceptance: Expanding the cognitive-behavioral tradition* (pp. 30–45). New York: The Guilford Press.

Roemer, L., Salters, K., Raffa, S. D., & Orsillo, S. M. (2005). Fear and avoidance of internal experiences in GAD: Preliminary tests of a conceptual model. *Cognitive Therapy and Research, 29*, 71–88.

Ruiz, F. J. (2010). A review of Acceptance and Commitment Therapy (ACT) empirical evidence: Correlational, experimental psychopathology, component and outcome studies. *International Journal of Psychology and Psychological Therapy, 10*(1), 125–162.

Sandoz, E. K., Wilson, K. G., & DuFrene, T. (2011). *Acceptance and Commitment Therapy for Eating Disorders*. Oakland, CA: New Harbinger Publications.

Santanello, A. W., & Gardner, F. L. (2007). The role of experiential avoidance in the relationship between maladaptive perfectionism and worry. *Cognitive Therapy and Research, 31*, 319–332.

Segal, Z. V., Williams, J. M. G., & Teasdale, J. D. (2012). *Mindfulness-Based Cognitive Therapy for Depression*. New York: Guilford Press.

Sidman, M. (1971). Reading and auditory-visual equivalences. *Journal of Speech and Hearing Research, 14*, 5–13.

Skinner, B. F. (1938). *The Behavior of Organisms: An Experimental Analysisý*. New York: Appleton-Century-Crofts, Inc.

Skinner, B. F. (1957). *Verbal Behavior*. New York: Appleton-Century-Crofts, Inc.

Skinner, B. F. (1966). An operant analysis of problem solving. In B. Kleinmuntz (Ed.), *Problem-solving: Research, method, and theory*. New York: John Wiley and Sons, Inc. 225–257.

Skinner, B. F. (1969). *Contingencies of Reinforcement: A Theoretical Analysis*. New York: Appleton.

Skinner, B. F. (1984). The operational analysis of psychological terms. *Behavioral and Brain Sciences, 7*(4), 547–553.

Stewart, S. H., Zvolensky, M. J., & Eifert, G. H. (2002). The relations of anxiety sensitivity, experiential avoidance, and alexithymic coping to young adults' motivations for drinking. *Behavior Modification, 26*(2), 274–296. doi: 10.1177/0145445502026002007.

Strosahl, K., Robinson, P., & Gustavsson, T. (2012). *Brief Interventions for Radical Change*. Oakland, CA: New Harbinger Publications.

Strosahl, K. D., Hayes, S. C., Bergan, J., & Romano, P. (1998). Assessing the field effectiveness of acceptance and commitment therapy: An example of the manipulated training research method. *Behavior Therapy, 29*, 35–63.

Toarmino, D., Pistorello, J., & Hayes, S. C. (1997). Validation of the Acceptance and Action Questionnaire. Unpublished manuscript.

Törneke, N. (2010). *Learning RFT*. Oakland, CA: New Harbinger Publications.

Tull, M. T., & Gratz, K. L. (2008). Further examination of the relationship between anxiety sensitivity and depression: The mediating role of experiential avoidance and difficulties engaging in goal-directed behavior when distressed. *Journal of Anxiety Disorders, 22*, 199–210.

Tull, M. T., Gratz, K. L., Salters, K., & Roemer, L. (2004). The role of experiential avoidance in posttraumatic stress symptoms and symptoms of depression, anxiety, and somatization. *Journal of Nervous & Mental Disease, 192*, 754–761.

Watson, J. B. (1913). Psychology as the behaviorist views it. *Psychological Review, 20*(2), 158–177. doi: 10.1037/h0074428.

Watson, J. B., & Rayner, R. (1920). Conditioned emotional reactions. *Journal of Experimental Psychology, 3*(1), 1–14. doi: 10.1037/h0069608.

Wegner, D., & Gold, D. (1995). Fanning old flames: Emotional and cognitive effects of suppressing thoughts of a past relationship. *Journal of Personality and Social Psychology, 68*(5), 782.

Whitaker, R. (2011). *Anatomy of an Epidemic: Magic Bullets, Psychiatric Drugs, and the Astonishing Rise of Mental Illness in America*. New York: Random House LLC.

Wilson, K. G., & DuFrene, T. (2009). *Mindfulness for Two*. Oakland, CA: New Harbinger Publications.

Wilson, K. G., Khorakiwala, D., & Hayes, S. C. (1991, May). Change in acceptance and commitment therapy. In K. G. Wilson (Chair) (Ed.), *Radical behavioral psychotherapy process research*. Symposium conducted at the meeting of the Association for Behavior Analysis Atlanta.

Wolpe, J. (1973). *The Practice of Behavior Therapy*. New York: Pergamon Press.

Zettle, R. D. (2005). The evolution of a contextual approach to therapy: From comprehensive distancing to ACT. *International Journal of Behavioral Consultation & Therapy, 1*(2), 77–89.

Zettle, R. D., & Hayes, S. C. (1982). Rule-governed behavior: A potential theoretical framework for cognitive-behavioral therapy. In P. C. Kendall (Ed.), *Advances in cognitive-behavioral research and therapy* (pp. 73–118). New York: Academic Press.

Part II

Depression

Bohlmeijer, E. T., Fledderus, M., Rokx, T. A. J. J., & Pieterse, M. E. (2011). Efficacy of an early intervention based on acceptance and commitment therapy for adults with depressive symptomatology: Evaluation in a randomized controlled trial. *Behaviour Research and Therapy, 49*(1), 62–67.

Bohlmeijer, E. T., & Hulsbergen, M. (2008). *Voluit Leven. Mindfulness of de kunst van het ervaren, nu als praktisch hulpboek* [*Living to the Full. Mindfulness or the Art of Acceptance, Now as a Practical Help Book*]. Amsterdam: Boom.

Bohlmeijer, E. T., Lamers, S. M., & Fledderus, M. (2015). Flourishing in people with depressive symptomatology increases with acceptance and commitment therapy. Post-hoc analyses of a randomized controlled trial. *Behaviour Research and Therapy, 65,* 101–106. doi: 10.1016/j.brat.2014.12.014.

Butler, A. C., Chapman, J. E., Forman, E. M., & Beck, A. T. (2006). The empirical status of cognitive-behavioral therapy: A review of meta-analyses. *Clinical Psychology Review, 26*(1), 17–31.

Carlbring, P., Hägglund, M., Luthström, A., Dahlin, M., Kadowaki, Å., Vernmark, K., & Andersson, G. (2013). Internet-based behavioral activation and acceptance-based treatment for depression: A randomized controlled trial. *Journal of Affective Disorders, 148*(2), 331–337.

Cuijpers, P., Smit, F., Oostenbrink, J., De Graaf, R., Ten Have, M., & Beekman, A. (2007). Economic costs of minor depression: A population-based study. *Acta Psychiatrica Scandinavica, 115,* 229–236.

Dougher, M. J., & Hackbert, L. (1994). A behavior-analytic account of depression and a case report using acceptance-based procedures. *The Behavior Analyst, 17*(2), 321.

Fledderus, M., Bohlmeijer, E. T., Fox, J. P., Schreurs, K. M., & Spinhoven, P. (2013). The role of psychological flexibility in a self-help acceptance and commitment therapy intervention for psychological distress in a randomized controlled trial. *Behaviour Research and Therapy, 51*(3), 142–151.

Fledderus, M., Bohlmeijer, E. T., & Pieterse, M. E. (2010). Does experiential avoidance mediate the effects of maladaptive coping styles on psychopathology and mental health? *Behavior Modification, 34*(6), 503–519.

Fledderus, M., Bohlmeijer, E. T., Pieterse, M. E., & Schreurs, K. M. G. (2012). Acceptance and commitment therapy as guided self-help for psychological distress and positive mental health: A randomized controlled trial. *Psychological Medicine, 42*(3), 485–495.

Folke, F., Parling, T., & Melin, L. (2012). Acceptance and commitment therapy for depression: A preliminary randomized clinical trial for unemployed on long-term sick leave. *Cognitive and Behavioral Practice, 19*(4), 583–594.

Forman, E. M., Herbert, J. D., Moitra, E., Yeomans, P. D., & Geller, P. A. (2007). A randomized controlled effectiveness trial of acceptance and commitment therapy and cognitive therapy for anxiety and depression. *Behavior Modification, 31*(6), 772–799.

Forman, E. M., Shaw, J. A., Goetter, E. M., Herbert, J. D., Park, J. A., & Yuen, E. K. (2012). Long-term follow-up of a randomized controlled trial comparing acceptance and commitment therapy and standard cognitive behavior therapy for anxiety and depression. *Behavior Therapy, 43*(4), 801–811.

Gird, S., & Zettle, R. D. (2010). Differential response to a dysphoric mood induction procedure as a function of level of experiential avoidance. *The Psychological Record, 59*(4), 3.

Gotlib, I. H., & Hammen, C. L. (Eds.) (2009). *Handbook of Depression.* New York: The Guilford Press.

Hayes, L., Boyd, C. P., & Sewell, J. (2011). Acceptance and commitment therapy for the treatment of adolescent depression: A pilot study in a psychiatric outpatient setting. *Mindfulness, 2*(2), 86–94.

Hayes, S. C., Luoma, J. B., Bond, F. W., Masuda, A., & Lillis, J. (2006). Acceptance and commitment therapy: Model, processes, and outcomes. *Behavior Research and Therapy, 44,* 1–25.

Hosman, C., Jane-Llopis, E., & Saxena, S. (Eds.). (2005). *Prevention of Mental Disorders: Effective Interventions and Policy Options*. Oxford: Oxford University Press.

Kanter, J. W., Baruch, D. E., & Gaynor, S. T. (2006). Acceptance and commitment therapy and behavioral activation for the treatment of depression: Description and comparison. *The Behavior Analyst, 29*(2), 161.

Lappalainen, P., Granlund, A., Siltanen, S., Ahonen, S., Vitikainen, M., Tolvanen, A., & Lappalainen, R. (2014). ACT Internet-based vs face-to-face? A randomized controlled trial of two ways to deliver acceptance and commitment therapy for depressive symptoms: An 18-month follow-up. *Behaviour Research and Therapy, 61*, 43–54.

Lappalainen, P., Kaipainen, K., Lappalainen, R., Hoffrén, H., Myllymäki, T., Kinnunen, M. L., & Korhonen, I. (2013). Feasibility of a personal health technology-based psychological intervention for men with stress and mood problems: Randomized controlled pilot trial. *JMIR Research Protocols, 2*(1).

Lappalainen, R., Lehtonen, T., Skarp, E., Taubert, E., Ojanen, M., & Hayes, S. C. (2007). The impact of CBT and ACT models using psychology trainee therapists: A preliminary controlled effectiveness trial. *Behavior Modification, 31*(4), 488–511.

Livheim, F., Hayes, L., Ghaderi, A., Magnusdottir, T., Högfeldt, A., Rowse, J., ... & Tengström, A. (2014). The effectiveness of acceptance and commitment therapy for adolescent mental health: Swedish and Australian pilot outcomes. *Journal of Child and Family Studies, 24*, 1016–1030.

Peterson, C. L., & Zettle, R. D. (2009). Treating inpatients with comorbid depression and alcohol use disorders: A comparison of acceptance and commitment therapy and treatment as usual. *The Psychological Record, 59*, 521–536.

Segal, Z. V., Williams, J. M. G., & Teasdale, J. D. (2012). *Mindfulness-Based Cognitive Therapy for Depression*. New York: Guilford Press.

Tamannaeifar, S., Gharraee, B., Birashk, B., & Habibi, M. (2014). A comparative effectiveness of acceptance and commitment therapy and group cognitive therapy for major depressive disorder. *Zahedan Journal of Research in Medical Sciences, 16*(10), 60–63.

Zettle, R. D., & Hayes, S. C. (1986). Dysfunctional control by client verbal behavior: The context of reason giving. *Analysis of Verbal Behavior, 4*, 30–38.

Zettle, R. D., & Rains, J. C. (1989). Group cognitive and contextual therapies in treatment of depression. *Journal of Clinical Psychology, 45*(3), 436–445.

Zettle, R. D., Rains, J. C., & Hayes, S. C. (2011). Processes of change in acceptance and commitment therapy and cognitive therapy for depression: A mediation reanalysis of Zettle and Rains. *Behavior Modification, 35*(3), 265–283.

Anxiety

OCD

Abramowitz, J. S., Taylor, S., & McKay, D. (2009). Obsessive-compulsive disorder. *Lancet, 374*, 491–499.

Armstrong, A. B., Morrison, K. L., & Twohig, M. P. (2013). A preliminary investigation of acceptance and commitment therapy for adolescent obsessive-compulsive disorder. *Journal of Cognitive Psychotherapy, 27*(2), 175–190.

Bluett, E. J., Homan, K. J., Morrison, K. L., Levin, M. E., & Twohig, M. P. (2014). Acceptance and commitment therapy for anxiety and OCD spectrum disorders: An empirical review. *Journal of Anxiety Disorders, 28*(6), 612–624.

Brown, F. J., & Hooper, S. (2009). Acceptance and Commitment Therapy (ACT) with a learning disabled young person experiencing anxious and obsessive thoughts. *Journal of Intellectual Disabilities, 13*(3), 195–201.

Crosby, J. M., Dehlin, J. P., Mitchell, P. R., & Twohig, M. P. (2012). Acceptance and commitment therapy and habit reversal training for the treatment of trichotillomania. *Cognitive and Behavioral Practice, 19*(4), 595–605.

Dehlin, J. P., Morrison, K. L., & Twohig, M. P. (2013). Acceptance and commitment therapy as a treatment for scrupulosity in obsessive compulsive disorder. *Behavior Modification, 37*(3), 409–430.

Fals-Stewart, W., Marks, A. P., & Schafer, J. (1993). A comparison of behavioral group therapy and individual behavior therapy in treating obsessive-compulsive disorder. *Journal of Nervous and Mental Disease, 181*, 189–193.

Fine, K. M., Walther, M. R., Joseph, J. M., Robinson, J., Ricketts, E. J., Bowe, W. E., & Woods, D. W. (2012). Acceptance-enhanced behavior therapy for trichotillomania in adolescents. *Cognitive and Behavioral Practice, 19*(3), 463–471.

Flessner, C. A., Busch, A. M., Heideman, P. W., & Woods, D. W. (2008). Acceptance-Enhanced Behavior Therapy (AEBT) for trichotillomania and chronic skin picking exploring the effects of component sequencing. *Behavior Modification, 32*(5), 579–594.

Foa, E. B., Liebowitz, M. R., Kozak, M. J., Davies, S., Campeas, R., Franklin, M. E., . . . & Tu, X. (2005). Randomized, placebo-controlled trial of exposure and ritual prevention, clomipramine, and their combination in the treatment of obsessive-compulsive disorder. *American Journal of Psychiatry, 162*, 151–161.

Franklin, M. E., Best, S. H., Wilson, M. A., Loew, B., & Compton, S. N. (2011). Habit reversal training and acceptance and commitment therapy for Tourette syndrome: A pilot project. *Journal of Developmental and Physical Disabilities, 23*(1), 49–60.

Hayes, S. C. (1987). A contextual approach to therapeutic change. In N. S. Jacobson (Ed.), *Psychotherapists in clinical practice: Cognitive and behavioral perspectives* (pp. 327–387). New York, NY: Guilford Press.

Levitt, J. T., Brown, T. A., Orsillo, S. M., & Barlow, D. H. (2004). The effects of acceptance versus suppression of emotion on subjective and psychophysiological response to carbon dioxide challenge in patients with panic disorder. *Behavior Therapy, 35*, 747–766.

Olatunji, B. O., Deacon, B. J., & Abramowitz, J. S. (2009). Is hypochondriasis an anxiety disorder? *The British Journal of Psychiatry, 194*(6), 481–482.

Tolin, D. F. (2009). Alphabet Soup: ERP, CT, and ACT for OCD. *Cognitive and Behavioral Practice, 16*(1), 40–48.

Twohig, M. P., Morrison, K. L., & Bluett, E. J. (2014). Acceptance and commitment therapy for obsessive compulsive disorder and obsessive compulsive spectrum disorders: A review. *Current Psychiatry Reviews, 10*(4), 296–307.

Twohig, M. P., Hayes, S. C., & Masuda, A. (2006a). Increasing willingness to experience obsessions: Acceptance and commitment therapy as a treatment for obsessive-compulsive disorder. *Behavior Therapy, 37*, 3–13.

Twohig, M. P., Hayes, S. C., & Masuda, A. (2006b). A preliminary investigation of acceptance and commitment therapy as a treatment for chronic skin picking. *Behaviour Research and Therapy, 44*, 1513–1522.

Twohig, M. P., Hayes, S. C., Plumb, J. C., Pruitt, L. D., Collins, A. B., Hazlett-Stevens, H., & Woidneck, M. R. (2010). A randomized clinical trial of acceptance and commitment therapy versus progressive relaxation training for obsessive-compulsive disorder. *Journal of Consulting and Clinical Psychology, 78*(5), 705.

Twohig, M. P., & Whittal, M. L. (2009). A case of obsessive-compulsive disorder. *Cognitive and Behavioral Practice, 16*(1), 3–6.

Twohig, M. P., Whittal, M. L., Cox, J. M., & Gunter, R. (2010). An initial investigation into the processes of change in ACT, CT, and ERP for OCD. *International Journal of Behavioral Consultation and Therapy, 6*(1), 67–83.

Twohig, M. P., & Woods, D. W. (2004). A preliminary investigation of acceptance and commitment therapy and habit reversal as a treatment of trichotillomania. *Behavior Therapy, 35*, 803–820.

Vakili, Y., & Gharraee, B. (2014). The effectiveness of acceptance and commitment therapy in treating a case of obsessive compulsive disorder. *Iranian Journal of Psychiatry, 9*(2), 115–117.

Wetterneck, C. T., Lee, E. B., Smith, A. H., & Hart, J. M. (2013). Courage, self-compassion, and values in obsessive-compulsive disorder. *Journal of Contextual Behavioral Science, 2*(3), 68–73.

Woods, D. W., Wetterneck, C. T., & Flessner, C. A. (2006). A controlled evaluation of acceptance and commitment therapy plus habit reversal for trichotillomania. *Behaviour Research and Therapy, 44*, 639–656.

GAD

Avdagic, E., Morrissey, S. A., & Boschen, M. J. (2014). A randomised controlled trial of acceptance and commitment therapy and cognitive-behaviour therapy for generalised anxiety disorder. *Behaviour Change, 31*(2), 110–130.

Brown, T. A., Barlow, D. H., & Liebowitz, M. R. (1994). The empirical basis of generalized anxiety disorder. *American Journal of Psychiatry, 151*, 1272–1280.

Fuchs, C., Lee, J. K., Roemer, L., & Orsillo, S.M. (2013). Using mindfulness- and acceptance-based treatments with clients from nondominant cultural and/or marginalized backgrounds: Client considerations, meta-analysis findings and Introduction to the Special Series. *Cognitive and Behavioral Practice, 20*, 1–12.

Hayes, S. A., Orsillo, S. M., & Roemer, L. (2010). Changes in proposed mechanisms of action during an acceptance-based behavior therapy for generalized anxiety disorder. *Behaviour Research and Therapy, 48*(3), 238–245.

Hayes-Skelton, S. A., Roemer, L., & Orsillo, S. M. (2013). A randomized clinical trial comparing an acceptance-based behavior therapy to applied relaxation for generalized anxiety disorder. *Journal of Consulting and Clinical Psychology, 81*(5), 761.

Kessler, R. C., Walters, E. E., & Wittchen, H.-U. (2004). Epidemiology. In R. G. Heimberg, C. L. Turk, & D. S. Mennin (Eds.), *Generalized anxiety disorder: Advances in research and practice* (pp. 29–50). New York: Guilford.

Linehan, M. (1993). *Cognitive-Behavioral Treatment of Borderline Personality Disorder*. New York: Guilford Press.

Orsillo, S. M., Roemer, L., & Barlow, D. H. (2003). Integrating acceptance and mindfulness into existing cognitive-behavioral treatment for GAD: A case study. *Cognitive and Behavioral Practice, 10*(3), 222–230.

Roemer, L., & Orsillo, S. M. (2002). Expanding our conceptualization of and treatment for generalized anxiety disorder: Integrating mindfulness/acceptance based approaches with existing cognitive-behavioral models. *Clinical Psychology: Science and Practice, 9*(1), 54–68.

Roemer, L., & Orsillo, S. M. (2007). An open trial of an acceptance-based behavior therapy for generalized anxiety disorder. *Behavior Therapy, 38*(1), 72–85.

Roemer, L., Orsillo, S. M., & Salters-Pedneault, K. (2008). Efficacy of an acceptance-based behavior therapy for generalized anxiety disorder: Evaluation in a randomized controlled trial. *Journal of Consulting and Clinical Psychology, 76*(6), 1083.

Roemer, L., Salters, K., Raffa, S. D., & Orsillo, S. M. (2005). Fear and avoidance of internal experiences in GAD: Preliminary tests of a conceptual model. *Cognitive Therapy and Research, 29*(1), 71–88.

Segal, Z. V., Williams, J. M. G., & Teasdale, J. D. (2002). *Mindfulness-Based Cognitive Therapy for Depression: A New Approach to Preventing Relapse.* New York: Guilford Press.

Sobczak, L. R., & West, L. M. (2013). Clinical considerations in using mindfulness- and acceptance-based approaches with diverse populations: Addressing challenges in service delivery in diverse community settings. *Cognitive and Behavioral Practice, 20*, 13–22. doi: 10.1016/j.cbpra.2011.08.005.

Waters, A. M., & Craske, M. G. (2005). Generalized anxiety disorder. In M. M. Antony, D. R. Ledley, R. G. Heimberg (Eds.) *Improving outcomes and preventing relapse in cognitive behavioral therapy* (pp. 77–127). New York: Guilford.

Wetherell, J. L., Liu, L., Patterson, T. L., Afari, N., Ayers, C. R., Thorp, S. R., & Petkus, A. J. (2011). Acceptance and commitment therapy for generalized anxiety disorder in older adults: A preliminary report. *Behavior Therapy, 42*(1), 127–134.

Yonkers, K. A., Warshaw, M. G., Massion, A. O., & Keller, M. B. (1996). Phenomenology and course of generalized anxiety disorder. *British Journal of Psychiatry, 168*, 308–313.

Social anxiety

Block, J. A., & Wulfert, E. (2000). Acceptance or change: Treating socially anxious college students with ACT or CBGT. *The Behavior Analyst Today, 1*(2), 1–55.

Craske, M. G., Niles, A. N., Burklund, L. J., Wolitzky-Taylor, K. B., Vilardaga, J. C. P., Arch, J. J., & Lieberman, M. D. (2014). Randomized controlled trial of cognitive behavioral therapy and acceptance and commitment therapy for social phobia: Outcomes and moderators. *Journal of Consulting and Clinical Psychology, 82*(6), 1034.

Dalrymple, K. L., & Herbert, J. D. (2007). Acceptance and commitment therapy for generalized social anxiety disorder: A pilot study. *Behavior Modification, 31*(3), 343–368.

Dalrymple, K. L., Morgan, T. A., Lipschitz, J. M., Martinez, J. H., Tepe, E., & Zimmerman, M. (2014). An integrated, acceptance-based behavioral approach for depression with social anxiety: Preliminary results. *Behavior Modification*, doi: 10.1177/0145445513518422.

Eng, W., Coles, M. E., Heimberg, R. G., & Safren, S. A. (2005). Domains of life satisfaction in social anxiety disorder: Relation to symptoms and response to cognitive-behavioral therapy. *Journal of Anxiety Disorders, 19*, 143–156.

England, E. L., Herbert, J. D., Forman, E. M., Rabin, S. J., Juarascio, A., & Goldstein, S. P. (2012). Acceptance-based exposure therapy for public speaking anxiety. *Journal of Contextual Behavioral Science, 1*(1), 66–72.

Fleming, J. E., & Kocovski, N. L. (2013). *The Mindfulness and Acceptance Workbook for Social Anxiety and Shyness: Using Acceptance and Commitment Therapy to Free Yourself from Fear and Reclaim Your Life*. Oakland, CA: New Harbinger Publications.

Herbert, J. D., & Cardaciotto, L. A. (2005). An acceptance and mindfulness-based perspective on social anxiety disorder. In *Acceptance and mindfulness-based approaches to anxiety* (pp. 189–212). New York: Springer.

Hofmann, S. G., & Bögels, S. M. (2006). Recent advances in the treatment of social phobia: Introduction to the special issue. *Journal of Cognitive Psychotherapy, 20*, 3–5.

Kashdan, T. B., Farmer, A. S., Adams, L. M., Ferssizidis, P., Mcknight, P. E., & Nezlek, J. B. (2013). Distinguishing healthy adults from people with social anxiety disorder: evidence for the value of experiential avoidance and positive emotions in everyday social interactions. *Journal of Abnormal Psychology, 122*(3), 645–655. http://doi.org/10.1037/a0032733.

Kashdan, T. B., Goodman, F. R., Machell, K. A., Kleiman, E. M., Monfort, S. S., Ciarrochi, J., & Nezlek, J. B. (2014). A contextual approach to experiential avoidance and social anxiety: Evidence from an experimental interaction and daily interactions of people with social anxiety disorder. *Emotion, 14*(4), 769–781. http://doi.org/10.1037/a0035935.

Kocovski, N. L., Fleming, J. E., Hawley, L. L., Huta, V., & Antony, M. M. (2013). Mindfulness and acceptance-based group therapy versus traditional cognitive behavioral group therapy for social anxiety disorder: A randomized controlled trial. *Behaviour Research and Therapy, 51*(12), 889–898.

Kocovski, N. L., Fleming, J. E., & Rector, N. A. (2009). Mindfulness and acceptance-based group therapy for social anxiety disorder: An open trial. *Cognitive and Behavioral Practice, 16*(3), 276–289.

Niles, A. N., Burklund, L. J., Arch, J. J., Lieberman, M. D., Saxbe, D., & Craske, M. G. (2014). Cognitive mediators of treatment for social anxiety disorder: Comparing acceptance and commitment therapy and cognitive behavioral therapy. *Behavior Therapy, 45*(5), 664–677.

Ossman, W. A., Wilson, K. G., Storaasli, R. D., & McNeill, J. W. (2006). A preliminary investigation of the use of acceptance and commitment therapy in group treatment for social phobia. *International Journal of Psychology and Psychological Therapy, 6*(3), 397–416.

Yadegari, L., Hashemiyan, K., & Abolmaali, K. (2014). Effect of acceptance and commitment therapy on young people with social anxiety. *International Journal of Scientific Research in Knowledge, 2*(8), pp. 395–403.

PTSD and panic disorder

American Psychiatric Association. (2000). *The Diagnostic and Statistical Manual of Mental Disorders* (4th ed., text rev.). Washington, DC: Author.

Batten, S. V., & Hayes, S. C. (2005). Acceptance and commitment therapy in the treatment of comorbid substance abuse and post-traumatic stress disorder: A case study. *Clinical Case Studies, 4*(3), 246–262.

Casselman, R. B., & Pemberton, J. R. (2015). ACT-based parenting group for veterans with PTSD: Development and preliminary outcomes. *The American Journal of Family Therapy, 43*(1), 57–66.

Eifert, G. H., & Heffner, M. (2003). The effects of acceptance versus control contexts on avoidance of panic-related symptoms. *Journal of Behavior Therapy and Experimental Psychiatry, 34*(3), 293–312.

Feldner, M. T., Zvolensky, M. J., Eifert, G. H., & Spira, A. P. (2003). Emotional avoidance: An experimental test of individual differences and response suppression using biological challenge. *Behaviour Research and Therapy, 41*(4), 403–411.

Kazdin, A. E. (1998). *Research Design in Clinical Psychology*. Boston: Allyn & Bacon.

Keller, M. B., Yonkers, K. A., Warshaw, M. G., Pratt, L. A., Gollan, J. K., Massion, A. O., & Lavori, P. W. (1994). Remission and relapse in subjects with panic disorder and panic with agoraphobia: A prospective short-interval naturalistic follow-up. *The Journal of Nervous and Mental Disease, 182*(5), 290–296.

Kessler, R. C., McGonagle, K. A., Zhao, S., Nelson, C. B., Hughes, M., Eshleman, S., & Kendler, K. S. (1994). Lifetime and 12-month prevalence of DSM-III-R psychiatric disorders in the United States: Results from the National Comorbidity Survey. *Archives of General Psychiatry, 51*(1), 8–9.

Levitt, J. T., Brown, T. A., Orsillo, S. M., & Barlow, D. H. (2004). The effects of acceptance versus suppression of emotion on subjective and psychophysiological response to carbon dioxide challenge in patients with panic disorder. *Behavior Therapy, 35*(4), 747–766.

López, F. J. C. (2000). Acceptance and commitment therapy (ACT) in panic disorder with agoraphobia: A case study. *Psychology in Spain, 4*(1), 120–128.

Meuret, A. E., Twohig, M. P., Rosenfield, D., Hayes, S. C., & Craske, M. G. (2012). Brief acceptance and commitment therapy and exposure for panic disorder: A pilot study. *Cognitive and Behavioral Practice, 19*(4), 606–618.

Meuret, A. E., Wolitzky-Taylor, K. B., Twohig, M. P., & Craske, M. G. (2012). Coping skills and exposure therapy in panic disorder and agoraphobia: Latest advances and future directions. *Behavior Therapy, 43*(2), 271–284.

Ojserkis, R., McKay, D., Badour, C. L., Feldner, M. T., Arocho, J., & Dutton, C. (2014). Alleviation of moral disgust, shame, and guilt in posttraumatic stress reactions: An evaluation of comprehensive distancing. *Behavior Modification*, doi: 10.1177/0145445514543465.

Orsillo, S. M., & Batten, S. V. (2005). Acceptance and commitment therapy in the treatment of posttraumatic stress disorder. *Behavior Modification, 29*(1), 95–129.

Rothbaum, B. O., Meadows, E. A., Resick, P., & Foy, D. W. (2000). Cognitive-behavioral therapy. In E. B. Foa, T. M. Keane, & M. J. Freidman (Eds.), *Effective treatments for PTSD: Practice guidelines from the International Society for Traumatic Stress Studies* (pp. 320–325). New York: Guilford.

Thompson, B. L., Luoma, J. B., & LeJeune, J. T. (2013). Using acceptance and commitment therapy to guide exposure-based interventions for posttraumatic stress disorder. *Journal of Contemporary Psychotherapy, 43*(3), 133–140.

Twohig, M. P. (2009). Acceptance and commitment therapy for treatment-resistant posttraumatic stress disorder: A case study. *Cognitive and Behavioral Practice, 16*(3), 243–252.

Woidneck, M. R., Morrison, K. L., & Twohig, M. P. (2013). Acceptance and commitment therapy for the treatment of posttraumatic stress among adolescents. *Behavior Modification*, doi: 10.1177/0145445513510527.

General anxiety disorders

Arch, J. J., & Craske, M. G. (2008). Acceptance and commitment therapy and cognitive behavioral therapy for anxiety disorders: Different treatments, similar mechanisms? *Clinical Psychology: Science and Practice, 15*(4), 263–279.

Arch, J. J., Eifert, G. H., Davies, C., Vilardaga, J. C. P., Rose, R. D., & Craske, M. G. (2012). Randomized clinical trial of cognitive behavioral therapy (CBT) versus acceptance and commitment therapy (ACT) for mixed anxiety disorders. *Journal of Consulting and Clinical Psychology, 80*(5), 750.

Arch, J. J., Wolitzky-Taylor, K. B., Eifert, G. H., & Craske, M. G. (2012). Longitudinal treatment mediation of traditional cognitive behavioral therapy and acceptance and commitment therapy for anxiety disorders. *Behaviour Research and Therapy, 50*(7), 469–478.

Barlow, D. H., Gorman, J. M., Shear, M. K., & Woods, S. W. (2000). Cognitive-behavioral therapy, imipramine, or their combination for panic disorder: A randomized controlled trial. *Journal of the American Medical Association, 283*, 2529–2536. doi: 10.1001/jama.283.19.2529.

Brown, L. A., Forman, E. M., Herbert, J. D., Hoffman, K. L., Yuen, E. K., & Goetter, E. M. (2011). A randomized controlled trial of acceptance-based behavior therapy and cognitive therapy for test anxiety: A pilot study. *Behavior Modification, 35*(1), 31–53.

Brown, T. A., & Barlow, D. H. (1995). Long-term outcome in cognitive-behavioral treatment of panic disorder: Clinical predictors and alternative strategies for assessment. *Journal of Consulting and Clinical Psychology, 63*, 754–765. doi: 10.1037/0022-006X.63.5.754.

Codd, R. T., Twohig, M. P., Crosby, J. M., & Enno, A. (2011). Treatment of three anxiety disorder cases with acceptance and commitment therapy in a private practice. *Journal of Cognitive Psychotherapy, 25*(3), 203–217.

Craske, M. G. (2003). *Origins of Phobias and Anxiety Disorders: Why More Women Than Men?* Oxford, England: Elsevier.

Davies, C. D., Niles, A. N., Pittig, A., Arch, J. J., & Craske, M. G. (2015). Physiological and behavioral indices of emotion dysregulation as predictors of outcome from cognitive behavioral therapy and acceptance and commitment therapy for anxiety. *Journal of Behavior Therapy and Experimental Psychiatry, 46*, 35–43.

Eifert, G. H., Forsyth, J. P., Arch, J., Espejo, E., Keller, M., & Langer, D. (2009). Acceptance and commitment therapy for anxiety disorders: Three case studies exemplifying a unified treatment protocol. *Cognitive and Behavioral Practice, 16*(4), 368–385.

Eilenberg, T., Kronstrand, L., Fink, P., & Frostholm, L. (2013). Acceptance and commitment group therapy for health anxiety: Results from a pilot study. *Journal of Anxiety Disorders, 27*(5), 461–468.

Graham, C. D., Gillanders, D., Stuart, S., & Gouick, J. (2014). An acceptance and commitment therapy (ACT)–based intervention for an adult experiencing post-stroke anxiety and medically unexplained symptoms. *Clinical Case Studies*, doi: 10.1177/1534650114539386.

Hoffmann, D., Halsboe, L., Eilenberg, T., Jensen, J. S., & Frostholm, L. (2014). A pilot study of processes of change in group-based acceptance and commitment therapy for health anxiety. *Journal of Contextual Behavioral Science 3*(3), 189–195.

Meyer, J. M., Farrell, N. R., Kemp, J. J., Blakey, S. M., & Deacon, B. J. (2014). Why do clinicians exclude anxious clients from exposure therapy? *Behaviour Research and Therapy, 54*, 49–53.

Rothman, D. K. (2004). New approach to test anxiety. *Journal of College Student Psychotherapy, 18*, 45–60.

Swain, J., Hancock, K., Hainsworth, C., & Bowman, J. (2014). Mechanisms of change: Exploratory outcomes from a randomised controlled trial of acceptance and commitment therapy for anxious adolescents. *Journal of Contextual Behavioral Science, 4*(1), 56–67.

Tolin, D. F. (2010). Is cognitive behavioral therapy more effective than other therapies? A meta-analytic review. *Clinical Psychology Review, 30*, 710–720. doi: 10.1016/j.cpr.2010.05.003.

Wolitzky-Taylor, K. B., Arch, J. J., Rosenfield, D., & Craske, M. G. (2012). Moderators and non-specific predictors of treatment outcome for anxiety disorders: A comparison of cognitive behavioral therapy to acceptance and commitment therapy. *Journal of Consulting and Clinical Psychology, 80*(5), 786.

Zeidner, M. (1998). *Test Anxiety: The State of the Art.* New York: Plenum Press.

Zettle, R. D. (2003). Acceptance and commitment therapy (ACT) vs. systematic desensitization in treatment of mathematics anxiety. *The Psychological Record, 53*(2), 3.

Serious mental health issues

BPD

Chapman, A. L., Gratz, K. L., & Brown, M. Z. (2006). Solving the puzzle of deliberate self-harm: The experiential avoidance model. *Behaviour Research and Therapy, 44*(3), 371–394.

Chapman, A. L., Specht, M. W., & Cellucci, T. (2005). Borderline personality disorder and deliberate self-harm: Does experiential avoidance play a role? *Suicide and Life-Threatening Behavior, 35*(4), 388–399.

Gratz, K. L., & Gunderson, J. G. (2006). Preliminary data on an acceptance-based emotion regulation group intervention for deliberate self-harm among women with borderline personality disorder. *Behavior Therapy, 37*(1), 25–35.

Gunderson, J. G. (2009). *Borderline Personality Disorder: A Clinical Guide.* Arlington: American Psychiatric Press.

Iverson, K. M., Follette, V. M., Pistorello, J., & Fruzzetti, A. E. (2012). An investigation of experiential avoidance, emotion dysregulation, and distress tolerance in young adult outpatients with borderline personality disorder symptoms. *Personality Disorders: Theory, Research, and Treatment, 3*(4), 415.

Morton, J., Snowdon, S., Gopold, M., & Guymer, E. (2012). Acceptance and commitment therapy group treatment for symptoms of borderline personality disorder: A public sector pilot study. *Cognitive and Behavioral Practice, 19*(4), 527–544.

Strosahl, K. D. (2004). ACT with the multi-problem patient. In S.C. Hayes & K.D. Strosahl (Eds.) *A practical guide to acceptance and commitment therapy* (pp. 209–245). New York: Springer US.

Psychosis

Bach, P., Gaudiano, B. A., Hayes, S. C., & Herbert, J. D. (2013). Acceptance and commitment therapy for psychosis: Intent to treat, hospitalization outcome and mediation by believability. *Psychosis, 5*(2), 166–174.

Bach, P., & Hayes, S. C. (2002). The use of acceptance and commitment therapy to prevent the rehospitalization of psychotic patients: A randomized controlled trial. *Journal of Consulting and Clinical Psychology, 70*(5), 1129–1139.

Bach, P., Hayes, S. C., & Gallop, R. (2012). Long term effects of brief acceptance and commitment therapy for psychosis. *Behavior Modification, 36*, 167–183.

Bacon, T., Farhall, J., & Fossey, E. (2014). The active therapeutic processes of acceptance and commitment therapy for persistent symptoms of psychosis: Clients' perspectives. *Behavioural and Cognitive Psychotherapy, 42*(4), 402–420.

Bloy, S., Oliver, J. E., & Morris, E. (2011). Using acceptance and commitment therapy with people with psychosis a case study. *Clinical Case Studies, 10*(5), 347–359.

Garcia, J. M., & Perez, M. (2001). ACT as a treatment for psychotic symptoms. The case of auditory hallucinations. *Analisis y Modificacion de Conducta, 27*(113), 455–472.

García Montes, J. M., Luciano Soriano, C. M., Hernández López, M., & Zaldívar Basurto, F. (2004). Aplicación de la terapia de aceptación y Compromiso (ACT) a sintomatología delirante: un estudio de caso. [Application of acceptance and commitment therapy (ACT) in delusional symptomathology: A case study]. *Psicothema, 6*(1), 117–124.

Gaudiano, B. A. (2005). Cognitive behavior therapies for psychotic disorders: Current empirical status and future directions. *Clinical Psychology: Science and Practice, 12*(1), 33–50.

Gaudiano, B. A., & Herbert, J. D. (2006a). Acute treatment of inpatients with psychotic symptoms using acceptance and commitment therapy: Pilot results. *Behaviour Research and Therapy, 44*(3), 415–437.

Gaudiano, B. A., & Herbert, J. D. (2006b). Believability of hallucinations as a potential mediator of their frequency and associated distress in psychotic inpatients. *Behavioural and Cognitive Psychotherapy, 34*(4), 497–502.

Gaudiano, B. A., Herbert, J. D., & Hayes, S. C. (2010). Is it the symptom or the relation to it? Investigating potential mediators of change in acceptance and commitment therapy for psychosis. *Behavior Therapy, 41*, 543–554.

Gaudiano, B. A., Nowlan, K., Brown, L. A., Epstein-Lubow, G., & Miller, I. W. (2013). An open trial of a new acceptance-based behavioral treatment for major depression with psychotic features. *Behavior Modification, 37*(3), 324–355.

Knapp, M., Mangalore, R., & Simon, J. (2004). The global costs of schizophrenia. *Schizophrenia Bulletin, 30*(2), 279.

Morris, E. M., Garety, P., & Peters, E. (2014). Psychological flexibility and nonjudgemental acceptance in voice hearers: Relationships with omnipotence and distress. *Australian and New Zealand Journal of Psychiatry*, doi: 10.1177/0004867414535671.

Oliver, J. E., McLachlan, K., Jose, P. E., & Peters, E. (2012). Predicting changes in delusional ideation: The role of mindfulness and negative schemas. *Psychology and Psychotherapy: Theory, Research and Practice, 85*(3), 243–259.

Oliver, J. E., O'Connor, J. A., Jose, P. E., McLachlan, K., & Peters, E. (2012). The impact of negative schemas, mood and psychological flexibility on delusional ideation: Mediating and moderating effects. *Psychosis, 4*(1), 6–18.

O'Neill, J., & Weil, T. M. (2014). Training deictic relational responding in people diagnosed with schizophrenia. *The Psychological Record, 64*(2), 301–310.

Pankey, J., & Hayes, S. C. (2003). Acceptance and commitment therapy for psychosis. *International Journal of Psychology and Psychological Therapy, 3*(2), 311–328.

Polk, K., Hambright, J., & Webster, M. (2009). The matrix life manual. Retrieved from http://www.drkevinpolk.com/20312.html

Pratt, S. I., & Mueser, K. T. (2002). Schizophrenia. In M. M. Antony, & D. H. Barlow (Eds.), *Handbook of assessment and treatment planning for psychological disorders* (pp. 375–414). New York: Guilford.

Shawyer, F., Farhall, J., Mackinnon, A., Trauer, T., Sims, E., Ratcliff, K.,...& Copolov, D. (2012). A randomised controlled trial of acceptance-based cognitive behavioural therapy for command hallucinations in psychotic disorders. *Behaviour Research and Therapy, 50*(2), 110–121.

Tarrier, N., Barrowclough, C., & Bamrah, J. S. (1991). Prodromal signs of relapse in schizophrenia. *Social Psychiatry and Psychiatric Epidemiology, 26*, 157–161.

Veiga-Martínez, C., Pérez-Álvarez, M., & García-Montes, J. M. (2008). Acceptance and commitment therapy applied to treatment of auditory hallucinations. *Clinical Case Studies, 7*(2), 118–135.

Vilardaga, R., Estévez, A., Levin, M. E., & Hayes, S. C. (2012). Deictic relational responding, empathy, and experiential avoidance as predictors of social anhedonia: Further contributions from relational frame theory. *Psychological Record, 62*(3), 409.

Villatte, M., Monestès, J. L., McHugh, L., Freixa i Baqué, E., & Loas, G. (2010). Adopting the perspective of another in belief attribution: Contribution of relational frame theory to the understanding of impairments in schizophrenia. *Journal of Behavior Therapy and Experimental Psychiatry, 41*(2), 125–134.

Villatte, M., Monestès, J. L., McHugh, L., Freixa i Baque, E., Loas, G., & Loas, A. (2008). Assessing deictic relational responding in social anhedonia: A functional approach to the development of theory of mind impairments. *International Journal of Behavioral Consultation and Therapy, 4*(4), 360–373.

Villatte, M., Monestès, J. L., McHugh, L., & Loas, G. (2011). Assessing perspective taking in schizophrenia using relational frame theory. *The Psychological Record, 60*(3), 3.

White, R., Gumley, A., McTaggart, J., Rattrie, L., McConville, D., Cleare, S., & Mitchell, G. (2011). A feasibility study of acceptance and commitment therapy for emotional dysfunction following psychosis. *Behaviour Research and Therapy, 49*(12), 901–907.

Wykes, T., Steel, C., Everitt, B., & Tarrier, N. (2008). Cognitive behaviour therapy for schizophrenia: Effect sizes, clinical models, and methodological rigor. *Schizophrenia Bulletin, 34*, 523–537.

Substance abuse

Batten, S. V., & Hayes, S. C. (2005). Acceptance and commitment therapy in the treatment of comorbid substance abuse and post-traumatic stress disorder a case study. *Clinical Case Studies, 4*(3), 246–262.

Becker, W. C., Sullivan, L. E., Tetrault, J. M., Desai, R. A., & Fiellin, D. A. (2008). Non-medical use, abuse and dependence on prescription opioids among US adults: Psychiatric, medical and substance use correlates. *Drug and Alcohol Dependence, 94*(1), 38–47.

Chutuape, M. A., Jasinski, D. R., Fingerhood, M. I., & Stitzer, M. L. (2001). One-, three-, and six-month outcomes after brief inpatient opioid detoxification. *The American Journal of Drug and Alcohol Abuse, 27*(1), 19–44.

Clausen, T., Waal, H., Thoresen, M., & Gossop, M. (2009). Mortality among opiate users: Opioid maintenance therapy, age and causes of death. *Addiction, 104*(8), 1356–1362.

Compton, P., Charuvastra, V. C., & Ling, W. (2001). Pain intolerance in opioid-maintained former opiate addicts: Effect of long-acting maintenance agent. *Drug and Alcohol Dependence, 63*(2), 139–146.

Corkery, J. M., Schifano, F., Ghodse, A. H., & Oyefeso, A. (2004). The effects of methadone and its role in fatalities. *Human Psychopharmacology: Clinical and Experimental, 19*(8), 565–576.

González-Menéndez, A., Fernández García, P., Rodríguez Lamelas, F., & Villagrá Lanza, P.(2014). Long-term outcomes of acceptance and commitment therapy in drug-dependent female inmates: A randomized controlled trial. *International Journal of Clinical and Health Psychology, 14*(1), 18–27.

Hayes, S. C., Wilson, K. G., Gifford, E. V., Bissett, R., Piasecki, M., Batten, S. V., ... & Gregg, J. (2004). A preliminary trial of twelve-step facilitation and acceptance and commitment therapy with polysubstance-abusing methadone-maintained opiate addicts. *Behavior Therapy, 35*(4), 667–688.

Lejuez, C. W., Paulson, A., Daughters, S. B., Bornovalova, M. A., & Zvolensky, M. J. (2006). The association between heroin use and anxiety sensitivity among inner-city individuals in residential drug use treatment. *Behaviour Research and Therapy, 44*(5), 667–677.

Magura, S., & Rosenblum, A. (2001). Leaving methadone treatment: Lessons learned, lessons forgotten, lessons ignored. *The Mount Sinai Journal of Medicine, New York, 68*(1), 62–74.

Pope, H. G., & Yurgelun-Todd, D. (2004). Residual cognitive effects of long-term cannabis use. In D. Castle, & R. Murray (Eds.), *Marijuana and madness: Psychiatry and neurobiology* (pp. 198–210). New York: Cambridge University Press.

Smout, M. F., Longo, M., Harrison, S., Minniti, R., Wickes, W., & White, J. M. (2010). Psychosocial treatment for methamphetamine use disorders: A preliminary randomized controlled trial of cognitive behavior therapy and acceptance and commitment therapy. *Substance Abuse, 31*(2), 98–107.

Stotts, A. L., Dodrill, C. L., & Kosten, T. R. (2009). Opioid dependence treatment: Options in pharmacotherapy. *Expert Opinion on Pharmacotherapy, 10*(11), 1727–1740.

Stotts, A. L., Green, C., Masuda, A., Grabowski, J., Wilson, K., Northrup, T. F., ... & Schmitz, J. M. (2012). A stage I pilot study of acceptance and commitment therapy for methadone detoxification. *Drug and Alcohol Dependence, 125*(3), 215–222.

Substance Abuse and Mental Health Services Administration. (2005). Results from the 2004 national survey on drug use and health: National findings (Office of Applied Studies, NSDUH, Series H-28, DHHS Publication No. SMA 05-4062). Rockville, MD.

Tapert, S. F., Aaron, G. A., Sedlar, G. R., & Brown, S. A. (2001). Adolescent substance abuse and sexual risk-taking behavior. *Journal of Adolescent Health, 28,* 181–189.

Twohig, M. P., Schoenberger, D., & Hayes, S. C. (2007). A preliminary investigation of acceptance and commitment therapy as a treatment for marijuana dependence. *Journal of Applied Behavior Analysis, 40,* 619–632.

Villagrá Lanza, P., Fernández García, P., Rodríguez Lamelas, F., & González Menéndez, A. (2014). Acceptance and commitment therapy versus cognitive behavioral therapy in the treatment of substance use disorder with incarcerated women. *Journal of Clinical Psychology, 70*(7), 644–657. Retrieved from http://doi.org/10.1002/jclp.22060

Smoking

Bricker, J. B., Bush, T., Zbikowski, S. M., Mercer, L. D., & Heffner, J. L. (2014). Randomized trial of telephone-delivered acceptance and commitment therapy versus cognitive behavioral therapy for smoking cessation: A pilot study. *Nicotine & Tobacco Research, 16*(11), 1446–1454. doi: 10.1093/ntr/ntu102.

Bricker, J. B., Mann, S. L., Marek, P. M., Liu, J., & Peterson, A. V. (2010). Telephone-delivered acceptance and commitment therapy for adult smoking cessation: A feasibility study. *Nicotine & Tobacco Research, 12*(4), 454–458.

Bricker, J., Wyszynski, C., Comstock, B., & Heffner, J. L. (2013). Pilot randomized controlled trial of web-based acceptance and commitment therapy for smoking cessation. *Nicotine & Tobacco Research, 15*(10), 1756–1764. doi: 10.1093/ntr/ntt056.

Bricker, J. B., Mull, K. E., Kientz, J. A., Vilardaga, R., Mercer, L. D., Akioka, K. J., & Heffner, J. L. (2014). Randomized, controlled pilot trial of a smartphone app for smoking cessation using acceptance and commitment therapy. *Drug and Alcohol Dependence, 143,* 87–94.

Brown, R. A., Palm, K. M., Strong, D. R., Lejuez, C. W., Kahler, C. W., Zvolensky, M. J., . . . & Gifford, E. V. (2008). Distress tolerance treatment for early-lapse smokers: Rationale, program description, and preliminary findings. *Behavior Modification, 32*(3), 302–332.

Fiore, M. C., Jaén, C. R., Baker, T. B., Bailey, W. C., Benowitz, N. L., Curry, S. J., & Wewers, M. E. (2008). *Treating Tobacco Use and Dependence: 2008 Update-Clinical Practice Guideline.* Rockville, MD: U.S. Department of Health and Human Services, Public Health Service.

Gifford, E. V., Kohlenberg, B. S., Hayes, S. C., Antonuccio, D. O., Piasecki, M. M., Rasmussen-Hall, M. L., & Palm, K. M. (2004). Acceptance-based treatment for smoking cessation. *Behavior Therapy, 35*(4), 689–705.

Gifford, E. V., Kohlenberg, B. S., Hayes, S. C., Pierson, H. M., Piasecki, M. P., Antonuccio, D. O., & Palm, K. M. (2011). Does acceptance and relationship focused behavior therapy contribute to bupropion outcomes? A randomized controlled trial of functional analytic psychotherapy and acceptance and commitment therapy for smoking cessation. *Behavior Therapy, 42*(4), 700–715.

Hernández-López, M., Luciano, M. C., Bricker, J. B., Roales-Nieto, J. G., & Montesinos, F. (2009). Acceptance and commitment therapy for smoking cessation: A preliminary study of its effectiveness in comparison with cognitive behavioral therapy. *Psychology of Addictive Behaviors, 23*(4), 723.

Irvin, J. E., & Brandon, T. E. (2000). The increasing recalcitrance of smokers in clinical trials. *Nicotine & Tobacco Research, 5*, 27–35.

Niaura, R., & Abrams, D. B. (2002). Smoking cessation: Progress, priorities, and prospectus. *Journal of Consulting and Clinical Psychology, 70*, 494–509.

Schimmel-Bristow, A., Bricker, J. B., & Comstock, B. (2012). Can acceptance & commitment therapy be delivered with fidelity as a brief telephone-intervention? *Addictive Behaviors, 37*(4), 517–520.

Stead, L. F., Perera, R., & Lancaster, T. (2013). Telephone counselling for smoking cessation. *Cochrane Database of Systematic Reviews 2013,* 8. doi: 10.1002/14651858.CD002850.pub3.

Eating behaviour

Baer, R. A., Fischer, S., & Huss, D. B. (2005). Mindfulness and acceptance in the treatment of disordered eating. *Journal of Rational-Emotive and Cognitive-Behavior Therapy, 23*(4), 281–300.

Berman, M. I., Boutelle, K. N., & Crow, S. J. (2009). A case series investigating acceptance and commitment therapy as a treatment for previously treated, unremitted patients with anorexia nervosa. *European Eating Disorders Review, 17*(6), 426–434.

Birmingham, C. L., Su, J., Hlynsky, J. A., Goldner, E. M., & Gao, M. (2005). The mortality rate from anorexia nervosa. *International Journal of Eating Disorders, 38*(2), 143–146. Retrieved from http://dx.doi.org/ 10.1002/eat.20164.

Butryn, M. L., Thomas, J. G., & Lowe, M. R. (2009). Reductions in internal disinhibition during weight loss predict better weight loss maintenance. *Obesity, 17*(5), 1101–1103.

Butryn, M. L., Webb, V., & Wadden, T. A. (2011). Behavioral treatment of obesity. *The Psychiatric Clinics of North America, 34*(4), 841–859. http://doi.org/10.1016/ j.psc.2011.08.006

Ciarrochi, J., Bailey, A., & Harris, R. (2014). *The Weight Escape.* Melbourne: Penguin Australia.

Fairburn, C. G. (2008). *Cognitive Behavior Therapy and Eating Disorders Cognitive Behavior Therapy and Eating Disorders* (pp. xii, 324). New York: Guilford Press.

Forman, E. M., & Butryn, M. L. (2015). A new look at the science of weight control: How acceptance and commitment strategies can address the challenge of self-regulation. *Appetite, 84*, 171–180.

Forman, E. M., Butryn, M. L., Hoffman, K. L., & Herbert, J. D. (2009). An open trial of an acceptance-based behavioral intervention for weight loss. *Cognitive and Behavioral Practice, 16*(2), 223–235.

Forman, E. M., Butryn, M. L., Juarascio, A. S., Bradley, L. E., Lowe, M. R., Herbert, J. D., & Shaw, J. A. (2013). The mind your health project: A randomized controlled trial of an innovative behavioral treatment for obesity. *Obesity, 21*(6), 1119–1126.

Forman, E. M., Herbert, J. D., Moitra, E., Yeomans, P. D., & Geller, P. A. (2007). A randomized controlled effectiveness trial of acceptance and commitment therapy and cognitive therapy for anxiety and depression. *Behavior Modification, 31*(6), 772–799.

Forman, E. M., Hoffman, K. L., Juarascio, A. S., Butryn, M. L., & Herbert, J. D. (2013). Comparison of acceptance-based and standard cognitive-based coping strategies for craving sweets in overweight and obese women. *Eating Behaviors, 14*(1), 64–68.

Forman, E. M., Hoffman, K. L., McGrath, K. B., Herbert, J. D., Brandsma, L. L., & Lowe, M. R. (2007). A comparison of acceptance-and control-based strategies for coping with food cravings: An analog study. *Behaviour Research and Therapy, 45*(10), 2372–2386.

Heffner, M., Sperry, J., Eifert, G. H., & Detweiler, M. (2002). Acceptance and commitment therapy in the treatment of an adolescent female with anorexia nervosa: A case example. *Cognitive and Behavioral Practice, 9*, 232–236.

Hill, M. L., Masuda, A., Melcher, H., Morgan, J. R., & Twohig, M. P. (2014). Acceptance and commitment therapy for women diagnosed with binge eating disorder: A case-series study. *Cognitive and Behavioral Practice.* doi: 10.1016/j.cbpra.2014.02.005.

Hill, M. L., Masuda, A., Moore, M., & Twohig, M. P. (2014). Acceptance and commitment therapy for individuals with problematic emotional eating: A case-series study. *Clinical Case Studies*, doi: 10.1177/1534650114547429.

Hooper, N., Sandoz, E. K., Ashton, J., Clarke, A., & McHugh, L. (2012). Comparing thought suppression and acceptance as coping techniques for food cravings. *Eating Behaviors, 13*(1), 62–64.

Jenkins, K. T., & Tapper, K. (2013). Resisting chocolate temptation using a brief mindfulness strategy. *British Journal of Health Psychology, 19*(3), 509–522. doi: 10.1111/bjhp.12050.

Juarascio, A., Kerrigan, S., Goldstein, S. P., Shaw, J., Forman, E. M., Butryn, M., & Herbert, J. D. (2013). Baseline eating disorder severity predicts response to an acceptance and commitment therapy-based group treatment. *Journal of Contextual Behavioral Science, 2*(3), 74–78.

Juarascio, A., Shaw, J., Forman, E., Timko, C. A., Herbert, J., Butryn, M., & Lowe, M. (2013a). Acceptance and commitment therapy as a novel treatment for eating disorders: An initial test of efficacy and mediation. *Behavior Modification, 37*(4), 459–489. doi: 10.1177/0145445513478633.

Juarascio, A., Shaw, J., Forman, E. M., Timko, C. A., Herbert, J. D., Butryn, M. L., & Lowe, M. (2013b). Acceptance and commitment therapy for eating disorders: Clinical applications of a group treatment. *Journal of Contextual Behavioral Science, 2*(3), 85–94.

Juarascio, A. S., Forman, E. M., & Herbert, J. D. (2010). Acceptance and commitment therapy versus cognitive therapy for the treatment of comorbid eating pathology. *Behavior Modification, 34*(2), 175–190.

Juarascio, A. S., Schumacher, L. M., Shaw, J., Forman, E. M., & Herbert, J. D. (2014). Acceptance-based treatment and quality of life among patients with an eating disorder. *Journal of Contextual Behavioral Science, 4*(1), 42–47.

Katterman, S. N., Goldstein, S. P., Butryn, M. L., Forman, E. M., & Lowe, M. R. (2014). Efficacy of an acceptance-based behavioral intervention for weight gain prevention in young adult women. *Journal of Contextual Behavioral Science, 3*(1), 45–50.

Lillis, J., Dahl, J., & Weineland, S. (2014). *The Diet Trap.* New Harbinger.

Masuda, A., & Latzman, R. D. (2012). Psychological flexibility and self-concealment as predictors of disordered eating symptoms. *Journal of Contextual Behavioral Science, 1*(1), 49–54.

Masuda, A., Price, M., Anderson, P. L., & Wendell, J. W. (2010). Disordered eating-related cognition and psychological flexibility as predictors of psychological health among college students. *Behavior Modification, 34*(1), 3–15.

Merwin, R. M., Timko, C. A., Moskovich, A. A., Ingle, K. K., Bulik, C. M., & Zucker, N. L. (2010). Psychological inflexibility and symptom expression in anorexia nervosa. *Eating Disorders, 19*(1), 62–82.

Merwin, R. M., Zucker, N. L., & Timko, C. A. (2013). A pilot study of an acceptance-based separated family treatment for adolescent anorexia nervosa. *Cognitive and Behavioral Practice, 20*(4), 485–500.

Merwin, R. M., Zucker, N. L., Lacy, J. L., & Elliott, C. A. (2010). Interoceptive awareness in eating disorders: Distinguishing lack of clarity from non-acceptance of internal experience. *Cognition and Emotion, 24*(5), 892–902.

Niemeier, H. M., Leahey, T., Palm Reed, K., Brown, R. A., & Wing, R. R. (2012). An acceptance-based behavioral intervention for weight loss: A pilot study. *Behavior Therapy, 43*(2), 427–435.

Ogden, C. L., Carroll, M. D., Curtin, L. R., McDowell, M. A., Tabak, C. J., & Flegal, K. M. (2006). Prevalence of overweight and obesity in the United States, 1999–2004. *JAMA, 295*(13), 1549–1555.

Orsillo, S. M., & Batten, S. V. (2002). ACT as treatment of a disorder of excessive control: Anorexia. *Cognitive and Behavioral Practice, 9*(3), 253–259.

Pearson, A. N., Follette, V. M., & Hayes, S. C. (2012). A pilot study of acceptance and commitment therapy as a workshop intervention for body dissatisfaction and disordered eating attitudes. *Cognitive and Behavioral Practice, 19*(1), 181–197.

Powers, P. S., Rosemurgy, A., Boyd, F., & Perez, A. (1997). Outcome of gastric restriction procedures: Weight, psychiatric diagnoses, and satisfaction. *Obesity Surgery, 7*(6), 471–477.

Rafiee, M., Sedrpoushan, N., & Abedi, M. R. (2013). Study the effect of acceptance and commitment therapy on reducing depression symptoms and body image dissatisfaction in obese women in Isfahan city (2012–13). *Journal of Social Science for Policy Implications, 1*(2), 25.

Tapper, K., Shaw, C., Ilsley, J., Hill, A. J., Bond, F. W., & Moore, L. (2009). Exploratory randomised controlled trial of a mindfulness-based weight loss intervention for women. *Appetite, 52*(2), 396–404.

Wadden, T. A., & Butryn, M. L. (2003). Behavioral treatment of obesity. *Endocrinology and Metabolism Clinics of North America, 32*(4), 981–1003.

Weineland, S., Arvidsson, D., Kakoulidis, T. P., & Dahl, J. (2012). Acceptance and commitment therapy for bariatric surgery patients: A pilot RCT. *Obesity Research & Clinical Practice, 6*(1), e21–e30.

Pain

Alonso, M. A., López, A., Losada, A., & González, J. L. (2013). Acceptance and commitment therapy and selective optimization with compensation for older people with chronic pain: A pilot study. *Behavioral Psychology-Psicologia Conductual, 21*(1), 59–79.

Baranoff, J., Hanrahan, S. J., & Connor, J. P. (2014). The roles of acceptance and catastrophizing in rehabilitation following anterior cruciate ligament reconstruction. *Journal of Science and Medicine in Sport, 18*(3), 250–254.

Baranoff, J., Hanrahan, S. J., Kapur, D., & Connor, J. P. (2013). Acceptance as a process variable in relation to catastrophizing in multidisciplinary pain treatment. *European Journal of Pain, 17*(1), 101–110.

Baranoff, J., Hanrahan, S. J., Kapur, D., & Connor, J. P. (2014). Six month post-treatment deterioration in acceptance (CPAQ-8) and cognitions following multidisciplinary pain treatment. *Journal of Behavioral Medicine, 37*(3), 469–479.

Buhrman, M., Skoglund, A., Husell, J., Bergström, K., Gordh, T., Hursti, T., . . . & Andersson, G. (2013). Guided internet-delivered acceptance and commitment therapy for chronic pain patients: A randomized controlled trial. *Behaviour Research and Therapy, 51*(6), 307–315.

Carrasquillo, N., & Zettle, R. D. (2014). Comparing a brief self-as-context exercise to control-based and attention placebo protocols for coping with induced pain. *The Psychological Record, 64*(4), 659–669.

Dahl, J., Wilson, K. G., & Nilsson, A. (2004). Acceptance and commitment therapy and the treatment of persons at risk for long-term disability resulting from stress and pain symptoms: A preliminary randomized trial. *Behavior Therapy, 35*(4), 785–801.

Dindo, L., Recober, A., Marchman, J. N., Turvey, C., & O'Hara, M. W. (2012). One-day behavioral treatment for patients with comorbid depression and migraine: A pilot study. *Behaviour Research and Therapy, 50*(9), 537–543.

Esteve, R., Ramírez-Maestre, C., & López-Martínez, A. E. (2007). Adjustment to chronic pain: The role of pain acceptance, coping strategies, and pain-related cognitions. *Annals of Behavioral Medicine, 33*(2), 179–188.

Feldner, M. T., Hekmat, H., Zvolensky, M. J., Vowles, K. E., Secrist, Z., & Leen-Feldner, E. W. (2006). The role of experiential avoidance in acute pain tolerance: A laboratory test. *Journal of Behavior Therapy and Experimental Psychiatry, 37*(2), 146–158.

Forsyth, L., & Hayes, L. L. (2014). The effects of acceptance of thoughts, mindful awareness of breathing, and spontaneous coping on an experimentally induced pain task. *The Psychological Record, 64*(3), 447–455.

Ghomian, S., & Shairi, M. R. (2014). The effectiveness of acceptance and commitment therapy for children with chronic pain (chact) on the function of 7 to 12 year-old children. *International Journal of Pediatrics, 2*(3.1), 195–203.

Gutiérrez, O., Luciano, C., Rodríguez, M., & Fink, B. C. (2004). Comparison between an acceptance-based and a cognitive-control-based protocol for coping with pain. *Behavior Therapy, 35*(4), 767–783.

Hann, K. E., & McCracken, L. M. (2014). A systematic review of randomized controlled trials of acceptance and commitment therapy for adults with chronic pain: Outcome domains, design quality, and efficacy. *Journal of Contextual Behavioral Science 3*(4), 217–227.

Hayes, S. C., Bissett, R. T., Korn, Z., Zettle, R. D., Rosenfarb, I. S., Cooper, L. D., & Grundt, A. M. (1999). The impact of acceptance versus control rationales on pain tolerance. *The Psychological Record, 49*(1), 3.

Johnston, M., Foster, M., Shennan, J., Starkey, N. J., & Johnson, A. (2010). The effectiveness of an acceptance and commitment therapy self-help intervention for chronic pain. *The Clinical Journal of Pain, 26*(5), 393–402.

Kehoe, A., Barnes-Holmes, Y., Barnes-Holmes, D., Cochrane, A., & Stewart, I. (2007). Breaking the pain barrier: Understanding and treating human suffering. *The Irish Psychologist, 33*(11), 288–297.

Keogh, E., Bond, F. W., Hanmer, R., & Tilston, J. (2005). Comparing acceptance- and control-based coping instructions on the cold-pressor pain experiences of healthy men and women. *European Journal of Pain, 9*(5), 591–598.

Kratz, A. L., Davis, M. C., & Zautra, A. J. (2007). Pain acceptance moderates the relation between pain and negative affect in female osteoarthritis and fibromyalgia patients. *Annals of Behavioral Medicine, 33*(3), 291–301.

Ljótsson, B., Atterlöf, E., Lagerlöf, M., Andersson, E., Jernelöv, S., Hedman, E., … & Wicksell, R. K. (2014). Internet-delivered acceptance and values-based exposure treatment for fibromyalgia: A pilot study. *Cognitive Behaviour Therapy, 43*(2), 93–104.

Masedo, A. I., & Rosa Esteve, M. (2007). Effects of suppression, acceptance and spontaneous coping on pain tolerance, pain intensity and distress. *Behaviour Research and Therapy, 45*(2), 199–209.

McCracken, L. M. (1998). Learning to live with the pain: Acceptance of pain predicts adjustment in persons with chronic pain. *Pain, 74*(1), 21–27.

McCracken, L. M. (2005). Social context and acceptance of chronic pain: The role of solicitous and punishing responses. *Pain, 113*(1), 155–159.

McCracken, L. M., & Eccleston, C. (2003). Coping or acceptance: What to do about chronic pain? *Pain, 105*(1), 197–204.

McCracken, L. M., & Eccleston, C. (2005). A prospective study of acceptance of pain and patient functioning with chronic pain. *Pain, 118*(1), 164–169.

McCracken, L. M., & Marin, F. M. (2014). Current and future trends in psychology and chronic pain: Time for a change? *Pain Management, 4*(2), 113–121.

McCracken, L. M., & Velleman, S. C. (2010). Psychological flexibility in adults with chronic pain: A study of acceptance, mindfulness, and values-based action in primary care. *Pain, 148*(1), 141–147.

McCracken, L. M., & Vowles, K. E. (2008). A prospective analysis of acceptance of pain and values-based action in patients with chronic pain. *Health Psychology, 27*(2), 215.

McCracken, L. M., & Vowles, K. E. (2014). Acceptance and commitment therapy and mindfulness for chronic pain: Model, process, and progress. *American Psychologist, 69*(2), 178.

McCracken, L. M., & Yang, S. Y. (2006). The role of values in a contextual cognitive-behavioral approach to chronic pain. *Pain, 123*(1), 137–145.

McCracken, L. M., MacKichan, F., & Eccleston, C. (2007). Contextual cognitive-behavioral therapy for severely disabled chronic pain sufferers: Effectiveness and clinically significant change. *European Journal of Pain, 11*(3), 314–322.

McCracken, L. M., Sato, A., & Taylor, G. J. (2013). A trial of a brief group-based form of acceptance and commitment therapy (ACT) for chronic pain in general practice: Pilot outcome and process results. *The Journal of Pain, 14*(11), 1398–1406.

McCracken, L. M., Spertus, I. L., Janeck, A. S., Sinclair, D., & Wetzel, F. T. (1999). Behavioral dimensions of adjustment in persons with chronic pain: Pain-related anxiety and acceptance. *Pain, 80*(1), 283–289.

McCracken, L. M., Vowles, K. E., & Eccleston, C. (2005). Acceptance-based treatment for persons with complex, long standing chronic pain: A preliminary analysis of treatment outcome in comparison to a waiting phase. *Behaviour Research and Therapy, 43*(10), 1335–1346.

McCracken, L. M., Vowles, K. E., & Gauntlett-Gilbert, J. (2007). A prospective investigation of acceptance and control-oriented coping with chronic pain. *Journal of Behavioral Medicine, 30*(4), 339–349.

McCracken, L. M., & Zhao-O'Brien, J. (2010). General psychological acceptance and chronic pain: There is more to accept than the pain itself. *European Journal of Pain, 14*(2), 170–175.

McMullen, J., Barnes-Holmes, D., Barnes-Holmes, Y., Stewart, I., Luciano, C., & Cochrane, A. (2008). Acceptance versus distraction: Brief instructions, metaphors and exercises in increasing tolerance for self-delivered electric shocks. *Behaviour Research and Therapy, 46*(1), 122–129.

Mo'tamedi, H., Rezaiemaram, P., & Tavallaie, A. (2012). The effectiveness of a group-based acceptance and commitment additive therapy on rehabilitation of female outpatients with chronic headache: Preliminary findings reducing 3 dimensions of headache impact. *Headache: The Journal of Head and Face Pain, 52*(7), 1106–1119.

Paez-Blarrina, M., Luciano, C., Gutiérrez-Martínez, O., Valdivia, S., Ortega, J., & Rodríguez-Valverde, M. (2008). The role of values with personal examples in altering the functions of pain: Comparison between acceptance-based and cognitive-control-based protocols. *Behaviour Research and Therapy, 46*(1), 84–97.

Páez-Blarrina, M., Luciano, C., Gutiérrez-Martínez, O., Valdivia, S., Rodríguez-Valverde, M., & Ortega, J. (2008). Coping with pain in the motivational context of values comparison between an acceptance-based and a cognitive control-based protocol. *Behavior Modification, 32*(3), 403–422.

Pinto-Gouveia, J., Costa, J., & Marôco, J. (2013). The first 2 years of rheumatoid arthritis: The influence of acceptance on pain, physical limitation and depression. *Journal of Health Psychology, 20*(1), 102–112. doi: 10.1177/1359105313499807.

Steiner, J. L., Bogusch, L., & Bigatti, S. M. (2013). Values-based action in fibromyalgia: Results from a randomized pilot of acceptance and commitment therapy. *Health Psychology Research, 1*(3), e34.

Takahashi, M., Muto, T., Tada, M., & Sugiyama, M. (2002). Acceptance rationale and increasing pain tolerance: Acceptance-based and FEAR-based practice. *Japanese Journal of Behavior Therapy, 28*(1), 35–46.

Thompson, M., & McCracken, L. M. (2011). Acceptance and related processes in adjustment to chronic pain. *Current Pain and Headache Reports, 15*(2), 144–151.

Thorsell, J., Finnes, A., Dahl, J., Lundgren, T., Gybrant, M., Gordh, T., & Buhrman, M. (2011). A comparative study of 2 manual-based self-help interventions, acceptance and commitment therapy and applied relaxation, for persons with chronic pain. *The Clinical Journal of Pain, 27*(8), 716–723.

Trompetter, H. R., Bohlmeijer, E. T., Veehof, M. M., & Schreurs, K. M. (2014). Internet-based guided self-help intervention for chronic pain based on acceptance and commitment therapy: A randomized controlled trial. *Journal of Behavioral Medicine, 38*(1), 66–80.

Vowles, K. E., & McCracken, L. M. (2008). Acceptance and values-based action in chronic pain: A study of treatment effectiveness and process. *Journal of Consulting and Clinical Psychology, 76*(3), 397.

Vowles, K. E., Fink, B. C., & Cohen, L. L. (2014). Acceptance and commitment therapy for chronic pain: A diary study of treatment process in relation to reliable change in disability. *Journal of Contextual Behavioral Science, 3*(2), 74–80.

Vowles, K. E., & McCracken, L. M. (2010). Comparing the role of psychological flexibility and traditional pain management coping strategies in chronic pain treatment outcomes. *Behaviour Research and Therapy, 48*(2), 141–146.

Vowles, K. E., McCracken, L. M., & Eccleston, C. (2007). Processes of change in treatment for chronic pain: The contributions of pain, acceptance, and catastrophizing. *European Journal of Pain, 11*(7), 779–787.

Vowles, K. E., McCracken, L. M., & Eccleston, C. (2008). Patient functioning and catastrophizing in chronic pain: The mediating effects of acceptance. *Health Psychology, 27*(2S), S136.

Vowles, K. E., McCracken, L. M., & O'Brien, J. Z. (2011). Acceptance and values-based action in chronic pain: A three-year follow-up analysis of treatment effectiveness and process. *Behaviour Research and Therapy, 49*(11), 748–755.

Vowles, K. E., McNeil, D. W., Gross, R. T., McDaniel, M. L., Mouse, A., Bates, M., ... & McCall, C. (2007). Effects of pain acceptance and pain control strategies on physical impairment in individuals with chronic low back pain. *Behavior Therapy, 38*(4), 412–425.

Vowles, K. E., Sowden, G., & Ashworth, J. (2014). A comprehensive examination of the model underlying acceptance and commitment therapy for chronic pain. *Behavior Therapy, 45*(3), 390–401.

Vowles, K. E., Wetherell, J. L., & Sorrell, J. T. (2009). Targeting acceptance, mindfulness, and values-based action in chronic pain: Findings of two preliminary trials of an outpatient group-based intervention. *Cognitive and Behavioral Practice, 16*(1), 49–58.

Vowles, K. E., Witkiewitz, K., Sowden, G., & Ashworth, J. (2014). Acceptance and commitment therapy for chronic pain: Evidence of mediation and clinically significant change following an abbreviated interdisciplinary program of rehabilitation. *The Journal of Pain, 15*(1), 101–113.

Wetherell, J. L., Afari, N., Rutledge, T., Sorrell, J. T., Stoddard, J. A., Petkus, A. J., ... & Hampton Atkinson, J. (2011). A randomized, controlled trial of acceptance and commitment therapy and cognitive-behavioral therapy for chronic pain. *Pain, 152*(9), 2098–2107.

Wicksell, R. K., Ahlqvist, J., Bring, A., Melin, L., & Olsson, G. L. (2008). Can exposure and acceptance strategies improve functioning and life satisfaction in people with chronic pain and whiplash-associated disorders (WAD)? A randomized controlled trial. *Cognitive Behaviour Therapy, 37*(3), 169–182.

Wicksell, R. K., Dahl, J., Magnusson, B., & Olsson, G. L. (2005). Using acceptance and commitment therapy in the rehabilitation of an adolescent female with chronic pain: A case example. *Cognitive and Behavioral Practice, 12*(4), 415–423.

Wicksell, R. K., Kemani, M., Jensen, K., Kosek, E., Kadetoff, D., Sorjonen, K., & Olsson, G. L. (2012). Acceptance and commitment therapy for fibromyalgia: A randomized controlled trial. *European Journal of Pain, 17*(4), 599–611.

Wicksell, R. K., Melin, L., Lekander, M., & Olsson, G. L. (2008). Evaluating the effectiveness of exposure and acceptance strategies to improve functioning and quality of life in longstanding pediatric pain: Arandomized controlled trial. *Pain, 141*(3), 248–257.

Wicksell, R. K., Melin, L., & Olsson, G. L. (2006). Exposure and acceptance in the rehabilitation of adolescents with idiopathic chronic pain: A pilot study. *European Journal of Pain, 11*(3), 267–274.

Wicksell, R. K., Olsson, G. L., & Hayes, S. C. (2010). Psychological flexibility as a mediator of improvement in acceptance and commitment therapy for patients with chronic pain following whiplash. *European Journal of Pain, 14*(10), 1059–e1.

Wicksell, R. K., Olsson, G. L., & Hayes, S. C. (2011). Mediators of change in acceptance and commitment therapy for pediatric chronic pain. *Pain, 152*(12), 2792–2801.

Zettle, R. D., & Rains, J. C. (1989). Group cognitive and contextual therapies in treatment of depression. *Journal of Clinical Psychology, 45*(3), 436–445.

Other health conditions

Andersson, G., Baguley, D., McKenna, L., & McFerran, D. (2005). *Tinnitus: A Multidisciplinary Approach*. London: Whurr.

Beyenburg, S., Mitchell, A. J., Schmidt, D., Elger, C. E., & Reuber, M. (2005). Anxiety in patients with epilepsy: Systematic review and suggestions for clinical management. *Epilepsy & Behavior, 7*(2), 161–171.

Ciarrochi, J., Fisher, D., & Lane, L. (2011). The link between value motives, value success, and well-being among people diagnosed with cancer. *Psycho-Oncology, 20*(11), 1184–1192.

Dahl, J., & Lundgren, T. (2005). Behavior analysis of epilepsy: Conditioning mechanisms, behavior technology and the contribution of ACT. *The Behavior Analyst Today, 6*(3), 191–202.

Davis, A., & El Rafie, E. A. (2000). Epidemiology of tinnitus. In R. S. Tyler (Ed.), *Tinnitus handbook* (pp. 1–23). San Diego: Singular Thomson Learning.

Elger, C. E., & Schmidt, D. (2008). Modern management of epilepsy: A practical approach. *Epilepsy & Behavior, 12*(4), 501–539.

Fernández, M. D., Luciano, C., & Valdivia-Salas, S. (2012). Impact of acceptance-based nursing intervention on postsurgical recovery: Preliminary findings. *The Spanish Journal of Psychology, 15*(3), 1361–1370.

Feros, D. L., Lane, L., Ciarrochi, J., & Blackledge, J. T. (2011). Acceptance and commitment therapy (ACT) for improving the lives of cancer patients: A preliminary study. *Psycho-Oncology, 22*(2), 459–464.

Gholamhosseini, S., & Mojtabaie, M. (2015). Effectiveness of acceptance and commitment therapy (ACT) to reduce the symptoms of anxiety in women with breast cancer. *Journal of Social Issues & Humanities, 3*(1), 154–157.

Gregg, J. A., Callaghan, G. M., Hayes, S. C., & Glenn-Lawson, J. L. (2007). Improving diabetes self-management through acceptance, mindfulness, and values: A randomized controlled trial. *Journal of Consulting and Clinical Psychology, 75*(2), 336.

Hawkes, A. L., Chambers, S. K., Pakenham, K. I., Patrao, T. A., Baade, P. D., Lynch, B. M., ... & Courneya, K. S. (2013). Effects of a telephone-delivered multiple health behavior change intervention (Can Change) on health and behavioral outcomes in survivors of colorectal cancer: A randomized controlled trial. *Journal of Clinical Oncology, 31*(18), 2313–2321.

Hawkes, A. L., Pakenham, K. I., Chambers, S. K., Patrao, T. A., & Courneya, K. S. (2014). Effects of a multiple health behavior change intervention for colorectal cancer survivors on psychosocial outcomes and quality of life: A randomized controlled trial. *Annals of Behavioral Medicine*, 1–12.

Hawkes, A. L., Pakenham, K. I., Courneya, K. S., Gollschewski, S., Baade, P., Gordon, L. G., … & Chambers, S. K. (2009). A randomised controlled trial of a tele-based lifestyle intervention for colorectal cancer survivors ("Can Change"): Study protocol. *BMC Cancer, 9*(1), 286.

Hawkes, A. L., Patrao, T. A., Green, A., & Aitken, J. F. (2012). Can prevent: A telephone-delivered intervention to reduce multiple behavioural risk factors for colorectal cancer. *BMC Cancer, 12*(1), 560.

Heffner, M., Eifert, G. H., Parker, B. T., Hernandez, D. H., & Sperry, J. A. (2003). Valued directions: Acceptance and commitment therapy in the treatment of alcohol dependence. *Cognitive and Behavioral Practice, 10*(4), 378–383.

Henry, J. A., Zaugg, T. L., Myers, P. J., & Schechter, M. A. (2008). The role of audiologic evaluation in progressive audiologic tinnitus management. *Trends in Amplification, 12*, 188.

Hesser, H., Gustafsson, T., Lundén, C., Henrikson, O., Fattahi, K., Johnsson, E., … & Andersson, G. (2012). A randomized controlled trial of internet-delivered cognitive behavior therapy and acceptance and commitment therapy in the treatment of tinnitus. *Journal of Consulting and Clinical Psychology, 80*(4), 649.

Hesser, H., Pereswetoff-Morath, C. E., & Andersson, G. (2009). Consequences of controlling background sounds: The effect of experiential avoidance on tinnitus interference. *Rehabilitation Psychology, 54*(4), 381.

Hesser, H., Westin, V., Hayes, S. C., & Andersson, G. (2009). Clients' in-session acceptance and cognitive defusion behaviors in acceptance-based treatment of tinnitus distress. *Behaviour Research and Therapy, 47*(6), 523–528.

Hodges, L. J., & Humphris, G. M. (2009). Fear of recurrence and psychological distress in head and neck cancer patients and their carers. *Psycho-Oncology, 18*(8), 841–848.

Hulbert-Williams, N. J., Storey, L., & Wilson, K. G. (2014). Psychological interventions for patients with cancer: Psychological flexibility and the potential utility of acceptance and commitment therapy. *European Journal of Cancer Care, 24*(1), 15–27.

Kangas, M., & McDonald, S. (2011). Is it time to act? The potential of acceptance and commitment therapy for psychological problems following acquired brain injury. *Neuropsychological Rehabilitation, 21*(2), 250–276.

Karekla, M., & Constantinou, M. (2010). Religious coping and cancer: Proposing an acceptance and commitment therapy approach. *Cognitive and Behavioral Practice, 17*(4), 371–381.

Kortte, K. B., Veiel, L., Batten, S. V., & Wegener, S. T. (2009). Measuring avoidance in medical rehabilitation. *Rehabilitation Psychology, 54*(1), 91.

Lundgren, T., Dahl, J., & Hayes, S. C. (2008). Evaluation of mediators of change in the treatment of epilepsy with acceptance and commitment therapy. *Journal of Behavioral Medicine, 31*(3), 225–235.

Lundgren, T., Dahl, J., Melin, L., & Kies, B. (2006). Evaluation of acceptance and commitment therapy for drug refractory epilepsy: A randomized controlled trial in South Africa: A pilot study. *Epilepsia, 47*(12), 2173–2179.

Lundgren, T., Dahl, J., Yardi, N., & Melin, L. (2008). Acceptance and commitment therapy and yoga for drug-refractory epilepsy: A randomized controlled trial. *Epilepsy & Behavior, 13*(1), 102–108.

Macmillan (2006). *Worried Sick: The Emotional Impact of Cancer.* London UK: Macmillan Cancer Support.

Masuda, A., Cohen, L. L., Wicksell, R. K., Kemani, M. K., & Johnson, A. (2011). A case study: Acceptance and commitment therapy for pediatric sickle cell disease. *Journal of Pediatric Psychology, 36*(4), 398–408.

Metzler, C. W., Biglan, A., Noell, J., Ary, D. V., & Ochs, L. (2001). A randomized controlled trial of a behavioral intervention to reduce high-risk sexual behavior among adolescents in STD clinics. *Behavior Therapy, 31*(1), 27–54.

Mittan, R. J. (2009). Psychosocial treatment programs in epilepsy: A review. *Epilepsy & Behavior, 16*(3), 371–380.

Montesinos, F., & Luciano, M. C. (2005). Treatment of relapse fear in breast cancer patients through an ACT-based protocol. In *Comunicación presentada en 9th European Congress of Psychology*, Granada, España.

Montesinos, F. M., Hernández, B. M., & Luciano, M. C. S. (2001). Application of acceptance and commitment therapy (ACT) in cancer patients. *Analisis y Modificacion de Conducta, 27*, 503–524.

Páez, M., Luciano, M. C., & Gutiérrez, O. (2007). Psychological treatment for breast cancer: Comparison between acceptance based and cognitive control based strategies. *Psicooncología, 4*, 75–95.

Pakenham, K. I., & Fleming, M. (2011). Relations between acceptance of multiple sclerosis and positive and negative adjustments. *Psychology & Health, 26*(10), 1292–1309.

Rost, A. D., Wilson, K., Buchanan, E., Hildebrandt, M. J., & Mutch, D. (2012). Improving psychological adjustment among late-stage ovarian cancer patients: Examining the role of avoidance in treatment. *Cognitive and Behavioral Practice, 19*(4), 508–517.

Sheppard, S. C., Forsyth, J. P., Hickling, E. J., & Bianchi, J. (2010). A novel application of acceptance and commitment therapy for psychosocial problems associated with multiple sclerosis: Results from a half-day workshop intervention. *International Journal of MS Care, 12*(4), 200–206.

Soo, C., Tate, R. L., & Lane-Brown, A. (2011). A systematic review of acceptance and commitment therapy (ACT) for managing anxiety: Applicability for people with acquired brain injury? *Brain Impairment, 12*(01), 54–70.

Stanton, A. L., Luecken, L. J., MacKinnon, D. P., & Thompson, E. H. (2013). Mechanisms in psychosocial interventions for adults living with cancer: Opportunity for integration of theory, research, and practice. *Journal of Consulting and Clinical Psychology, 81*(2), 318.

Watson, E. K., Rose, P. W., Neal, R. D., Hulbert-Williams, N., Donnelly, P., Hubbard, G., ... & Wilkinson, C. (2012). Personalised cancer follow-up: Risk stratification, needs assessment or both? *British Journal of Cancer, 106*(1), 1.

Westin, V., Hayes, S. C., & Andersson, G. (2008). Is it the sound or your relationship to it? The role of acceptance in predicting tinnitus impact. *Behaviour Research and Therapy, 46*(12), 1259–1265.

Westin, V. Z., Schulin, M., Hesser, H., Karlsson, M., Noe, R. Z., Olofsson, U., ... & Andersson, G. (2011). Acceptance and commitment therapy versus tinnitus retraining therapy in the treatment of tinnitus: A randomised controlled trial. *Behaviour Research and Therapy, 49*(11), 737–747.

Whiting, D. L., Deane, F. P., Ciarrochi, J., McLeod, H. J., & Simpson, G. K. (2014). Validating measures of psychological flexibility in a population with acquired brain injury. *Psychological Assessment*. Advance online publication. http://dx.doi.org/10.1037/pas0000050.

Whiting, D. L., Simpson, G. K., McLeod, H. J., Deane, F. P., & Ciarrochi, J. (2012). Acceptance and commitment therapy (ACT) for psychological adjustment after traumatic brain injury: Reporting the protocol for a randomised controlled trial. *Brain Impairment, 13*(03), 360–376.

Williams, J. D., Vaughan, F., Huws, J., & Hastings, R. P. (2014). Brain injury spousal caregivers' experiences of an acceptance and commitment (ACT) group. *Social Care and Neurodisability, 5*(1), 29–40.

Zaccara, G., Gangemi, P. F., & Cincotta, M. (2008). Central nervous system adverse effects of new antiepileptic drugs: A meta-analysis of placebo-controlled studies. *Seizure, 17*(5), 405–421.

Work

Atkins, P., & Parker, S. (2011). Understanding individual compassion in organizations: The role of appraisals and psychological flexibility. *Academy of Management Review, 37*(4), 524–526.

Bethay, J. S., Wilson, K. G., Schnetzer, L. W., Nassar, S. L., & Bordieri, M. J. (2013). A controlled pilot evaluation of acceptance and commitment training for intellectual disability staff. *Mindfulness, 4*(2), 113–121.

Biglan, A., Layton, G. L., Jones, L. B., Hankins, M., & Rusby, J. C. (2011). The value of workshops on psychological flexibility for early childhood special education staff. *Topics in Early Childhood Special Education, 32*(4). doi: 10.1177/0271121411425191.

Bond, F. W., & Bunce, D. (2000). Mediators of change in emotion-focused and problem-focused worksite stress management interventions. *Journal of Occupational Health Psychology, 5*(1), 156.

Bond, F. W., & Bunce, D. (2003). The role of acceptance and job control in mental health, job satisfaction, and work performance. *Journal of Applied Psychology, 88*(6), 1057.

Bond, F. W., & Flaxman, P. E. (2006). The ability of psychological flexibility and job control to predict learning, job performance, and mental health. *Journal of Organizational Behavior Management, 26*(1–2), 113–130.

Bond, F. W., Flaxman, P. E., & Bunce, D. (2008). The influence of psychological flexibility on work redesign: Mediated moderation of a work reorganization intervention. *Journal of Applied Psychology, 93*(3), 645.

Bond, F. W., Lloyd, J., & Guenole, N. (2013). The work-related acceptance and action questionnaire: Initial psychometric findings and their implications for measuring psychological flexibility in specific contexts. *Journal of Occupational and Organizational Psychology, 86*(3), 331–347.

Brinkborg, H., Michanek, J., Hesser, H., & Berglund, G. (2011). Acceptance and commitment therapy for the treatment of stress among social workers: A randomized controlled trial. *Behaviour Research and Therapy, 49*(6), 389–398.

Bunce, D., & West, M. A. (1996). Stress management and innovation interventions at work. *Human Relations, 49*(2), 209–232.

Donaldson-Feilder, E., & Bond, F. W. (2004). Psychological acceptance and emotional intelligence in relation to workplace well-being. *British Journal of Guidance and Counselling, 34,* 187–203.

Flaxman, P. E., & Bond, F. W. (2010a). A randomised worksite comparison of acceptance and commitment therapy and stress inoculation training. *Behaviour Research and Therapy, 48*(8), 816–820.

Flaxman, P. E., & Bond, F. W. (2010b). Worksite stress management training: Moderated effects and clinical significance. *Journal of Occupational Health Psychology, 15*(4), 347.

Hayes, S. C., & Smith, S. (2005). *Get Out of Your Mind and into Your Life: The New Acceptance and Commitment Therapy.* Oakland, CA: New Harbinger.

Jeffcoat, T., & Hayes, S. C. (2012). A randomized trial of ACT bibliotherapy on the mental health of K-12 teachers and staff. *Behaviour Research and Therapy, 50*(9), 571–579.

Kishita, N., & Shimada, H. (2011). Effects of acceptance-based coping on task performance and subjective stress. *Journal of Behavior Therapy and Experimental Psychiatry, 42*(1), 6–12.

Kurz, A. S., Bethay, J. S., & Ladner-Graham, J. M. (2014). Mediating the relation between workplace stressors and distress in ID support staff: Comparison between the roles of psychological inflexibility and coping styles. *Research in Developmental Disabilities, 35*(10), 2359–2370.

Lloyd, J., Bond, F. W., & Flaxman, P. E. (2013). The value of psychological flexibility: Examining psychological mechanisms underpinning a cognitive behavioural therapy intervention for burnout. *Work & Stress, 27*(2), 181–199.

Ly, K. H., Asplund, K., & Andersson, G. (2014). Stress management for middle managers via an acceptance and commitment-based smartphone application: A randomized controlled trial. *Internet Interventions, 1*(3), 95–101.

McConachie, D. A. J., McKenzie, K., Morris, P. G., & Walley, R. M. (2014). Acceptance and mindfulness-based stress management for support staff caring for individuals with intellectual disabilities. *Research in Developmental Disabilities, 35*(6), 1216–1227.

McCracken, L. M., & Yang, S. Y. (2008). A contextual cognitive-behavioral analysis of rehabilitation workers' health and well-being: Influences of acceptance, mindfulness, and values-based action. *Rehabilitation Psychology, 53*(4), 479.

Moran, D. J. (2011). ACT for leadership: Using acceptance and commitment training to develop crisis-resilient change managers. *International Journal of Behavioral Consultation and Therapy, 7*(1), 68–77.

Noone, S. J., & Hastings, R. P. (2009). Building psychological resilience in support staff caring for people with intellectual disabilities: Pilot evaluation of an acceptance-based intervention. *Journal of Intellectual Disabilities, 13*(1), 43–53.

Noone, S. J., & Hastings, R. P. (2010). Using acceptance and mindfulness-based workshops with support staff caring for adults with intellectual disabilities. *Mindfulness, 1*(2), 67–73.

Onwezen, M. C., van Veldhoven, M. J. P. M., & Biron, M. (2014). The role of psychological flexibility in the demands–exhaustion–performance relationship. *European Journal of Work and Organizational Psychology, 23*(2), 163–176.

VanStelle, S. E., Koerber, J. L., & Fox, E. J. (2010). Expansion of OBM: How RFT and ACT can influence our field. *OBM Network News, 24*(3), 11–14.

The ACT variety

Academia

Blanco, C., Okuda, M., Wright, C., Hasin, D. S., Grant, B. F., Liu, S. M., & Olfson, M. (2008). Mental health of college students and their non-college-attending peers: Results from the national epidemiologic study on alcohol and related conditions. *Archives of General Psychiatry, 65*(12), 1429–1437.

Chase, J. A., Houmanfar, R., Hayes, S. C., Ward, T. A., Vilardaga, J. P., & Follette, V. (2013). Values are not just goals: Online ACT-based values training adds to goal setting in improving undergraduate college student performance. *Journal of Contextual Behavioral Science, 2*(3), 79–84.

Cook, D., & Hayes, S. (2010). Acceptance-based coping and the psychological adjustment of Asian and Caucasian Americans. *IJBCT, 6*(3), 186–97.

Glick, D. M., Millstein, D. J., & Orsillo, S. M. (2014). A preliminary investigation of the role of psychological inflexibility in academic procrastination. *Journal of Contextual Behavioral Science, 3*(2), 81–88.

Hayes, S. C., & Smith, S. (2005). *Get Out of Your Mind and into Your Life: The New Acceptance and Commitment Therapy*. Oakland, CA: New Harbinger.

Levin, M. E., Pistorello, J., Seeley, J. R., & Hayes, S. C. (2014). Feasibility of a prototype web-based acceptance and commitment therapy prevention program for college students. *Journal of American College Health, 62*(1), 20–30.

Muto, T., Hayes, S. C., & Jeffcoat, T. (2011). The effectiveness of acceptance and commitment therapy bibliotherapy for enhancing the psychological health of Japanese college students living abroad. *Behavior Therapy, 42*(2), 323–335.

Clinical

Beilby, J. M., Byrnes, M. L., & Yaruss, J. S. (2012). Acceptance and commitment therapy for adults who stutter: Psychosocial adjustment and speech fluency. *Journal of Fluency Disorders, 37*(4), 289–299.

Clarke, S., Kingston, J., James, K., Bolderston, H., & Remington, B. (2014). Acceptance and commitment therapy group for treatment-resistant participants: A randomised controlled trial. *Journal of Contextual Behavioral Science, 3*(3), 179–188.

Cullinan, C. C., & Gaynor, S. T. (2014). Treatment of agoraphobia in a pregnant woman: A combination of exposure and acceptance and commitment therapy. *Clinical Case Studies*, doi: 10.1177/1534650114539729.

Dalrymple, K. L., Fiorentino, L., Politi, M. C., & Posner, D. (2010). Incorporating principles from acceptance and commitment therapy into cognitive-behavioral therapy for insomnia: A case example. *Journal of Contemporary Psychotherapy, 40*(4), 209–217.

Gómez, M. J., Luciano, C., Páez-Blarrina, M., Ruiz, F. J., Valdivia-Salas, S., & Gil-Luciano, B. (2014). Brief ACT protocol in at-risk adolescents with conduct disorder and impulsivity. *International Journal of Psychology and Psychological Therapy, 14*(3), 307–332.

Hertenstein, E., Thiel, N., Lueking, M., Kuelz, A. K., Schramm, E., Baglioni, C., & Nissen, C. (2014). Quality of life improvements after acceptance and commitment therapy in nonresponders to cognitive behavioral therapy for primary insomnia. *Psychotherapy and Psychosomatics, 83*(6), 371–373.

Paul, R. H., Marx, B. P., & Orsillo, S. M. (2000). Acceptance-based psychotherapy in the treatment of an adjudicated exhibitionist: A case example. *Behavior Therapy, 30*(1), 149–162.

Peterson, B. D., Eifert, G. H., Feingold, T., & Davidson, S. (2009). Using acceptance and commitment therapy to treat distressed couples: A case study with two couples. *Cognitive and Behavioral Practice, 16*(4), 430–442.

Razzaque, R. (2013). An acceptance and commitment therapy based protocol for the management of acute self-harm and violence in severe mental illness. *Journal of Psychiatric Intensive Care, 9*(02), 72–76.

Twohig, M. P., & Crosby, J. M. (2010). Acceptance and commitment therapy as a treatment for problematic internet pornography viewing. *Behavior Therapy, 41*(3), 285–295.

Yadavaia, J. E., Hayes, S. C., & Vilardaga, R. (2014). Using acceptance and commitment therapy to increase self-compassion: A randomized controlled trial. *Journal of Contextual Behavioral Science, 3*(4), 248–257.

Zarling, A., Lawrence, E., & Marchman, J. (2014). A randomized controlled trial of acceptance and commitment therapy for aggressive behavior. *Journal of Consulting and Clinical Psychology*. Advance online publication. http://dx.doi.org/10.1037/a0037946.

Component

Arch, J. J., & Craske, M. G. (2006). Mechanisms of mindfulness: Emotion regulation following a focused breathing induction. *Behaviour Research and Therapy, 44*(12), 1849–1858.

Crocker, J., Niiya, Y., & Mischkowski, D. (2008). Why does writing about important values reduce defensiveness? Self-affirmation and the role of positive other-directed feelings. *Psychological Science, 19*(7), 740–747.

Deacon, B. J., Fawzy, T. I., Lickel, J. J., & Wolitzky-Taylor, K. B. (2011). Cognitive defusion versus cognitive restructuring in the treatment of negative self-referential thoughts: An investigation of process and outcome. *Journal of Cognitive Psychotherapy, 25*(3), 218–232.

De Young, K. P., Lavender, J. M., Washington, L. A., Looby, A., & Anderson, D. A. (2010). A controlled comparison of the word repeating technique with a word association task. *Journal of Behavior Therapy and Experimental Psychiatry, 41*(4), 426–432.

Foody, M., Barnes-Holmes, Y., Barnes-Holmes, D., & Luciano, C. (2013). An empirical investigation of hierarchical versus distinction relations in a self-based ACT exercise. *International Journal of Psychology and Psychological Therapy, 13*(3), 373–388.

Hayes, S. C., Luoma, J. B., Bond, F. W., Masuda, A., & Lillis, J. (2006). Acceptance and commitment therapy: Model, processes and outcomes. *Behaviour Research and Therapy, 44*(1), 1–25.

Healy, H. A., Barnes-Holmes, D., Barnes-Holmes, Y., Keogh, C., Luciano, C., & Wilson, K. (2008). An experimental test of a cognitive defusion exercise. *The Psychological Record, 58*, 623–640.

Heppner, W. L., Kernis, M. H., Lakey, C. E., Campbell, W. K., Goldman, B. M., Davis, P. J., & Cascio, E. V. (2008). Mindfulness as a means of reducing aggressive behavior: Dispositional and situational evidence. *Aggressive Behavior, 34*(5), 486–496.

Hinton, M. J., & Gaynor, S. T. (2010). Cognitive defusion for psychological distress, dysphoria, and low self-esteem: A randomized technique evaluation trial of vocalizing strategies. *International Journal of Behavioral Consultation and Therapy, 6*(3), 164–185.

Hooper, N., Davies, N., Davies, L., & McHugh, L. (2011). Comparing thought suppression and mindfulness as coping techniques for spider fear. *Consciousness and Cognition, 20*(4), 1824–1830.

Hooper, N., & McHugh, L. (2013). Cognitive defusion versus thought distraction in the mitigation of learned helplessness. *Psychological Record, 63*(1), 209–217.

Hooper, N., Sandoz, E. K., Ashton, J., Clarke, A., & McHugh, L. (2012). Comparing thought suppression and acceptance as coping techniques for food cravings. *Eating Behaviors, 13*(1), 62–64.

Kashdan, T. B., & Mcknight, P. E. (2013). Commitment to a purpose in life: an antidote to the suffering by individuals with social anxiety disorder. *Emotion, 13*(6), 1150–1159. http://doi.org/10.1037/a0033278.

Kishita, N., Muto, T., Ohtsuki, T., & Barnes-Holmes, D. (2014). Measuring the effect of cognitive defusion using the implicit relational assessment procedure: An experimental analysis with a highly socially anxious sample. *Journal of Contextual Behavioral Science, 3*(1), 8–15.

Levin, M. E., Hildebrandt, M. J., Lillis, J., & Hayes, S. C. (2012). The impact of treatment components suggested by the psychological flexibility model: A meta-analysis of laboratory-based component studies. *Behavior Therapy, 43*(4), 741–756.

Low, C. A., Stanton, A. L., & Bower, J. E. (2008). Effects of acceptance-oriented versus evaluative emotional processing on heart rate recovery and habituation. *Emotion, 8*(3), 419.

Luciano, C., Molina, F., Gutiérrez-Martínez, O., Barnes-Holmes, D., Valdivia-Salas, S., Cabello, F., & Wilson, K. G. (2010). The impact of acceptance-based versus avoidance-based protocols on discomfort. *Behavior Modification, 34*(2), 94–119.

Marcks, B. A., & Woods, D. W. (2005). A comparison of thought suppression to an acceptance-based technique in the management of personal intrusive thoughts: A controlled evaluation. *Behaviour Research and Therapy, 43*(4), 433–445.

Marcks, B. A., & Woods, D. W. (2007). Role of thought-related beliefs and coping strategies in the escalation of intrusive thoughts: An analog to obsessive-compulsive disorder. *Behaviour Research and Therapy, 45*(11), 2640–2651.

Masuda, A., Feinstein, A. B., Wendell, J. W., & Sheehan, S. T. (2010). Cognitive defusion versus thought distraction: A clinical rationale, training, and experiential exercise in altering psychological impacts of negative self-referential thoughts. *Behavior Modification, 34*(6), 520–538. doi: 10.1177/0145445510379632.

Masuda, A., Hayes, S. C., Sackett, C. F., & Twohig, M. P. (2004). Cognitive defusion and self-relevant negative thoughts: Examining the impact of a ninety year old technique. *Behaviour Research and Therapy, 42*(4), 477–485.

Masuda, A., Hayes, S. C., Twohig, M. P., Drossel, C., Lillis, J., & Washio, Y. (2009). A parametric study of cognitive defusion and the believability and discomfort of negative self-relevant thoughts. *Behavior Modification, 33*, 250–262.

Masuda, A., Twohig, M. P., Stormo, A. R., Feinstein, A. B., Chou, Y. Y., & Wendell, J. W. (2010). The effects of cognitive defusion and thought distraction on emotional discomfort and believability of negative self-referential thoughts. *Journal of Behavior Therapy and Experimental Psychiatry, 41*(1), 11–17.

Titchener, E. B. (1916). *A Text-book of Psychology*. New York: MacMillan.

Weger, U. W., Hooper, N., Meier, B. P., & Hopthrow, T. (2012). Mindful maths: Reducing the impact of stereotype threat through a mindfulness exercise. *Consciousness and Cognition, 21*(1), 471–475.

Yovel, I., Mor, N., & Shakarov, H. (2014). Examination of the core cognitive components of cognitive behavioral therapy and acceptance and commitment therapy: An analogue investigation. *Behavior Therapy. 45*(4), 482–494.

Exercise and sport

Bernier, M., Thienot, E., Cordon, R., & Fournier, J. F. (2009). Mindfulness and acceptance approaches in sport performance. *Journal of Clinical Sport Psychology, 25*(4), 320.

Burton, N. W., Pakenham, K. I., & Brown, W. J. (2010). Feasibility and effectiveness of psychosocial resilience training: A pilot study of the READY program. *Psychology, Health & Medicine, 15*(3), 266–277.

Butryn, M. L., Forman, E., Hoffman, K., Shaw, J., & Juarascio, A. (2011). A pilot study of acceptance and commitment therapy for promotion of physical activity. *Journal of Physical Activity and Health, 8*(4), 516.

Fernández, R., Secades, R., Terrados, N., García, E., & García, J. M. (2004). Efecto de la hipnosis y de la terapia de aceptación y compromiso (ACT) en la mejora de la fuerza física en piragüistas. *International Journal of Clinical and Health Psychology, 4*(3), 481–493.

Gardner, F. L., & Moore, Z. E. (2004). A mindfulness-acceptance-commitment-based approach to athletic performance enhancement: Theoretical considerations. *Behavior Therapy, 35*(4), 707–723.

Gardner, F. L., & Moore, Z. E. (2007). *The Psychology of Enhancing Human Performance: The Mindfulness-Acceptance-Commitment (MAC) Approach*. New York, NY: Springer Publishing Co.

Goodwin, C. L., Forman, E. M., Herbert, J. D., Butryn, M. L., & Ledley, G. S. (2011). A pilot study examining the initial effectiveness of a brief acceptance-based behavior therapy for modifying diet and physical activity among cardiac patients. *Behavior Modification, 36*(2), 199–217. doi: 10.11770145445511427770.

Ivanova, E., Jensen, D., Cassoff, J., Gu, F., & Knäuper, B. (2014). Acceptance and commitment therapy improves exercise tolerance in sedentary women. *Medicine and Science in Sports and Exercise.* doi: 10.1249/MSS.0000000000000536.

Lutkenhouse, J. M. (2007). The case of Jenny: A freshman collegiate athlete experiencing performance dysfunction. *Journal of Clinical Sport Psychology, 1*(2), 166–180.

Moffitt, R., & Mohr, P. (2014). The efficacy of a self-managed acceptance and commitment therapy intervention DVD for physical activity initiation. *British Journal of Health Psychology, 20*(1), 115–129.

Ruiz, F. J. (2006). Aplicación de la Terapia de Aceptación y Compromiso (ACT) para el incremento del rendimiento ajedrecístico. Un estudio de caso. *International Journal of Psychology and Psychological Therapy, 6*, 77–97.

Ruiz, F. J., & Luciano, C. (2009). [Acceptance and Commitment Therapy (ACT) and improving chess performance in promising young chess-players]. *Psicothema, 21*(3), 347–352.

Ruiz, F. J., & Luciano, C. (2012). Improving international-level chess players' performance with an acceptance-based protocol: Preliminary findings. *Psychological Record, 62*(3), 447.

Schwanhausser, L. (2009). Application of the mindfulness-acceptance-commitment (MAC) protocol with an adolescent springboard diver. *Journal of Clinical Sport Psychology, 4*, 377–395.

Parenting

Blackledge, J. T., & Hayes, S. C. (2006). Using acceptance and commitment training in the support of parents of children diagnosed with autism. *Child & Family Behavior Therapy, 28*(1), 1–18.

Brown, F. L., Whittingham, K., Boyd, R. N., McKinlay, L., & Sofronoff, K. (2014). Improving child and parenting outcomes following paediatric acquired brain injury: A randomised controlled trial of Stepping Stones Triple P plus acceptance and commitment therapy. *Journal of Child Psychology and Psychiatry, 55*(10), 1172–1183.

Brown, F. L., Whittingham, K., McKinlay, L., Boyd, R., & Sofronoff, K. (2013). Efficacy of Stepping Stones Triple P plus a stress management adjunct for parents of children with an acquired brain injury: The protocol of a randomised controlled trial. *Brain Impairment, 14*(02), 253–269.

Casselman, R. B., & Pemberton, J. R. (2015). ACT-based parenting group for veterans with PTSD: Development and preliminary outcomes. *The American Journal of Family Therapy, 43*(1), 57–66.

Coyne, L. W., McHugh, L., & Martinez, E. R. (2011). Acceptance and commitment therapy (ACT): Advances and applications with children, adolescents, and families. *Child and Adolescent Psychiatric Clinics of North America, 20*(2), 379–399.

DeMyer, M. K. (1979). *Parents and Children in Autism*. Washington, DC: VH Winston.

Evans, T., Whittingham, K., & Boyd, R. (2012). What helps the mother of a preterm infant become securely attached, responsive and well-adjusted? *Infant Behavior and Development, 35*(1), 1–11.

Moyer, D. N., & Sandoz, E. K. (2014). The role of psychological flexibility in the relationship between parent and adolescent distress. *Journal of Child and Family Studies, 24*(5), 1406–1418.

Murrell, A. R., & Scherbarth, A. J. (2006). State of the research & literature address: ACT with children, adolescents and parents. *International Journal of Behavioral Consultation and Therapy, 2*(4), 531–543.

Murrell, A. R., Steinberg, D. S., Connally, M. L., Hulsey, T., & Hogan, E. (2014). Acting out to ACTing on: A preliminary investigation in youth with ADHD and co-morbid disorders. *Journal of Child and Family Studies*, 1–8. doi: 10.1007/s10826-014-0020-7.

Whittingham, K. (2014). Parenting in context. *Journal of Contextual Behavioral Science, 3*(3), 212–215.

Whittingham, K., & Douglas, P. (2014). Optimizing parent-infant sleep from birth to 6 months: A new paradigm. *Infant Mental Health Journal, 35*(6), 614–623.

Whittingham, K., Sanders, M., McKinlay, L., & Boyd, R. N. (2013). Stepping Stones Triple P and acceptance and commitment therapy for parents of children with cerebral palsy: Trial protocol. *Brain Impairment, 14*(02), 270–280.

Whittingham, K., Sanders, M., McKinlay, L., & Boyd, R. N. (2014). Interventions to reduce behavioral problems in children with cerebral palsy: An RCT. *Pediatrics*, doi: 10.1542/peds.2013-3620.

Whittingham, K., Wee, D., Sanders, M. R., & Boyd, R. (2013). Predictors of psychological adjustment, experienced parenting burden and chronic sorrow symptoms in parents of children with cerebral palsy. *Child: Care, Health and Development, 39*(3), 366–373.

Training

Brock, M. J., Robb, H. B., Walser, R. D., & Batten, S. V. (2015, in press). Recognizing common clinical mistakes in ACT: A quick analysis and call to awareness. *Journal of Contextual Behavioral Science*, doi: 10.1016/j.jcbs.2014.11.003.

Kennedy, A. E., Whiting, S. W., & Dixon, M. R. (2014). Improving novel food choices in preschool children using acceptance and commitment therapy. *Journal of Contextual Behavioral Science, 3*(4), 228–235.

Luoma, J. B., Hayes, S. C., Twohig, M. P., Roget, N., Fisher, G., Padilla, M., & Kohlenberg, B. (2007). Augmenting continuing education with psychologically focused group consultation: Effects on adoption of group drug counseling. *Psychotherapy: Theory, Research, Practice, Training, 44*(4), 463.

Luoma, J. B., & Vilardaga, J. P. (2013). Improving therapist psychological flexibility while training acceptance and commitment therapy: A pilot study. *Cognitive Behaviour Therapy, 42*(1), 1–8.

Pakenham, K. I. (2014). Effects of acceptance and commitment therapy (ACT) training on clinical psychology trainee stress, therapist skills and attributes, and ACT processes. *Clinical Psychology & Psychotherapy*. doi: 10.1002/cpp.1924.

Richards, R., Oliver, J. E., Morris, E., Aherne, K., Iervolino, A. C., & Wingrove, J. (2011). Acceptance and commitment therapy training for clinicians: An evaluation. *The Cognitive Behaviour Therapist, 4*(03), 114–121.

Stafford-Brown, J., & Pakenham, K. I. (2012). The effectiveness of an ACT informed intervention for managing stress and improving therapist qualities in clinical psychology trainees. *Journal of Clinical Psychology, 68*(6), 592–513.

Varra, A. A., Hayes, S. C., Roget, N., & Fisher, G. (2008). A randomized control trial examining the effect of acceptance and commitment training on clinician willingness to use evidence-based pharmacotherapy. *Journal of Consulting and Clinical Psychology, 76*(3), 449.

Wardley, M. N., Flaxman, P. E., Willig, C., & Gillanders, D. (2014). Feel the feeling: Psychological practitioners' experience of acceptance and commitment therapy well-being training in the workplace. *Journal of Health Psychology*, doi: 10.1177/1359105314557977.

Stigma

Crisp, A. H., Gelder, M. G., Nix, S., Meltzer, H. I., & Rowlands, O. J. (2000). Stigmatisation of people with mental illnesses. *British Journal of Psychiatry, 177*, 4–7.

Gilbert, P. (2010). *Compassion Focused Therapy: Distinctive Features.* New York, NY: Routledge.

Graham, J. R., West, L., & Roemer, L. (2013). The experience of racism and anxiety symptoms in an African American sample: Moderating effects of trait mindfulness. *Mindfulness, 4*, 332–341. doi: 10.1007/s12671-012-0133-2.

Hayes, S. C., Bissett, R., Roget, N., Padilla, M., Kohlenberg, B. S., Fisher, G., ... & Niccolls, R. (2004). The impact of acceptance and commitment training and multicultural training on the stigmatizing attitudes and professional burnout of substance abuse counselors. *Behavior Therapy, 35*(4), 821–835.

Lillis, J., & Hayes, S. C. (2007). Applying acceptance, mindfulness, and values to the reduction of prejudice: A pilot study. *Behavior Modification, 31*(4), 389–411.

Lillis, J., Hayes, S. C., Bunting, K., & Masuda, A. (2009). Teaching acceptance and mindfulness to improve the lives of the obese: A preliminary test of a theoretical model. *Annals of Behavioral Medicine, 37*(1), 58–69.

Luoma, J. B., Kohlenberg, B. S., Hayes, S. C., Bunting, K., & Rye, A. K. (2008). Reducing self-stigma in substance abuse through acceptance and commitment therapy: Model, manual development, and pilot outcomes. *Addiction Research & Theory, 16*(2), 149–165.

Luoma, J. B., Kohlenberg, B. S., Hayes, S. C., & Fletcher, L. (2012). Slow and steady wins the race: A randomized clinical trial of acceptance and commitment therapy targeting shame in substance use disorders. *Journal of Consulting and Clinical Psychology, 80*(1), 43.

Macrae, C. N., Bodenhausen, G. V., Milne, A. B., & Jetten, J. (1994). Out of mind but back in sight: Stereotypes on the rebound. *Journal of Personality & Social Psychology, 67*, 808–817.

Maslach, C., Jackson, S. E., & Leiter, M. P. (1986). *Maslach Burnout Inventory.* Palo Alto: Routledge/Taylor & Francis Group.

Masuda, A., Hayes, S. C., Fletcher, L. B., Seignourel, P. J., Bunting, K., Herbst, S. A., & Lillis, J. (2007). Impact of acceptance and commitment therapy versus education on stigma toward people with psychological disorders. *Behaviour Research and Therapy, 45*(11), 2764–2772.

Masuda, A., Hill, M. L., Morgan, J., & Cohen, L. L. (2012). A psychological flexibility-based intervention for modulating the impact of stigma and prejudice: A descriptive review of empirical evidence. *Psychology, Society & Education, 4*(2), 211–223.

Masuda, A., Price, M., Anderson, P. L., Schmertz, S. K., & Calamaras, M. R. (2009). The Role of Psychological Flexibility in Mental Health Stigma and Psychological Distress for the Stigmatizer. *Journal of Social and Clinical Psychology, 28*(10), 1244–1262.

Skinta, M. D., Lezama, M., Wells, G., & Dilley, J. W. (2014, in press). Acceptance and compassion-based group therapy to reduce HIV stigma. *Cognitive and Behavioral Practice.* doi: 10.1016/j.cbpra.2014.05.006.

West, L. M., Graham, J. R., & Roemer, L. (2013). Functioning in the face of racism: Preliminary findings on the buffering role of values clarification in a Black American sample. *Journal of Contextual Behavioral Science, 2*(1), 1–8.

Part III

A-Tjak, J. G. L., Davis, M. L., Morina, N., Powers, M. B., Smits, J. A. J., & Emmelkamp, P. M. G. (2015). A meta-analysis of the efficacy of acceptance and commitment therapy for clinically relevant mental and physical health problems. *Psychotherapy and Psychosomatics, 84*(1), 30–36.

Öst, L. G. (2014). The efficacy of acceptance and commitment therapy: An updated systematic review and meta-analysis. *Behaviour Research and Therapy, 61*, 105–121.

Further Resources

Anxiety

Eifert, G. H., & Forsyth, J. P. (2005). *Acceptance and Commitment Therapy for Anxiety Disorders: A Practitioner's Treatment Guide to Using Mindfulness, Acceptance, and Values-Based Behavior Change.* Oakland, CA: New Harbinger Publications.

Fleming, J. E., & Kocovski, N. L. (2013). *The Mindfulness and Acceptance Workbook for Social Anxiety and Shyness: Using Acceptance and Commitment Therapy to Free Yourself from Fear and Reclaim Your Life.* Oakland, CA: New Harbinger Publications.

Hershfield, J., & Corboy, T. (2013). *The Mindfulness Workbook for OCD: A Guide to Overcoming Obsessions and Compulsions Using Mindfulness and Cognitive Behavioral Therapy.* Oakland, CA: New Harbinger Publications.

Orsillo, S. M., & Roemer, L. (Eds.). (2005). *Acceptance and Mindfulness-Based Approaches to Anxiety: New Directions in Conceptualization and Treatment.* New York: Kluwer Academic/Plenum (Springer).

Orsillo, S. M., & Roemer, L. (2011). *The Mindful Way Through Anxiety.* New York, NY: Guilford Press.

Roemer, L., & Orsillo, S. M. (2009). *Mindfulness- and Acceptance-Based Behavioral Therapies in Practice.* New York: Guilford Press.

Walser, R., & Westrup, D. (2007). *Acceptance & Commitment Therapy for the Treatment of Post-Traumatic Stress Disorder & Trauma-Related Problems: A Practitioner's Guide to Using Mindfulness & Acceptance Strategies.* Oakland, CA: New Harbinger.

Woods, D. W., & Twohig, M. P. (2008). *Trichotillomania: An ACT-Enhanced Behavior Therapy Approach Therapist Guide.* Oxford: Oxford University Press.

Psychosis

Bach, P. A., Gaudiano, B., Pankey, J., Herbert, J. D., & Hayes, S. C. (2006). Acceptance, Mindfulness, Values, and Psychosis: Applying Acceptance and Commitment Therapy (ACT) to the Chronically Mentally Ill. In R. A. Baer (Ed), *Mindfulness-Based Treatment Approaches: Clinician's Guide to Evidence Base and Applications.* (pp. 93–116). San Diego, CA: Elsevier Academic Press.

Morris, E. M., Johns, L. C., & Oliver, J. E. (Eds.). (2013). *Acceptance and Commitment Therapy and Mindfulness for Psychosis.* John Wiley & Sons.

Depression

Hayes, L. L., Bach, P. A., & Boyd, C. P. (2010). Psychological treatment for adolescent depression: Perspectives on the past, present, and future. *Behaviour Change, 27*(1), 1–18. doi: 10.1375/bech.27.1.1.

Robinson, P., & Strosahl, K. D. (2008). *The Mindfulness and Acceptance Workbook for Depression: Using Acceptance and Commitment Therapy to Move through Depression and Create a Life Worth Living.* Oakland, CA: New Harbinger.

Saltzman, Amy. (2014). *A Still Quiet Place: A Mindfulness Program for Teaching Children and Adolescents to Ease Stress and Difficult Emotions.* Oakland, CA: New Harbinger Publications.

Teasdale, J. D., Williams, J. M. G., Segal, Z. V., & Kabat-Zinn, J. (2014). *The Mindful Way Workbook: An 8-Week Program to Free Yourself from Depression and Emotional Distress.* New York: The Guilford Press.

Twohig, M., & Hayes, S. C. (2008). *ACT Verbatim for Depression and Anxiety: Annotated Transcripts for Learning Acceptance and Commitment Therapy.* Oakland, CA: New Harbinger & Reno, NV: Context Press.

Zettle, R. (2007). *ACT for Depression: A Clinician's Guide to Using Acceptance & Commitment Therapy in Treating Depression.* Oakland, CA: New Harbinger.

Substance abuse

Hayes, S. C., & Levin, M. E. (Eds.). (2012). *Mindfulness and Acceptance for Addictive Behaviors: Applying Contextual CBT to Substance Abuse and Behavioral Addictions (1st ed.).* Oakland, CA: Context Press.

Eating behaviour

Ciarrochi, J., Bailey, A., & Harris, R. (2014). *The Weight Escape.* Melbourne: Penguin Australia.

Heffner, M., & Eifert, G. H. (2004). *The Anorexia Workbook: How to Accept Yourself, Heal Your Suffering, and Reclaim Your Life.* Oakland, CA: New Harbinger.

Lillis, J., Dahl, J., & Weineland, S. M. (2014). *The Diet Trap: Feed Your Psychological Needs and End the Weight Loss Struggle Using Acceptance and Commitment Therapy.* Oakland, CA: New Harbinger Publications.

Pearson, A. N., Heffner, M., & Follette, V. M. (2010). *Acceptance and Commitment Therapy for Body Image Dissatisfaction: A Practitioner's Guide to Using Mindfulness, Acceptance, and Values-Based Behavior Change Strategies.* Oakland, CA: New Harbinger Publications, Inc.

Sandoz, E. K., & DuFrene, T. (2014). *Living with Your Body and Other Things You Hate: How to Let Go of Your Struggle with Body Image Using Acceptance and Commitment Therapy.* Oakland, CA: New Harbinger.

Sandoz, E. K., Wilson, K. G., & DuFrene, T. (2011a). *Acceptance and Mindfulness Workbook for Bulimia and Related Difficulties.* Oakland, CA: New Harbinger Publications.

Sandoz, E. K., Wilson, K. G., & DuFrene, T. (2011b). *Acceptance and Commitment Therapy for Eating Disorders: A Process-Focused Guide to Treating Anorexia and Bulimia.* Oakland, CA: New Harbinger Publications.

Other health conditions

Gregg, J., Callaghan, G., & Hayes, S. C. (2007). *The Diabetes Lifestyle Book: Facing Your Fears and Making Changes for a Long and Healthy Life.* Oakland, CA: New Harbinger.

Pain

Burch, V. (2011). *Living Well with Pain and Illness*. London: Hachette UK.

Dahl, J., & Lundgren, T. (2006). *Living Beyond Your Pain: Using Acceptance and Commitment Therapy to Ease Chronic Pain*. Oakland, CA: New Harbinger Publications.

Dahl, J., Luciano, C., & Wilson, K. G. (2005). *Acceptance and Commitment Therapy for Chronic Pain*. Oakland, CA: New Harbinger Publications.

McCracken, L. M. (2006). *Contextual Cognitive-Behavioral Therapy for Chronic Pain*. Seattle: International Association for the Study of Pain.

McCracken, L. (Ed.). (2011). *Mindfulness and Acceptance in Behavioral Medicine: Current Theory and Practice*. Oakland, CA: New Harbinger Publications.

Work

Hayes, S. C., Bond, F. W., Barnes-Holmes, D., & Austin, J. (Eds.). (2013). *Acceptance and Mindfulness at Work: Applying Acceptance and Commitment Therapy and Relational Frame Theory to Organizational Behavior Management*. London/New York: Routledge.

Moran, D. J. (2013). *Building Safety Commitment*. IL: Valued Living Books.

The ACT variety

Coyne, L. W., & Murrell, A. R. (2009). *The Joy of Parenting: An Acceptance and Commitment Therapy Guide to Effective Parenting in the Early Years*. Oakland, CA: New Harbinger.

Greco, L., & Hayes, S. C. (Eds.). (2008). *Acceptance and Mindfulness Treatments for Children and Adolescents: A Practitioner's Guide*. Oakland, CA: New Harbinger.

McCurry, C. (2009). *Parenting Your Anxious Child with Mindfulness and Acceptance*. Oakland, CA: New Harbinger Publications.

Pistorello, J. (Ed.). (2013). *Mindfulness and Acceptance for Counseling College Students: Theory and Practical Applications for Intervention, Prevention, and Outreach*. Oakland, CA: Context Press.

Saltzman, Amy (2014). *A Still Quiet Place: A Mindfulness Program for Teaching Children and Adolescents to Ease Stress and Difficult Emotions*. Oakland, CA: New Harbinger Publications.

Whittingham, K. (2013). *Becoming Mum*. Brisbane: Pivotal Publishing.

General

Hayes, S. C., & Smith, S. (2005). *Get Out of Your Mind and into Your Life: The New Acceptance and Commitment Therapy*. Oakland, CA: New Harbinger.

Hayes, S. C., Strosahl, K. D., & Wilson, K. G. (2012). *Acceptance and Commitment Therapy: The Process and Practice of Mindful Change (2nd edition)*. New York, NY: The Guilford Press.

Kashdan, T., & Ciarrochi, J. (2013). *Mindfulness, Acceptance, and Positive Psychology: The Seven Foundations of Well-Being*. Oakland, CA: New Harbinger.

Luoma, J. B., Hayes, S. C., & Walser, R. D. (2007). *Learning ACT: An Acceptance & Commitment Therapy Skills-Training Manual for Therapists*. Oakland, CA: New Harbinger & Reno, NV: Context Press.

Masuda, A. (Ed.). (2014). *Mindfulness and Acceptance in Multicultural Competency: A Contextual Approach to Sociocultural Diversity in Theory and Practice*. Oakland, CA: New Harbinger Publications.

McHugh, L., & Stewart, I. (2012). *The Self and Perspective Taking: Contributions and Applications from Modern Behavioral Science*. Oakland, CA: New Harbinger Publications.

McKay, M., & Zurita Ona, P. (2013). *Advanced Training in ACT: Mastering Key In-Session Skills for Applying Acceptance and Commitment Therapy*. Oakland, CA: New Harbinger.

Polk, K. L., & Schoendorff, B. (Eds.). (2014). *The ACT Matrix: A New Approach to Building Psychological Flexibility Across Settings and Populations*. Oakland, CA: New Harbinger Publications.

Ramnero, J., & Törneke, N. (2008). *ABCs of Human Behavior: Behavioral Principles for the Practicing Clinician*. Oakland, CA: New Harbinger & Reno, NV: Context Press.

Stoddard, J. A., & Afari, N. (2014). *The Big Book of ACT Metaphors: A Practitioner's Guide to Experiential Exercises and Metaphors in Acceptance and Commitment Therapy*. Oakland, CA: New Harbinger Publications.

Tirch, D., Schoendorff, B., & Silberstein, L. R. (2014). *The ACT Practitioner's Guide to the Science of Compassion: Tools for Fostering Psychological Flexibility*. Oakland, CA: New Harbinger Publications.

Törneke, N. (2010). *Learning RFT: An Introduction to Relational Frame Theory and Its Clinical Applications*. Oakland, CA: New Harbinger Publications.

Westrup, D. (2014). *Advanced Acceptance and Commitment Therapy: The Experienced Practitioner's Guide to Optimizing Delivery*. Oakland, CA: New Harbinger Publications.

Wilson, K. G., & DuFrene, T. (2009). *Mindfulness for Two: An Acceptance and Commitment Therapy Approach to Mindfulness in Psychotherapy*. Oakland, CA: New Harbinger.

Index

Printed and bound by CPI Group (UK) Ltd, Croydon, CR0 4YY